CHARTING the
COURSE for
TREATING CHILDREN
with AUTISM

CHARTING the COURSE for TREATING CHILDREN with AUTISM

A Beginner's Guide for Therapists

Linda Kelly

Janice Plunkett D'Avignon

W. W. Norton & Company

New York • London

Most of the clinical case examples in this book are presented as composite cases. Where required, written releases have been obtained from the parents/guardians of the children or from the clients themselves.

For information about permission to reproduce selections from this book, write to Permissions, W. W. Norton & Company, Inc., 500 Fifth Avenue, New York, NY 10110

For information about special discounts for bulk purchases, please contact W. W. Norton Special Sales at specialsales@wwnorton.com or 800-233-4830

Manufacturing by Integrative Book
Book design by Molly Heron
Production manager: Leeann Graham

Library of Congress Cataloging-in-Publication Data

Kelly, Linda, 1961–
Charting the course for treating children with autism : a beginner's guide for therapists / Linda Kelly, Janice Plunkett D'Avignon. — First edition.
    pages cm
 "A Norton Professional Book."
 Includes bibliographical references and index.
  ISBN 978-0-393-70871-4 (hardcover)
1. Autism spectrum disorders in children—Treatment.
2. Children with autism spectrum disorders—Family relationships.
I. D'Avignon, Janice Plunkett. II. Title.
RJ506.A9K45 2014
618.92'85882—dc23

                                                        2013031746

W. W. Norton & Company, Inc.
500 Fifth Avenue, New York, N.Y. 10110
www.wwnorton.com

W. W. Norton & Company Ltd.
Castle House, 75/76 Wells Street, London W1T 3QT

1 2 3 4 5 6 7 8 9 0

THIS BOOK IS DEDICATED TO
Charlie and Stefanie MacDonald
to Marc, Robert, and Abigail Huard
and, of course, to Jack D'Avignon.

Contents

Acknowledgments

WE WOULD LIKE to acknowledge the following people at W. W. Norton for their support and encouragement throughout the writing of this book. First and foremost, we thank our editor Deborah Malmud for believing in us and in our vision. Her guidance will be forever appreciated. We would also like to recognize the direction given by Sophie Hagen, whose efficiency and knowledge kept us on track in the final stages. Thanks also to Ben Yarling for his assistance and help along the way. Lastly, we want to express our gratitude to Kevin Olsen for his enthusiasm and hard work.

We also want to acknowledge those whose involvement contributed to the final product: Dr. Nancy Rappaport for her professional advice and referral to W. W. Norton; Stefanie MacDonald for reading each chapter, reviewing the guides, and offering salient suggestions; Dr. Barry Velleman for his research assistance and valuable insights throughout this process; Dr. Andrea Giordani for her professional expertise and feedback on the chapters; and Nick Betancur for his assistance with formatting forms and being so generous with his time.

In addition, we want to express our appreciation to our loved ones for their faith and confidence in our ability to complete this project. We thank the following people, in alphabetical order: Aimée D'Avignon, Arsène D'Avignon, Jack D'Avignon, Marc D'Avignon, Victoria D'Avignon, Abigail Huard, Marc Huard, Michael Huard, Robert Huard, Marie Plunkett Hurley, Marguerite Levakis, Charlie

MacDonald, Stefanie Kelly MacDonald, Elaine Plunkett Murphy, Dr. Patricia Packard, Tom & Mary Plunkett, Lynne Rosenburg, and Dr. Barry Velleman.

Most of all, we are grateful to those individuals and families whose real-life experiences of living with autism spectrum disorder have served to inspire the writing of this book. And in conclusion, we thank the many leaders in the field for their wisdom and untiring dedication to bettering the lives of those who carry this diagnosis.

CHARTING the COURSE for TREATING CHILDREN with AUTISM

CHAPTER 1

Introduction to Autism Spectrum Disorders

I T IS OUR mutual desire to write this book in order to share with you our personal and professional experiences of working with high-functioning children on the autism spectrum. It is this shared interest that brought us together. We began by collaborating in our professional lives around our work with these children and their families. We came to realize that the more traditional therapeutic approach, relying on insight and intuition, simply would not work in treating this disorder. Instead, we discovered that, above all, therapists new to working with this population need to have a full understanding of how these children think and perceive their world. Also, we found that the parents/guardians of these children need ongoing training and support to learn how to parent them differently.

Because of the uniqueness of the children themselves and their impact on their families, we have found that it is crucial for the therapist to clearly define the parameters of the therapeutic relationship. Basic interview formats typically used for determining client–therapist compatibility are insufficient in preparing to treat this population of clients. Their needs are different and yours will be also. We have discovered that tools specific to the autism spectrum are needed for these tasks. We have provided them for you as reproducible forms in the appendices of this book and on an attached CD. Through the use of this information, you will be better prepared to determine "goodness of fit" and to chart the course of treatment for children diagnosed with autism spectrum disorder (ASD) and their families. Keep in mind that in addition to these tools, we recommend that you have a mentor experienced in the field or a designated colleague for consultations. They will be able to point out the differences in approaches between working with children diagnosed with ASD versus those with other diagnoses. Through this consultation, you may determine that the extent of the child's/family's challenges may or may not fit with your own therapeutic strengths. For instance, they may need someone who is skilled in working with school systems. This may not be an area of interest nor of expertise for you. Another possibility is that they may need extensive family work in therapy and that may or may not match your skills. Conferring with specialists in the field will support you and help to direct your therapeutic choices.

In a traditional therapy situation, especially working with children, a therapist may make use of pretend play or traditional toys. The child on the autism spectrum may have little use for pretend play as he or she tends to be routed in what is real and concrete. Making use of therapeutic tools, frequently relied upon in traditional child therapy, can take on a different meaning to the autistic child. For example, one such youngster was asked by his therapist to use a picture of a thermometer to self-monitor his anxiety levels. Unbeknownst to the therapist, this tool caused the child considerable anxiety each evening as he sought to determine what the weather temperature had been that day. For this child, limits in mental flexibility caused him to associate only one purpose for a thermometer, and he did not understand what was being asked of him.

This is because children on the spectrum do not spontaneously generate connections or insights into their experiences and do not generalize from one situation to another. Traditional interventions, parental and therapeutic, do not work with these children. For example, despite having been repeatedly chastised by his mother for invading his brother's room and not respecting personal space, one young boy decided he would visit a neighbor's house when the family was not at home. This made sense to him. In the literal mind of the high-functioning child on the spectrum, he could do this because the neighbor had a "welcome" mat on the front step and, under it, a house key! For him, there was no connection between invading his brother's privacy and invading the privacy of neighbors. In one instance, he was told specifically not to do it; and in the other instance, he was not told anything. He did not generalize from one situation to the other. In the autistic world, connections are made where there are not any, and connections are often not made where they exist. These traits are frustrating for the parents/guardians and confusing for the child.

While we will refer to some aspects of psychotherapeutic theory, for example, uses of cognitive-behavioral therapy (CBT) techniques or uses of reinforcement and behavioral contracts, as used in applied behavioral analysis, this is not the focus of our book. Rather, our intent is threefold. First, we will provide you with solid information and practical examples that will increase your understanding of this disability and how it affects the ASD child and his or her family. Secondly, we offer you specific tools for determining whether there is a "goodness of fit" between you and your potential ASD client. These include the following:

- *Initial Contact Form.* This form is meant for use in gathering preliminary and essential information needed in determining the possibility for "goodness of fit" between you and your potential client.
- *Developmental Guide.* This guide distinguishes areas of potential concern in the development of ASD children versus neurotypical development.
- *Family Profile Form.* This tool assists you in acquiring in-depth family history information from the parents/guardians and may be used as a final determinant of "goodness of fit."

Lastly, we are giving you the following tools for negotiating the construction of a clear and comprehensive therapeutic relationship and treatment plan.

- *Child Interview Form.* This series of guided questions is provided to elicit pertinent information from the child's perspective in the initial interview. The wording is tailored to the unique language needs of the ASD child/adolescent.
- *Autism Spectrum Descriptive Profile (ASDP).* These forms will support you with targeting problem areas and with identifying their intensity for the child and family. The ASDP is a checklist that measures functioning across four domains: social, learning, independent functioning, and positive attributes.

- *Collaborative Agreement Between Therapist and Parents/Guardians.* This agreement clearly delineates the participation of the therapist and defines mutual expectations.
- *Collaborative Agreement Between Therapist and Child.* Similar to the above, therapy-related expectations and the therapist's involvement in them are described in such a way to make it clear and comprehensible to the ASD child.
- *Thinking About Siblings: A Checklist.* This checklist has been created in an effort to assist you and the parents/guardians with the process of considering the particular needs of the siblings of the ASD child.
- *Skills and Behaviors: A Checklist for Therapists.* This tool is designed to elicit discussions and detect themes around behaviors and limitations that have the potential to compromise future quality of life for the ASD child. It defines the three most relevant areas of functioning that must be addressed now in order to pave the way for future success.

This book will deal exclusively with those aspects of the ASD diagnosis considered to be most prevalent in children determined to be high functioning. They, like their lower functioning cohorts, have long suffered and have a history of being misunderstood. Until recently their needs have not been identified, and therefore treatment options have been limited. It has only been over the last few years that the fields of psychology and education have come to learn that there is much potential to be realized in these youngsters. It is our hope that this book will contribute to a growing body of knowledge related to the development of treatment strategies that will include families in the process.

The parents/guardians of these children seek clarity, often asking the therapist, "What am I supposed to do next?" Their needs are complicated. They need to understand how this disorder affects *their* child, as it is completely unique to each child with ASD. They need to be able to communicate to others how best to interact with their child. They need to know what is typical and what is not typical for their child's social-emotional developmental level. They also need to know how to balance their responsibilities and time spent among the ASD child, his or her siblings, and other demands of family life. Most of all, they need to know how to interact with their own child. These are the challenges they will bring to you.

Typically, clients on the spectrum and their families require more time for interventions outside of the therapy sessions. For example, teacher consultations may be a necessary factor in treatment. School problems may be less disciplinary and more disability related than school personnel or even family members think. The instructional role of the therapist is a very real one when working with this population and demands a considerable investment of time. In determining the feasibility of taking on this client, you will need to consider how much time you will be able to invest and how much time is likely to be needed in order to appropriately treat the client.

We would like you to consider these initial impressions of parents/guardians of high-functioning children on the spectrum. Notice the pride and the hope they convey as they talk about the accomplishments of their little ones.

> *"Isn't he amazing? Only four years old and he can name all the presidents in order of terms and their political affiliations and more. He knows who they married, if they had children and their exact years of service!"*
>
> *"My ten-year-old loves numbers. You know, he can recite endless lists of prime numbers without ever missing even one!"*
>
> *"She is really like a little professor, don't you think? She is so smart! She just doesn't share the same interests as other children her age."*
>
> *"My daughter is a riot! She takes everything so literally. I said, 'Watch your head going down that passage way,' and you know what she said? 'How could I do that, Mama?'"*

Examples like this represent the formulations of hope and heartbreak when a parent comes to see them as part of a bigger picture. It is a picture that holds frustrations and fears, pride and problems, and opens up a roadway to be traveled. It is the beginning of a journey of learning how to parent a child who has been diagnosed as having ASD. Through your treatment, you will be helping them to change their perceptions and parenting approaches. This will start with ensuring that they understand the diagnosis.

Hearing the diagnosis from the specialist, be it the neurologist, psychologist, or pediatrician, is never easy. The age of diagnosis can be variable. It is not always expected and not always easy to detect. For some, it is known as "a hidden diagnosis" because, like the children described earlier, the child on the spectrum initially appears to be bright, even precocious. Although he or she may seem to be just a bit "quirky," this generally does not present as a concern in a young child. The "quirkiness" itself is a trait attributed to his or her intelligence, rather than to any kind of developmental deficit.

It has only been in recent times that those of us in the field of child development have come to know a bit more about the general diagnosis of ASD, and yet we still struggle to understand its many unique characterizations in the children it affects. What we do know is that when we see it, it is there and it goes beyond "quirkiness." It is a repertoire of behaviors, perceptions, and practices that sets these children apart from others. As they grow and develop, these differences become increasingly more obvious and troubling. The impact of the child's difficulties and differences takes its toll on family dynamics and relationships. The family balance is often lost. Parents/guardians who find themselves in this situation require direction and they are frequently unable to find it.

Part of the problem is that ASD manifests itself differently in each child on the spectrum. It can only be defined fully by three essential features: socialization and communication difficulties; the expression of narrow and exaggerated interests; and the demonstration of certain behaviors that seem compulsive in nature. The last category is broad and can range from a perseverative interest in a particular and peculiar topic, to the expression of stereotypical behaviors (e.g., hand-flapping, rocking, etc.). Examples of perseverative interests include things like the need to fill up pages by writing down random phone numbers or the need to list baseball statistics or other rote information (Fattig, 2008). Engaging in these tasks alleviates the social anxiety the ASD child experiences, but at the same time, it isolates him or her from neurotypical peers.

The ASD child's behaviors begin to interfere significantly with home and school functioning at different times in his or her life. It is then when parents will turn to therapists for help. They most likely have tried to address the problems on their own or with the support of others. Yet they may not have the information they need in order to connect the problems they are having with the specific characteristics of the diagnosis as it uniquely presents in their child. For example, a refusal to do homework may be connected less to oppositional/defiant behavior and more to the ASD perception that schoolwork should be done at school not at home. Often parents/guardians will not see how anxiety around issues like this one underlies and contributes to the confusion and frustration the child is experiencing.

Anxiety is actually the basis for behaviors that can appear to others to be obsessive-compulsive or inattentive in nature. Repetitive physical behaviors can range from flapping and rocking as mentioned earlier, to the more socially acceptable practice of playing with a ball. These behaviors are reported to be soothing to the child on the spectrum and can temporarily decrease anxiety. The more socially accepted behaviors are harder to detect as being indicative of anxiety. It is the frequency, duration, and intensity of these actions that parents/guardians need to pay attention to. Once recognized, it can be interpreted for what it is and the practice itself will serve as a gauge for parents/guardians to assess the child's level of anxiety.

Sometimes there can be an exaggerated need for sameness and conformity that may be interpreted as being characteristic of obsessive-compulsive disorder (OCD). And in some cases that is exactly what it is. Yet there are other instances in which repetitive and restrictive behaviors are instead compensatory strategies for maintaining functioning in the child's world. Unlike OCD, they are not driven by plaguing fears. For some children diagnosed with ASD, reliance on routines and sameness makes the world more manageable and frees them up to invest their energy in coping with all that cannot be predicted and managed (Attwood, 2007; Baron-Cohen, 1990). For an eloquent personal account by a 13-year-old autistic boy, the reader is referred to a book titled *The Reason I Jump* (Higashida, 2013).

Heightened levels of anxiety are inherent in this disorder and result from the inability to shift perspectives and accurately perceive how another person might be thinking or feeling. This is best described in the Theory of Mind literature (Baron-Cohen, Leslie, & Firth, 1985). As Tony Attwood (2007) describes it, there is a difficulty in "putting oneself in another person's shoes." This lack of insight is connected to a lack of skill in monitoring subtle communicative signals (e.g., reading body language and facial expressions). In addition, accepted rules for turn-taking and other conversational practices are not internalized and not applied. All of this leads to social isolation and rejection. Sadly, this situation only worsens as the child grows older. Seeing one's child increasingly rejected by peers is often a reason the parents/guardians will seek treatment.

Another important point for you to consider is that for many parents, the diagnosis of ASD was not given to their child until he or she was well into the school years. Instead, they were told that their child was struggling with any number of diagnoses sharing similar traits, much like the example of OCD given earlier. The result is a diagnostic history that is more akin to an alphabet soup than it is to a clear description of the child's actual profile. These other diagnoses may include attention-deficit/hyperactivity disorder (ADHD), generalized anxiety disorder (GAD), or nonverbal learning disorder (NVLD) (Klin, McPartland, & Volkmar, 2005).

This long list of possible diagnoses results from certain apparent crossovers. For each, there are behaviors that may resemble that diagnosis, but in reality it is a "close, but no cigar" situation. By the time the child enters school, parents want answers and actively seek them out. They suspect that there is something else going on as they watch their child struggle to keep up with the increasing demands of daily life. It is not surprising that many parents ultimately report relief in getting the diagnosis, as difficult as it is to hear. At least, there is a name for it. At last, there may be some answer on how to deal with it. And, just maybe, there really is hope.

Hope comes with knowledge. And over the years the understanding of ASD has increased as our knowledge base has expanded. At one time those who were diagnosed were classified as everything from being psychotic to being outrageous savants. Children on the spectrum were seen as being unreachable, unteachable, uncaring. Their inability to perceive how others feel was falsely interpreted as an inability *to* feel. Many children were seen as "troubled children" and were left to their own devices. Individuals on the spectrum are often perceived to be lacking empathy and sensitivity toward others. Their motives of intent are questioned and misunderstood. Alternatively, as explained by Tony Attwood at the 2012 Asperger's Association of New England (AANE) Conference in Boston, MA, those on the spectrum are typically kind and sensitive people who act out of misperceptions rather than maliciousness.

As a treating therapist, it is important for you to be familiar with the history associated with this diagnosis and how it continues to unfold. In the 1940s, autism was defined by child psychiatrist Dr. Leo Kanner. He saw it as a childhood disorder characterized by such aloofness and social isolation as to result in a breakdown of communications and a retreat into a "separate world." The stereotypical behaviors that are characteristic of many children on the spectrum were noted as being self-stimulatory. They were seen as being related to the self-stimulating behaviors of childhood schizophrenia. Autism itself became known as a particular form of childhood schizophrenia (Kanner, 1943).

Around this same time, Hans Asperger, a German psychiatrist working with young children, noted a peculiarity among certain members of his patients. He saw a group of young autistic boys as having seemingly advanced verbal skills but with a persistent and pervasive interest in one topic, exclusive of all others. These boys were unable to communicate well with peers, were unaware of social expectations, were rigid in their perceptions, and had unusual mannerisms. He saw them as having above-average intelligence and a good deal of potential. Surprisingly, although writing about ASDs at the same time, Asperger was unaware of Leo Kanner's work in the United States (Asperger, 1944).

In the 1970s parents of children on the spectrum were maligned by Chicago child psychologist Bruno Bettelheim (1972), who accused them of being uncaring and rejecting, thus *causing* the disorder in their children. Under the influence of Bettelheim, the term "refrigerator mothers" was used to describe the mothers of these children and, because they were viewed as being so damaging to their children, parents were not allowed to participate in the therapy offered to the children. Bettelheim ran a center for autistic children in which the children remained separate from parents while parents were required to undergo intensive psychoanalysis to resolve their issues relating to their inability to love their children. (The reader is referred to an excellent documentary entitled *Refrigerator Mothers*, which was produced by Kartemquin Films in 2003.)

In the 1980s, Lorna Wing, a British psychiatrist, became interested in the work of Hans Asperger, and she introduced the term *Asperger syndrome* to describe a particular group of children on the spectrum. Lorna Wing's research and teaching did much to change social and professional perceptions of autism (Wing, 1981). She and others, like British child psychiatrist Sir Michael Rutter and American child psychiatrist Russell Barkley, have paved the way for a more advanced and comprehensive understanding of children diagnosed with ASD.

As more has become known about the varieties of autism and the range of differences among those diagnosed with it, therapeutic treatments have also changed. Gone are most of the harsh punishment regimes of some behavior modification therapies. Also gone are the use of medications like LSD and electric shock treatments used in the 1960s and 1970s. New ways of understanding spectrum disorders have led to a variety of approaches to treating children and helping them to develop more effective coping skills, allowing them to become more integrated into general education classrooms and the community at large.

The work of current experts in the field is largely responsible for introducing those changes that have made the crucial differences. Temple Grandin, Tony Attwood, and Carol Gray are among those who have helped us to see that the diagnosis is only the beginning of understanding how these children think, feel, and function in our everyday world. They, and others like them, have helped us to see that there are many ways of working with ASD children. New strategies teach these children how to interpret, comprehend, and respond to situations and people whom they may find to be confusing and overwhelming. With the help of those in the field who are doing research and formulating theories and treatments, there is more information available to enhance and realize the potential for these children. We need only find what works for each child diagnosed with autism spectrum disorder. So let's begin that task and look at the first document, the Initial Contact Form. (You may review this form in its entirety in Appendix A.)

The Initial Contact Form will help you to gather the essential information necessary for you to begin to determine whether you will choose to work with this family. In addition, it will assist you in taking that first step toward discovering the unique aspects associated with this ASD child's profile. We will now review the information on this form in closer detail. The first section of the contact form is presented below.

INITIAL CONTACT FORM

I. GENERAL INFORMATION

Name of caller:_____

Date of call: _____

Relationship to child: parent _____ guardian _____

Insurance information:_____

Name of company:_____

Type of policy: _____

Alternative payment method: _____

Additional Notes: _____

_____

_____

    Upon receiving that first phone call from a parent/guardian of a high-functioning child on the spectrum, we recommend that you use this intake form or something similar. What is important here is to identify the relationship of the caller to the child and the provisions for payment of services. If the caller is a guardian rather than a parent, you will need to have legal documentation of guardianship for your records. If the caller is a parent, you will need to inquire whether a custodial arrangement exists.

    While each state may have its own laws governing child custody, typically, the parent with sole legal custody will have the right to seek all medical and mental health treatment for the child without consent from the noncustodial parent. When parents share custody in a joint legal arrangement, you should request the court documents to ascertain whether the other parent must be notified or otherwise involved in the initiation of treatment. When you are in doubt about a parent's legal rights, seek additional information from the caller. If you are unable to resolve this issue within the context of the initial phone call, you might choose to end the referral process here.

II. BACKGROUND INFORMATION

Mailing address: _____

Contact phone number: _____

Second parent/guardian name and contact information
(if applicable): _____

CHILD'S DIAGNOSES:

Diagnosis:	
Diagnosed by:	
Date of diagnosis:	

Diagnosis:	
Diagnosed by:	
Date of diagnosis:	

Diagnosis:	
Diagnosed by:	
Date of diagnosis:	

Current medical providers:

Name	
Specialty	
Prescribed medications	

Name	
Specialty	
Prescribed medications	

Current mental health provider:

Provider	
Dates	
Reason for treatment	

Current non–mental health therapists
(i.e., speech, occupational, physical):

Name of Therapist	Setting (school, home, etc.)	Dates	Reason for Treatment

Past counseling or other treatment:

Name of Therapist	Setting	Dates	Reason for Treatment

Source of this referral: _____

Additional Notes: _____

_____

In this second section, your goal is to get a good sense of how well the parent/guardian understands the child's *current* diagnosis(es). It is possible for there to be more than one diagnosis affecting the child's behavior. What you want to know is how the parent/guardian views the child's symptoms and how he or she relates them to the ASD diagnosis. The trick here is to get a cursory understanding of this information, without launching into a full-blown discussion.

With this initial call, you are getting information that will later help you to prioritize areas of need as you begin to think about formulating treatment goals. There may be so many issues presented in this call that you are beginning to feel uncomfortable about the prospect of taking this case. The constellation of diagnoses being reported may be so confusing that you will decide to refer this person to another therapist. But before making a final decision, you may want to run this by your designated colleague or mentor.

Getting information about medications, if any, is important. If there is a current prescriber who is part of a group practice, it may be that this person works only in collaboration with his or her own colleagues. In this case, you will want the parents/guardians to take the responsibility of researching alternative prescribers. If there is a therapist currently involved, you will want to know why present therapeutic treatment is being terminated. At this point, you should request authorization allowing you to speak with that therapist. Be prepared to explain to the caller why this consultation may be helpful to you. You may need this information for your initial assessment of the "goodness of fit" between you and this potential client. This will be one of the first places where you will set the parameters that define your role in this relationship (see Chapter 6).

Again, if there is another therapist involved, you will need to know the status of that relationship. If there is a therapeutic bond between that therapist and the child, you will need to ensure that the parents/guardians work with that person to establish a planned termination process. This may happen before your treatment begins or it can run concurrently in order to facilitate the transition.

If there is no current relationship, it is still important for you to know what worked and did not work in prior treatment. It is possible that from your conversation with the parent/guardian you may not feel the need to contact the other therapist. We caution you to get only what you need to know now in order to determine your willingness to work with this client and his or her family in the future.

It will be helpful for you to find out whether the child is involved in other forms of non–mental health therapies in or outside of school. It is not unusual for high-functioning children on the spectrum to have had some treatment from a speech and language therapist, an occupational or a physical therapist, and so on. If there is a history of privately obtained treatment in these areas, you are likely working with a more savvy and informed parent/guardian.

III. CURRENT CIRCUMSTANCES

What precipitated the call for treatment? **Ask about a specific event or incident that triggered this call.** _____

_____

_____

Obtain a brief explanation of how the child is functioning in the following areas:

School: _____

Home: _____

Extended Family Relationships: _____

Peer Relationships:_____

Legal Problems (if any): _____

Additional Notes:_____

Note: *You will be gathering more information later via the Family Profile Form (see Chapter 3).*

This third section is meant to unveil the motivating factors that prompted the need for an appointment with you. The events leading up to this phone call could be relatively unremarkable or could be traumatic in the lives of those involved. If it involves legal issues or complicated school conflicts, you want to be sure that the parents/guardians have other supports in place to help them in dealing with the presenting problem (i.e., a lawyer or an educational advocate, etc.). We also remind you that if their situation is serious enough, there may be court-related demands down the road and you are likely to be expected to appear and testify on behalf of your client. This again emphasizes the need for a designated mentor/colleague relationship with someone who has expertise in the field of high-functioning autism.

Once you have enough information about the reason for the call, you can then ask questions about the child's level of functioning. By investigating the child's ability to communicate, comprehend, and adapt to his or her present circumstances, you should be able to ensure that this child's functioning is indeed on the high end of the autism spectrum. You will also get an idea of how the child manages his or her behaviors across settings and how receptive he or she may be in working through problems within the confines of your office. Initially you may be working more often with the parents/guardians than with the child. With this disability, it is more important for the parents to learn how to interact with their child rather than for the child to be expected to understand the demands of the parents.

If at this point in the phone conversation you are considering accepting this client for treatment, it is a good time to explain that you are going to need more detailed information. You will need to tell the parent/guardian that you are sending home a Family Profile Form (see Chapter 3). We recommend that you require this form to be filled out and returned to you prior to setting the first appointment. The information you obtain will provide crucial details that may affect your decision to treat.

IV. REFLECTIONS ON THE CALL

Length of phone call: _____

Tone of the conversation (disorganized, methodical, angry, anxious, frustrated, etc.):_____

Quality of reciprocity in the conversation (interruptions, one-sided, talking over, perseverative, etc.):_____

Clarity of responses (on topic, direct answers, ability to listen and comprehend, logical presentation, etc.):_____

Final impressions after call (Was the caller a sympathetic person? Did the story make sense?):_____

The final section of the Initial Contact Form is designedly less structured. It is meant to trigger some thoughts about your feelings around the conversation you just had. All in all, how do you think it went? Did you find yourself confused or frustrated in your attempts to get basic information? If this was the case, what do you think was going on? What reasons can you assign to the confusion and frustration? Consider the tone of the call. If the parent was rapidly or loudly speaking, it may have been out of significant anxiety. If there was a precipitating event to the seeking of treatment, was the parent's/guardian's response consistent with the circumstances? Alternatively, was it exaggerated, disorganized, or otherwise unexpected?

Be aware that parents/guardians will sometimes present as if they themselves are on the spectrum. They may seem rigid in their thought processes and may perseverate on a given topic. The give and take of conversation may not be what you would expect. As explained further in Chapter 3, it is likely that one or more family members, perhaps a parent, may also exhibit some of the features of ASD. Be aware that it may simply be that this parent/guardian has for so long had to think in terms of meeting the needs of the ASD child, he or she has come to automatically think from that perspective. As Tony Attwood pointed out at a conference in Boston (2012), the difference in that instance is that the parent/guardian can shift away from that rigid thought pattern and the ASD child cannot.

As we conclude, you can see from the information in this chapter, that your decision to treat will be multifaceted and could be reached at one of a few points along the way. You may have all the information you need at the end of the initial phone call or you may want to wait until you have more information via the Family Profile Form. Ideally, you will have received this completed form *prior* to meeting. Alternatively, you may decide to have a preliminary meeting before reaching a final decision as to whether you and this client are compatible. After evaluating the considerations discussed in this chapter, that is, time, comfort level, caseload demands, and the client/family profile, you will be in the best position to determine whether you are able to chart an effective course of treatment for this particular ASD child and family.

CHAPTER 2

Typical Versus Autism Spectrum Disorder Development

How Do You Know?

IN WORKING WITH high-functioning children who have an ASD diagnosis (pervasive developmental disorder–not otherwise specified [PDD-NOS], Asperger syndrome, or ASD levels 1 or 2), you will often find that the diagnosis was not given until the child had reached school age. Those fortunate enough to have been diagnosed at a younger age were most likely recipients of early intervention services. Developmental delays in speech and language acquisition, and/or the lack of age-appropriate socialization practices by or before the age of 3 years, would have served as "red flags" to pediatric specialists.

Pediatricians, with the support of the American Association of Family Physicians and the American Academy of Pediatricians, are mandated under federal law to screen for developmental delays at designated times in the course of the child's early development. Specific screening tools, such as the Social Communication Questionnaire (SCQ) or the Modified Checklist for Autism in Toddlers (MCHAT), are used to identify "at-risk" children in order to provide early intervention services. It is the astute practitioner who through careful monitoring accurately diagnoses the high-functioning ASD child.

Why is this? Why do so many of these children end up with the "alphabet soup" list of diagnoses referred to in the previous chapter? Even with well-developed diagnostic tools available, many doctors will tell parents/guardians of high-functioning ASD children not to worry about the behavioral concerns they report. They advise them not to be concerned because "children develop at different rates." Hyperlexical talents or adult-like speech patterns are interpreted as signs of intellectual advancement. An unusual knowledge base, quirky behaviors, and unexpected anxieties are often concerns for parents but not always witnessed or understood by their pediatricians. Parental instincts indicating that something is askew are too often ignored.

With the child diagnosed with ASD, it is not uncommon initially to be assigned other diagnoses (i.e., ADHD or OCD). This occurs because certain characteristics of ASD resemble other disorders which may or may not actually be present. It is likely that the underlying ASD diagnosis is missed because, more often than not, early and precocious language acquisition masks the full manifestation of symptoms. Language acquisition is considered a sign of typical development, but the acquisition of language often focuses on the development of speech and not on the pragmatic or social uses of language across developmental stages. The development of pragmatic skills is an issue studied by Elsa Abele (2012) and will be discussed later in this chapter.

Looking at discrete aspects of the achievement of developmental milestones can be misleading. As pointed out by Nancy Wiseman in her guide for parents (2006), parents and pediatricians often miss the fullness that is essential to the developmental task itself. This happens when too much emphasis is placed on the specifics of development. For example, it is not enough to recognize that the infant can track faces, but does the infant track his or her caregiver's face in particular? Does the baby laugh spontaneously at the funny antics of another person? Does he or she seek out eye contact and initiate smiles and other prosocial behaviors? Does he or she laugh and play with family members, interacting in a give-and-take fashion? These are the components that qualify the accomplishments of development. It is through attention to these qualifiers that ASD behaviors are best identified and understood.

Attention to the components of developmental achievements and the surrounding circumstances associated with their emergence is crucial to understanding the world of the child on the spectrum. Underlying factors not readily interpreted may be prime motivators for the accomplishment, or lack thereof, for specific behaviors. For example, the *feel* of a rug or a wood floor may be a deterrent to the child learning to crawl or walk. As noted by many in the field, sensory issues are commonly experienced by children across the autism spectrum. Sensitivity to textures, smells, sounds, tastes, and touch may affect the manner in which a developmental milestone is approached and/or accomplished (Baranek, Linn, & David, 2008).

Coordination of motor movements and motor planning problems are not always reported when considering the achievement of an age-appropriate benchmark. And yet these features are critical "red flags" to recognizing the presence of ASD in the developing child. For example, ball playing may be accomplished in the child on the spectrum, but combining batting a ball and running bases may prove to be difficult due to visual-motor planning deficits. Adding to this is a level of anxiety that ASD children experience in playing games requiring sensory-motor coordination. For these children, motor planning and anxiety around not being able to predict the outcome of a game involving others are significant factors that need to be considered in reporting on developmental milestones.

Through understanding the differences between typical and atypical development across the domains most affected by autism, you will be better able to address the issues that are associated with these differences. Know that the domains are consistent across cultures, but the expectations associated with developmental tasks vary across cultures (Matson et al., 2011; Volkmar, 2005). As with human behavior in general, cultural variations must always be considered.

So let's begin by looking at the Developmental Guide (see Appendix B) to discuss the ways in which high-functioning children on the spectrum will likely differ from their peers as they grow and mature in the areas of physical, social-emotional, and communicative development. You will find specific examples of developmental milestones that we have chosen as being most representative across ages and within each of these three categories (Brisbane, 2006; North Carolina Department of Health and Human Services, 2007).

Physical Development

As you know, much of early physical development is based on growth charts. The extent and the rate of development are systematically measured and recorded throughout the first years of life, and specific benchmarks are targeted as markers of normal development. From **birth to 2 years of age**, crawling, walking, sleeping, eating, toileting, tolerating hygienic practices, and demonstrating fine motor abilities are all considered crucial aspects of typical development. Just being able to do these things is generally considered the measure of the accomplishment. For the child on the spectrum, it is *how* these milestones are manifested, as well as the peculiarities often associated with their emergence, that can provide important information. If it is recognized that milestones are being met with notable and unexpected peculiarities, there is a greater chance that early intervention will be implemented. Early intervention is important for the remediation of increasingly troublesome behaviors related to skill development.

Keeping this in mind, what you are more likely to encounter is the situation in which the parents/guardians saw unusual behaviors, wondered about them, and may even have asked about them repeatedly, only to be told there was nothing to worry about. But, in fact, there was something to worry about. Recent research on the physical development of children on the spectrum tells a different story. For example, Dr. Philip Teitelbaum, a longtime expert and researcher in the area of movement development, points to the differences and urges pediatricians to take note (Teitelbaum & Teitelbaum, 2008).

Toe-walking, asymmetrical crawling, or corkscrew-like rolling are all manners of movements that may be reported as part of the initial signs that something was different in the child's development (Teitelbaum & Teitelbaum, 2008). Unlike the developmental aspects of social and communicative skills, there is disagreement in the field as to whether differences in the development of gross motor skills are specific to ASD. Not all children on the spectrum evidence these differences and, indeed, the differences themselves can be observed across other developmental disabilities (Chawarska, Klin, & Volkmar, 2008). Nonetheless, these skill deficits have been reported often enough by caregivers of all levels of ASD children to warrant mention.

Sleep is another area of concern for parents/guardians of spectrum children. Interrupted sleep and disruptive sleep patterns are common to this population. It is said that sleep deprivation contributes to the behavioral dysregulation problems commonly seen in children on the spectrum. Children who are high-functioning ASD may experience greater problems with sleep than those who are lower functioning. It is possible that increased anxiety associated with social difficulties resulting from a lack of social awareness is a part of the sleep problem (Richdale & Prior, 1995). Teenagers have been known to report bedtime as a "worry time," a time to review the confusion and social rejection of the day. Recognizing problems with sleep patterns when the child is young and introducing strategies to facilitate relaxation are ways to decrease the chances for developing more ingrained sleep problems later on.

As you explore the development of your client, you will need to talk to the parents/guardians about their experiences as they watched their child grow and develop. Sometimes characteristics present back in the child's earliest days are precursors to similar behaviors still present in later childhood. For example, one little boy who started out as a "toe-walker" learned to navigate his way from one piece of furniture to another, holding on tightly so as not to fall. When he became a full-fledged walker, he continued this holding-on practice even though it was no longer necessary. Later, as a boy of school age, he was what his mother described as "super cautious" and not willing to engage in risky behaviors. Tree climbing, fence walking, hopping from stone to stone in a creek may be risky, but they are all examples of things that typical children attempt and enjoy. This is not necessarily true for the child on the autism spectrum who may find them to be anxiety provoking and sources of potential danger.

The inability to participate freely in expected childhood activities contributes to the increasing isolation from peers that is experienced by the ASD child. These difficulties can be traced back to the first 2 years of development. For example, researchers in the field agree that playing with puzzles, unzipping clothing, pointing, pinching, stacking, and so on are all areas in which the child may experience limitations as he or she attempts to perform fine motor tasks typical of children his or her age.

Problems with fine motor development may also affect the child's ability to use eating utensils. While this may be the case, issues with eating are more likely to be related to sensory intolerance. Sensitivity to textures, tastes, and smells is heightened in autistic children and can be a source of great conflict during mealtimes. For the toddler, refusal to eat can escalate into a full-blown tantrum, one that does not easily subside. All babies have tantrums, but it is the frequency, duration, and intensity of the meltdown that distinguishes a child's behavior as typical or not (Greene, 2010). For children on the spectrum, behavioral dysregulation is often an issue. It is one that can be traced back to the child's earliest years.

When thinking about your client's earliest years, you will want to figure out a sensitive way to broach the topic of toilet training with the parents/guardians. Be prepared to hear about toileting practices that may seem unusual or even bizarre. For example, one young mother blushingly shared with her therapist that her son was so disturbed by using a potty chair, she gave up on toilet training and let him wear pull-ups until he was in the first grade. Another parent once confided that even at the age of 10, her son squatted on the toilet rather than sitting on it directly. Talking about toileting as it relates to early development may cause some angst, as there may well be a connection to the present problems.

You should know that with this population there is a tendency to engage in unusual bathroom-related practices across development. At times this stems from a lack of appreciation for social practices, and other times it is related to sensory issues that become ingrained in routines. Examples of this can range from not using toilet paper to going to the bathroom in unexpected places (i.e., the sink, a trash container, or in a closet). Being aware of a propensity for unusual behaviors is important to your understanding of the child's unique profile and the family dynamics surrounding it.

As discussed earlier, sensory issues directly affect the *quality* of the achievement of a developmental milestone. Just as in toileting, this is also true in the learning of hygiene practices. Face washing, bathing, and tooth brushing may be resisted by the baby/toddler. To accomplish these tasks, the tasks themselves have to be modified. For instance, using fingers instead of toothbrushes with little ones is a way to do this. Bathing can be modified by avoiding full-body immersion in water and giving sponge baths instead. Other parents have substituted premoistened towelettes for face cloths. Again, all of these modifications are made in the effort to find some way to meet a developmental milestone.

Because of the long-standing duration of some unusual practices, parents/guardians may not fully recognize just how unusual and unexpected those practices are. Other parents/guardians *will* recognize that the way the child's needs are being met is unusual, and *these* caregivers may be embarrassed to talk about it. For them, the definition of "normal" is flexible and over time has come to include the unusual behaviors of their ASD child. Parents/guardians will need you to probe sensitively and support them in their disclosures. You will need to obtain this information about unusual practices in toileting and hygiene in order to determine behaviors to be targeted for change. As the child gets older, some practices will be more embedded than others and may be more resistant to intervention. Starting out by questioning early development is a good way to get a sense of how long the unusual practices have occurred and how much impact they have had. Your major treatment goals may well emerge from your understanding of how behaviors have developed over time and the extent to which they are impacting the child's social functioning.

In the age range of **2–4 years**, coordination of movement becomes more advanced. Typically developing youngsters are able to engage in more complex motor activities such as hopping and jumping (on two feet), skipping, pedaling a tricycle, and ball playing. Many of these skills are acquired through imitation and practice. Research on imitation and emulation of body movements with the use of objects has shown that this is an area of concern for children on the spectrum. Even when compared to children with other developmental disorders, deficits in these skills are seen as being specific to the functioning of ASD children (Rogers, Hepburn, Stackhouse, & Wehner, 2003).

Parents/guardians are likely to report that their child experienced difficulty in acquiring these more complex, coordinated motor skills. For some children there will be an accomplishment of sorts—the jumping up and down happens or the pedaling of the tricycle is mastered, but in an odd, uncoordinated, or clumsy fashion. Here again, it is *how* a milestone is achieved rather than the simple fact that it *was* achieved that matters. Without a smooth performance in the execution of motor skills, the child on the spectrum is ill prepared to move to the next of stage of development. It is in this next stage that we find these skills essential as the basis for interactive play with peers. For this reason, pediatric checklists that focus only on whether the task was accomplished are clearly insufficient in recognizing what could be early signs of autism.

Motor planning deficits, combined with continuing sensory sensitivities, contribute to developmental difficulties in the areas of eating, toileting, bathing, and dressing for the child in this age range. The neurotypical child can rely on the adequate development of skills in these areas to meet psychosocial needs for autonomy and initiation (Erikson, 1963). But if by the age of 4 years the child is not toileting himself or herself and not initiating actions that are indicative of good hygiene, he or she is missing skills critical to the development of future independence across stages (Kroeger & Sorensen-Burnworth, 2009).

When the 4-year-old child is failing to demonstrate accomplishments in the areas of hygiene and toileting, he or she begins to attract the attention of others. When this happens, the parents/guardians are faced with criticisms that result in embarrassment and feelings of inadequacy. At a time in life when one needs and wants to be recognized as competent in parenting, having these skills questioned serves to deepen self-doubt and to increase one's fears for the future in terms of one's own ability to parent the child. In some, it underlies an unwillingness to disclose. It is likely that this unwillingness itself is rooted in the earlier stage when the parents/guardians would first begin to experience judgment from others. Do not be surprised if you find that the history initially reported to you may not be all inclusive of the information you need to understand your client's profile. It will be up to you to establish a process to work through this deeply rooted resistance in order to get the notable details associated with the child's early developmental accomplishments.

When looking at physical development between the ages of **4 and 6 years**, remember that the parent/guardians will have had a variety of sources for feedback about the child's functionality by that time. There will have been preschool and, in some instances, primary school experiences that the parents/guardians should be able to address with you. In addition, the child's pediatrician will have been more exposed to the child and may have been asked about specific developmental concerns. Consider asking the parents/guardians directed questions such as: What kinds of activities did your child excel in? Were there play activities that your child avoided? Were there some activities that he or she engaged in to the exclusion of all others? What you are looking for is the beginnings of social isolation due to an inability to demonstrate smooth and coordinated motor skills. In terms of physical development, a lack of skills in this area will affect the child on the playground, in the neighborhood, at recess, and at gym.

With the increased expectations of this age range, an inability to demonstrate typical performance in play skills is connected to further social failures that we will be discussing later. As you will see, it is through play that the child learns other skills important for successful development across social-emotional and communicative stages of growth. For the purposes of this chapter, we have separated developmental aspects across three domains (physical, social-emotional, and communicative); however, it is the unique integration of these domains in which children on the spectrum most notably present as being different from their peers. This is a task we will address with you in Chapter 5.

It is during the **6–12 year** age range that typical children exhibit the integrated and coordinated physical skills necessary to their participation in social play. Bike riding, jump roping, and other activities that integrate hand-eye coordination with complex motor sequences are development typical to this stage. The school-age child is adept at putting these skills to work as a means of facilitating the developmental tasks of the stage. For the child on the spectrum, problems with executing complex motor sequences and with coordinating play skills can be a source of frustration and confusion leading to social failure and rejection.

For example, one high-functioning ASD young man was urged by well-meaning parents to join a park league baseball team. The thought was that by encouraging him to play ball with peers he would learn how to be "part of a team" and would spend less time in solitary play activities. On his first time up at bat, the boy hit the ball and then ran the bases in the opposite direction, making him the laughing stock of everyone on the field. In the child's mind, this ridicule and derision were incomprehensible. His goal was to fulfill the true purpose of the game: He wanted to cover the distance from home plate and back again after touching all the bases. This is a good example of the concrete and literal thinking and reasoning that is typical of individuals on the spectrum. For this boy, how he ran the bases made no difference at the time and yet it became a source of endless argument and obsession for him afterward. It caused him sleepless nights and constant distraction as he struggled to understand why his age-mates thought his behavior to be strange.

Being "different" becomes even more of a problem when the youngster enters the 12–18 year age range of adolescence. While most difficulties in this area are in social-emotional and communicative domains (see below), there are some studies that attest to problems associated with physical development in adolescence. Many of these center on the development of eating disorders in girls and body dysmorphic disorder (BDD) in boys. On a popular blog, http://www.wrongplanet.net, body image problems are discussed among young men, most of whom have been diagnosed with Asperger syndrome.

Researchers see a correlation between the OCD characteristics of teens on the spectrum and the development of bulimia, anorexia, and BDD. Tony Attwood (2007) and others have addressed the development of eating disorders in girls with Asperger diagnoses. In fact, Attwood reports that between 18% and 23% of adolescent girls who have anorexia also meet the diagnostic criteria for Asperger syndrome (Attwood, 2007).

The development of eating disorders remains an area of investigation in the field and it is one that you as a therapist should be alert to when you are working with teenagers on the spectrum. But that is just one of the number of issues you will be dealing with if your client is in the 12–18 year age range. As you will see, this period of development is critical for acquiring the skills necessary for successfully negotiating one's way to adulthood.

Social-Emotional Development

From **birth to 2 years**, the beginnings of crucial social-emotional behaviors emerge. Typically developing babies establish eye contact with their primary caregivers. They respond to their voices and to physical touch. They are soothed and aroused by them. It is during this time that a special bonding develops and the groundwork is laid for attachment formation. Attachment studies abound, and it is well documented that prosocial behaviors are intricately connected to this developmental phenomenon (Ainsworth, Blehar, Waters, & Wall, 1978; Bowlby, 1988; Harlow, 1959).

The growth of social-emotional responses begins in the first weeks of life. Instinctually babies imitate facial expressions and actions (i.e., imitating tongue protrusions or opening and closing of the mouth). They are drawn to areas of contrast, preferring the human face to anything else. These primitive responses account for the beginnings of both social connections and interactive responses. As the months progress, typical infants show enjoyment in turn-taking baby games. They smile and laugh while playing Peek-a-Boo or Patty Cake. They show preferences for caregivers and actively attempt to engage in forms of conversational exchanges based on babbling sounds and imitating conversational tones.

It is during this time that they establish what is known in the field as coordinated joint attention and social referencing. Joint attention refers to the child's need to share interest in an object with another person. By directing his or her gaze at an object of interest and then checking to see whether the other person is sharing this interest, the baby exhibits the first signs of social sharing. This fundamental skill has been proven to be critical to typical social-emotional development. As this ability of sharing attention with another person develops over the first years of life, so too does the capacity to see things from another perspective and the ability to relate to others in a socially enjoyable way. Establishing and developing joint attention is key to the DIR/Floortime therapeutic intervention first developed by Stanley Greenspan and his wife, Nancy Thorndike Greenspan. (*Note: Floortime is a popular approach to treating ASD and competes with the more often used applied behavioral analysis [ABA] method. For information on Floortime techniques, the reader is referred to* Engaging Autism, *by Greenspan and Wieder, 2006*).

Social referencing occurs when the child seeks information by looking to a trusted other for some understanding or communication of a particular event (Landa, 2000). Social referencing also involves being able to *perceive* another's interpretation of a situation. These two key factors are significant in pinpointing differences between typical and atypical development. In using social referencing, the child looks toward another person, generally his or her parent/caregiver for affective information about a situation or action (Hall, 2009). At times, the child is looking to know whether a behavior is acceptable (e.g., Is this something I can play with?). At other times, the child looks to the adult to determine an appropriate affective response (e.g., Is this something I should fear?). It is, in part, through this seeking and sharing of personal information that relational connections are formed.

Autistic children do not involve others socially in the same manner as neurotypical peers do. A lack of joint attention formation and social referencing accounts for differences in the exhibition of empathetic behaviors typically observed in children in the 2–4 year range of social-emotional growth. For instance, as Dr. Laura Hall (2009) reports in her book, *Autism Spectrum Disorders,* these children are just as likely to take pride in an accomplishment as their neurotypical counterparts but are *not* as likely to seek out the praise of others for their success (Sigman, Mundy, Sherman, & Ungerer, 1986). A lack of social sharing and a decreased demonstration of empathetic responses in the ASD population have been well documented (Sigman & Ruskin, 1999). It is our belief that these developmental limitations promote social isolation in these early years and lead to decreased opportunities for involvement in reciprocal play.

Maria Montessori is generally credited with saying that play is the work of the child. For children **from 4 to 6 years** of age, play represents the developmental milestone that is the gateway to all future social success. It is through play that the child processes the rules (written and unwritten) that govern social and behavioral expectations. Social reciprocity is established and social roles are explored. At this stage the child moves from parallel play to cooperative play. It is through engaging in pretend play or imaginative play that the child comes to understand the perspectives of others and relates to their experiences.

Also during this period of development, one finds that the typically developing child shifts his or her focus from an emphasis on the particulars of the play-time activity to the involvement of other participants (Attwood, 2007). Attwood states that "Very young children with Asperger Syndrome have a clear end-product in mind when playing with toys; however, they may fail to communicate this effectively to a playmate, or tolerate or incorporate the other child's suggestions, as this would produce an unanticipated outcome." He adds that "the young child with Asperger Syndrome often seeks predictability and control in play activities while typical peers seek spontaneity and collaboration" (Attwood, 2007, pp. 64–65).

When reviewing the history of your client, it is likely that the parents/guardians will report that it was during this time that they began to recognize a lack of mutual friendships in the child's life. They will talk about fewer invitations to parties for other children and fewer playdates when compared to their typical peers. They will explain that sometimes it was the spontaneity in these kinds of occasions that would upset their ASD child and result in a consistent refusal to go to parties. Sometimes the lack of friendships resulted from the rigidity associated with the child's need to predict outcomes. Whatever the reason, the end result is social rejection, and it is heartbreaking for all involved. This is a topic that will be difficult to explore with parents/guardians, and it will require extra sensitivity as you seek to understand the social isolation your client has experienced.

It is important to recognize that behavioral difficulties in sharing and cooperating are common to all children in this age group, not just ASD children. It is when these difficulties are exaggerated or carried beyond an expected maturational level that one begins to suspect that it may be related to ASD. It is here that limitations in Theory of Mind (the ability to see things from another person's perspective) and an overreliance on or a rigid interpretation of rules differentiate the ASD child from the typically developing one (Baron-Cohen, 1991). These are issues that take on even greater importance as the child moves to the next stage of development.

Parents/guardians will be reporting increasing difficulties with social-emotional issues when talking about their children in the **6–12 year** age range. Friendships have not been developing as expected, and the difference between the ASD child and his or her peers is becoming more apparent. During this time, invitations to parties and playdates are fewer because of these differences. This lack of invitation to participate in social gatherings is associated with specific behavioral traits exhibited by the child. He or she may be demonstrating a high interest in unusual topics or hobbies. She may be attached to wearing only specific articles of clothing because they are soft or have no buttons. He may be adhering to rigid manners of behaving, such as washing only specific parts of his body and not others. Continuing issues with sensory intolerance and rigid routines may be off-putting to typical peers. Noncompliance with socially accepted styles of dressing and good hygiene practices has increased social consequences for children in this age group. While these consequences are difficult for all, they are devastating for ASD children. Children on the spectrum are unable to understand these issues as they are perceived by others. Yet for the high-functioning autistic child, there is still an awareness of not fitting in. Sadly, as peers become less tolerant of differences, the greater the likelihood that the child on the spectrum will experience ridicule along with rejection.

Added to this, social demands increase during this time frame due to the prevalence of unwritten social rules. This combines with the fact that the use of social language is being required for peer acceptance. All of this results in the heightened frustration and increased anxiety experienced by both the ASD child and the family. It is not unusual for the child to respond to these circumstances with aggression, defiance, and hostility.

This negativity is closely tied to confusion. Behaviors resulting from misunderstandings/misperceptions on the part of the ASD child can result in faulty diagnostic interpretations, particularly in this age range. For instance, disruptive behaviors may be viewed as a discrete diagnostic category as opposed to being an inherent component of the ASD diagnosis itself. Another example is what Tony Attwood (2012) describes as "depression attacks" (i.e., brief and unexpected periods of depression) in those with Asperger syndrome. These may *not* be seen as ASD related but rather as a distinct mood disorder because their presentation can appear to be fleeting.

As you can see from all of the above, the demands of parenting a child on such a differing and unexpected path of development are huge. At a time when one expects parenting to be more routine and predictable, parenting is anything but that for these caregivers. Because the ASD child requires constant attention and support, the needs of other children in the family may not be recognized or met. At home, time and energy are consumed with handling crises and cajoling or even disciplining others into meeting the immediate needs of the ASD child. Outside of the home, the parents/guardians are often spending inordinate chunks of time in trying to resolve school issues.

Keeping these things in mind, it will be important to establish priorities to be addressed through your treatment plan. These will come first from determining typical versus atypical development and then differentiating with the parents which areas are ASD related and which areas can be attributed to "kids being kids." Troublesome behaviors, regardless of their roots, belong in your treatment plan based on their level of impact on individual and family functioning. That said, it is still important to determine what is ASD related so as to ensure the accuracy of the child's profile, to correctly identify goals for treatment, and to provide appropriate parent training.

If you are treating a child who is in the adolescent stage of development, generally considered to be around the ages of **12–18 years**, the issues he or she is facing will be more acutely apparent. By its very nature, the experience of adolescence and all that that involves is deeply connected to social experiences. It is during this time in typical development that identification with peers becomes central to the formation of a psychosocial identity. Through interactions with age-mates, the teenager begins to discern specific traits linked to his or her own personal beliefs and experiences that will eventually define his or her own unique identity.

Initially the typically developing adolescent will seek to be as much like peers as he or she can be. Young teens dress alike, talk alike, think alike, like the same songs, like the same celebrities, and in general see themselves as completely unique from adults and all others. They become self-conscious about appearances and hypervigilant about monitoring what others may be thinking of them. They attend to social nuances and are sensitive to the subtleties of nonverbal language.

Youngsters in the early adolescent stage tend to travel in groups and make the first step toward identity achievement by defining themselves as a member of a group. Early on in middle school one sees the formation of cliques and groups that define themselves by shared interests. There are sports-minded groups, studious groups, groups comprised of the popular kids, groups made up of the "geeky" kids, and on and on it goes. Through this adherence to group identities, a process of attaching to more overarching groups will sometimes happen (i.e., the "Goths," the "Emos," etc.). Through it all, the search for belong-ingness with peers is the one constant.

As you read this, it should become apparent to you just how difficult this period of development is for the young teen on the spectrum. It is all about connecting to people and doing it through the knowledge of social rules and practices, the very factors most affected by the individual's diagnosis and that lie at the core of ASD. To attach to a group, one has to have some understand-ing of the social functioning of the group itself. One has to be able to "speak the language" of the group. Whether it is teenage jargon or particular body gestures and signs, knowing the language is essential. For the youngster on the spectrum, the sophistication of abstract language is elusive and the use of nonverbal com-munication is next to impossible. So right from the start, the disadvantages for the ASD adolescent are enormous.

It is not always recognized that, like typical peers at the beginning of the adolescent years, the child on the spectrum also "wants to fit in" but does not know how. High-functioning ASD teens will work hard at trying to figure out a way to do this. In a moving account of living her life having been diagnosed with Asperger syndrome, Dr. Liane Holliday Willey in her book, *Pretending to be Normal* (1999, p. 42), says about her adolescent years, "I watched people like a scientist watches an experiment. Never did I feel like I was looking in a mirror. Always did I feel I was here and they were there." Willey comments on not caring much about being with people or belonging to groups, but that she was lucky to have had some good friends who coached her through her high school years.

Not all young teens are fortunate enough to have this experience. One young man spent so much time and effort trying to study the behaviors and language of his peers so that he would fit in that he became physically ill due to disrupted sleep and a loss of appetite. His anxiety was such that he obsessed constantly about the possible ways he could become part of a group. He did his best to attach himself to peers that he thought might want to befriend him. Sadly, he became the target of their cruelty, and time and time again they set him up for ridicule and social failure.

Things do not get easier as the teen on the spectrum approaches the later stages of adolescent development. It is during this period that identity formation is formalized through a series of moves toward autonomy and independence. Future planning is critical and the adolescent is now motivated by a need for defining his or her identity in terms of future outcomes. To do this requires a higher level of thought processing, one that involves the ability to entertain multiple variables and competing possibilities all the while weighing and measuring the acceptability and feasibility of a variety of choices. As classmates begin to explore life choices (i.e., college selections, areas for study, vocational pursuits, moving away, living independently), the gap between the child on the spectrum and peers grows wider.

Transitioning through adolescence is particularly difficult for ASD children because of the psychosocial demands of this period. Also, at this time, the adolescent is demonstrating an ability to shift mental sets and to engage in perspective taking. In typical development, empathy for others is firmly established and broadened to include empathy for social circumstances that the child has never experienced. It is here, in perspective taking and in the ability to think abstractly, that the ASD teenager is set apart. Rigid patterns of thinking and singular perspectives based on what has been learned or experienced are characteristic of autism and abundantly apparent in the high-functioning ASD adolescent child. As mentioned earlier, a lack of understanding or confusion around purpose can be seen by others as signs of oppositional or defiant behavior and can result in further social rejection.

For example, one young man was severely criticized by peers when he was asked whether he was going to participate in a drive to provide funds for the children of a firefighter who died while fighting a neighborhood fire. "Why would I do that?" he asked. The question was genuine. Unfortunately, it was perceived as being sarcastic and showing disdain for the plight of others. This was not the case. It was simply that the novelty of the situation was not part of the young man's cognitive set; he lacked experience in helping others in this specific way. Without being directly taught social practices in these situations, the ASD person is at a loss. You will find that in working with this population, much of your therapy will be directed to problem solving with your client (Greene, 2012). Finding ways for the child to recognize how social limitations affect others will help him or her to develop appropriate compensatory strategies.

Communicative Domain

Separating social-emotional and communicative domains is difficult and is addressed in *The Diagnostic and Statistical Manual of Mental Disorders*, fifth edition (*DSM-5*). The previously described triad of symptom groups found in the *DSM-IV-TR* (reciprocal social interactions; verbal/nonverbal communication; repetitive, restricted behaviors) has been collapsed into two domains for an ASD diagnosis: social-communicative and repetitive, restricted behaviors. Children who do not manifest the latter but have significant impairment in communications will receive a newly formulated diagnosis called social communication disorder (Loranger & Kaufmann, 2012). This change is provocative and has raised much discussion and dissension among clinicians in the field.

For the purposes of this book, we have chosen to focus on specific developmental tasks that include, but are not restricted to, only these two areas of functioning that are targeted by the *DSM-5* for this diagnosis. We have made this choice because it is a failure to succeed within and/or across these domains that lies at the heart of the referral to you for psychotherapeutic intervention.

The language profile of an individual on the spectrum is uniquely defined and is crucial to the understanding of how your client experiences his or her world. As Tony Attwood (2007) states, knowing the rules of conversing with a person on the spectrum is the basis for establishing optimal communications. The development of specific cognitive and language skills is different for each ASD child, but commonalities do exist. The need for measured and concise speech and avoiding ambiguity by making one's intentions clear are both examples Attwood gives as ways to enhance conversational meaning for individuals on the spectrum.

Familiarity with the client's *limitations* in pragmatic speech is also important. As Elsa Abele (2012), a prominent speech and language therapist with a recognized expertise in this area, points out:

A person may have the sounds and FORM of language and vocabulary and CONTENT of language, but, when putting the parts together to produce conversation or narratives (personal event, expository, procedural story) language breaks down. The person with pragmatic language deficits needs to learn first to use language for different purposes like greeting, requesting, or protesting. (Abele, 2012, p. 2)

She goes on to say that it is through direct instruction that the subtleties and unwritten rules of language are learned.

In the list of typical stages of speech and language development found in the Developmental Guide (see Appendix B), the early differences in the ASD child are significant. From **birth to age 2**, the growth of language is truly remarkable. The child moves from the primitive communications of the newborn to using words and gestures as the means of conveying intent. By the end of the first year, the child has mastered between two and eight words, by age 2 that number increases to about 200–300 words (Hall, 2009). Initial sounds of cooing and babbling are transformed into words and sounds with meaning. Practices involving interactions with babies (babbling back and forth with the infant, playing turn-taking games, etc.) become the basis of establishing conversational rules of give-and-take. Reciprocal social exchanges of language make up the foundational skills for future social growth.

For the ASD child, you are likely to find important early language differences being reported by the parent/guardians. They may or may not have recognized these differences at the time but have subsequently come to see a pattern of development. Alternatively, you may be the one who helps the parents/guardians to see this pattern for the first time. Studies show that children on the spectrum do not demonstrate preferential eye gaze or spontaneous social smiles. Pointing and gesturing to call attention to an object of interest (i.e., joint attention) is reduced and enjoyment is confined to solitary appreciation (Sigman et al., 1986). These deficits in language development lay the groundwork for larger problems in later social communications.

Between the ages of **2 to 4 years**, the typical child experiences what has been called "the language explosion." Since the 1960s, this amazing growth in expressive and receptive language skills has been an area of study for developmental theorists in the field of language acquisition. Erik Lenneberg (1967) detailed the growth of language development, noting that around 24 to 36 months of age the typical child's vocabulary increases up to approximately 1,000 spoken words and 2,000–3,000 words understood. The *how* and *why* of this "burst of development," as well as its links to social interactions with others, are still being debated today. What is agreed upon in the field of language acquisition is that communicative social language skills are in place around the age of 4.

For many children on the spectrum, language development takes a different route from that experienced by typical peers in this age category. For some, language expression is itself delayed or not observed. For others, early language is echolalic. Echolalia can be immediate or delayed. When a parent reports that the child's early speech consisted of repetitions of what he or she had just heard, that is immediate echolalia. For example, a parent asks the child, "Want a cookie?" and the child responds, "Want a cookie?" Delayed echolalia is characterized by the use of previously scripted material the child has heard on a video or television program.

Another developmental difference noted in the 2 to 4 year age category is found in pronoun usage. For some, pronouns are used, but in a mixed-up sort of way with third-person referents substituted for first-person pronouns. It can also be the case with children in this age group that there is a lack of recognition of the name or gender of other people (Fay, 1980; Just, Keller, Malave, Kana, & Varma, 2012).

Many children on the spectrum are reported to give odd rejoinders to WH . . . questions, perhaps because they are more focused on the less essential features of what is being asked than on the question itself. Reporting on studies describing these discrepancies, Hall gives an example of the WH . . . problem: "When asked 'Who took you for a car ride?' the student may respond, 'to the store' or 'red car'" (Hall, 2009, p. 156).

For high-functioning children, language is often developed early and it can be idiosyncratic in content, volume, and tone. Some children by the age of 4 are like "little professors." They have a pedantic tone to their speech and they "lecture" to all who will listen. They adhere to a rigid and restricted topic of conversation, never inviting rejoinders. Others may exhibit speech patterns that are flat or prosaic. By the age of 4 years many high-functioning children on the spectrum will be exhibiting oddities in prosody. Stresses on particular words of a sentence will be connected to the importance the child attaches to words or to word phrases as he or she understands them. Stresses on minor syllables in a word rather than on the major ones may be tied to a deficit in the awareness of how others hear the word being spoken, as suggested by findings connected to Theory of Mind (Baron-Cohen, 2001). From the information provided earlier, it becomes apparent that early language differences combine with processing differences as well as social-emotional comprehension deficits to lay the foundation for the lack of skill development in the pragmatic language of the high-functioning autistic child.

Another factor of consideration is that from **ages 4 to 6** the preschooler is increasingly exposed to the social world of peers. Communication skills among these children will vary with maturation and development. Gender differences in language development tend to blur dramatic distinctions in language production. Despite any lingering difficulties with speech and language acquisition, the child in this stage is exploring his or her social world and using language skills to master the give-and-take of peer interactions.

During this time period, social differences are being noted by parents/guardians and may come to the attention of teachers and health care professionals as well. Social language skills may not be where they should be, and speech and language therapy may be offered. Practicing conversational rules and social exchanges within the structure of small group settings may be offered through the school or community. Any information you can gather around how well these interventions were received by the child will help you to have a clearer idea of how well the child was able to adapt and use language tools effectively.

From the years **6 to 12**, the use of pragmatic language skills is crucial to the child's social, emotional, and cognitive well-being. It is during this time that the challenges associated with the demands of social language begin to impact all aspects of functioning. In *The Hidden Curriculum*, the authors describe the hidden curriculum as "the set of rules or guidelines that are often not directly taught but are assumed to be known." This includes understanding the subtleties of language present in metaphor, sarcasm, or jargon and it involves being able to "read" body language (Myles, Trautman, & Schelvan, 2004, p. 5). The authors point out that deficits in pragmatic language cause problems across school, home, and community domains.

Many language problems present in this stage of development are the same language problems carried over from previous stages. They are problems related to the inability to take another person's perspective and to the tendency to take a strict literal interpretation of anything said. Without the explicit learning of what to say and how to say it, children on the spectrum tend to be brutally honest in their responses to others. When asked by her aunt whether her (the aunt's) hair looked all right, one 10-year-old girl said, "I don't know. I can never tell if you combed it or not." Such frankness can be humorous to those who know and love these children. Yet it can be devastating to a relationship with someone unfamiliar with the characteristics of the diagnosis.

To enhance the development of awareness of others and of oneself as seen by others, Michelle Garcia Winner has developed an entire curriculum around the teaching of social skills (Garcia Winner & Crooke, 2004). Her Superflex curriculum is based on fun and literal figures that represent the concrete areas of need for the child to develop social awareness in thinking and communicating (Madrigal & Winner, 2008). Elsa Abele (2012) has developed a conversational hierarchy that teaches discrete skills necessary to conversing with peers. In her group-focused approach, Abele leads the child on the spectrum step by step through the pragmatics of language acquisition, teaching the child how to attend to context as well as content and to nonverbal as well as verbal cues of a listener. It would be to your advantage as the therapist to explore these interventions and familiarize yourself with them. You may find some of these techniques useful in your therapy.

Fortunately for the parents of children in the school-age bracket, programs like these are available for the support and development of social language skills. Unfortunately, not all school districts have personnel trained in the area of pragmatics. As the therapist you will want to know as much as you can about your client's language skills and the kinds of interventions he or she may have experienced. You will find that is in the area of social language development that your advice will be needed. Parents will look to you for finding ways to help their child acquire pragmatic skills that will increase the child's opportunities for social interactions with peers.

Once a typically developing child has reached adolescence (12–18 years), the basic accomplishments of the language acquisition process are well established. The task now is to use and understand the more sophisticated aspects of language. The typical adolescent understands varied uses of language subtleties and nonverbal language. He or she uses language to express abstract and sophisticated thoughts. Through the use of language, the adolescent's interests and experiences of the social world are broadened and enjoyed.

While the high-functioning ASD teenager has mastered grammar and syntax and has acquired an average to above-average vocabulary, he or she has not achieved the pragmatics of language functioning. It is that the *context* of language learning has not developed in these youngsters. Elsa Abele (2012) points out that the development of pragmatic language does not occur spontaneously with children on the spectrum. Instead, pragmatic language skills require explicit instruction.

Well into adolescence, and even into adulthood for some, rules of conversation that govern the speaker–listener relationship are not recognized, and monopolization of conversational topics continues to be a social language problem. The ASD adolescent is socially isolated due to his or her tendency to perseverate on a narrow/unusual topic of interest; to interpret questions literally; and to fail to appreciate humor, sarcasm, inference, and nonverbal expression.

To achieve social-emotional success as a teenager, one has to have the ability to identify with a group. In doing so, one has to engage in the language of the group and to share their topics of interest. The ASD teenager is unaware of the unwritten rules that govern adolescent groups and has not broken away from his or her idiosyncratic conversational style. His or her tendency is to focus solely on a preferred topic of interest while failing to recognize that others are not interested.

In a wonderful display of generalizing learning from the classroom to another situation (a learning trait you will find to be lacking in the ASD child), one 13-year-old girl on the spectrum was able to recognize the effects of having a singular interest that excluded the other person. It was the end of a testing session when the examiner began to engage in "self-talk" as she started checking off her list of testing protocols. The student said, "Sounds like One-Sided Sid is with us now." One-Sided-Sid is a Superflex cartoon character from the Social Thinking Curriculum who talks only about what is of interest to him to the exclusion of all others (Madrigal & Winner, 2008).

The concrete and literal interpretations of everyday language expressions can be surprising and even humorous. One mother reported that when she and her son finally got home after a very stressful day, she exclaimed, "Whew! This has been a very long day!" Her teenage son then replied, "Every day is exactly 24 hours. I don't think one can be longer than another, Mom."

Interpreting questions literally can also be troublesome for the teen. An older adolescent was driving and got stopped by a policeman for speeding. When he was pulled over, the policeman first asked whether he could see the young man's license. The ASD teen answered the question by saying, "No. You can't." (The boy thought it was a stupid question. How could he "see" it? It was tucked away in his wallet and not in plain view.) The irritated policeman, after finally getting the license, asked the driver whether he had been drinking. Now, having a diagnosis of Asperger syndrome and being one of those "Aspies" (a term preferred by some) who are rule bound, he responded, "Of course not, I am not 21." In his rule-governed autistic world, drinking before 21 is not allowed and he could not understand why he would even be asked that question. As a result, the young man was given a hefty fine for a minor speeding violation.

Later in this book, we will be talking more about the pros and cons of the concrete and literal interpretations that individuals on the spectrum exhibit. But for now, it is most important that you as the therapist are acutely aware that this lack of social language functioning and understanding of contextual language applications is a major source of increasing anxiety over the life span of the ASD individual. This anxiety can become a major obstacle for future success. Chapter 9 of this book will examine this issue further and help you to understand how developmental issues of childhood and adolescence across all domains are uniquely connected to the future for the person on the spectrum.

CHAPTER 3

Interviewing the Parents/Guardians

So FAR WE have outlined the basic characteristics of ASD and pointed out the developmental differences between children and adolescents diagnosed as being high functioning on the autism spectrum and those who are neurotypical. From Chapter 2, you should have a clear sense of just how different these children are and how these differences impact on family functioning. Your phone interview (as explained in Chapter 1) with one or both of the parents/guardians is key to understanding just what areas are most troublesome in their family life. Remember, this is a relatively new diagnosis and much needs to be learned about the many facets of this disability. Most important, keep in mind that each child is unique in his or her presentation of those diagnostic features that brought him or her to a clinician's attention.

In this chapter we will talk about your first meeting with the parents/guardians. We recommend that you mail a copy of the Family Profile Form (see Appendix C) and request that it be returned for your review prior to scheduling that first meeting. While some referrals will not result in a first meeting, others will. This chapter is largely based on the assumption that you have reached a decision to conduct a first interview. Once the form is returned, you may find that the form is incomplete or that some areas may be overemphasized, replete with unnecessary personal details. These are all important aspects to highlight as you read through the form and formulate your initial picture of this client and the family.

Questions not completed may indicate confusion on the part of the parents/guardians. There may be a lack of understanding in how to answer certain questions and/or they may perceive the information you are seeking to be irrelevant or too personal. In this case, a phone call may be warranted to gather more information before making any final decisions about moving forward with this family. Be prepared to probe sensitively for additional information, as you cannot predetermine the reasons for any omissions. Often these families are in crisis mode and parents/guardians may be feeling particularly vulnerable and cautious about sharing personal information.

When the opposite is true and too much information is given on the Family Profile Form, other factors need to be considered. There may be a current crisis related to the ASD child or another family member. Or this may be indicative of a tendency to disclose too much too soon. In cases like this, individuals may not follow through with treatment out of embarrassment connected to having provided too many details.

Understanding this possibility will be important as you initially gather information. Probing too deeply too soon may interfere with building the therapeutic trust needed to develop the client–therapist relationship. Parents/guardians of children on the spectrum have often learned through experience that others are judging them. They have been viewed as being too overprotective, too controlling, or lacking in parenting skills. They report often regretting disclosure and, as a result, new relationships are not easily formed or trusted.

Another possibility is that the parent/guardian filling out the form may also have characteristics of ASD. This may appear in an overemphasis of one particular aspect of the child's behavior. Or the parent might demonstrate rigidity in dealing with the child's unexpected actions. In some cases a parent who shows ASD characteristics may express them through an inability to perceive situations from another's point of view. This is not to say that the parent shares the diagnosis, although he or she may. It could also be that the parent/guardian has developed a certain rigidity of thinking as a way to adapt to the demands of parenting the ASD child. If you detect certain features in one of the caregivers that lead you to think there is something unusual about their presentation, make note of this for future reference. Differences in the way a form is filled out or in the manner in which the parents/guardians initially present may be important to determining "goodness of fit" and also to treatment down the road.

At this point in time, you could still be determining if there *will* be "treatment down the road." While you may need the actual face-to-face interview to make this decision, there will be times when the information you have compiled to this point is enough to support the decision against treatment. As a reminder to what was discussed in Chapter 1, you may feel that this case is too complicated or too uncomfortable. Or, because you are new to this disability, you may feel it is beyond your level of expertise. In these instances, remember that referring someone to another therapist should be done with particular sensitivity. As stated earlier, the parents/guardians' experiences have often been such as to make them feel vulnerable to (perceived) rejection.

Now that we have talked about the way that the Family Profile Form has been completed, let's look at each section and determine how to proceed using the form to guide you through your first interview. With the case examples and research provided throughout this chapter, you will be better prepared to move through the interview process. While the parents/guardians may have an intense need to be heard and validated, remember that you have a lot of ground to cover in a limited amount of time. The process will flow more efficiently if you set a structured timeline and adhere to it.

The first section of the Family Profile Form represented below addresses basic information.

FAMILY PROFILE FORM

I. GENERAL INFORMATION

Name of Child:_____

Name of Parent(s)/Guardian(s):_____

Child is yours by: birth ___ adoption ___ stepchild ___ other _____

Parent(s)/Guardian(s) are: married ___ unmarried ___ divorced ___ other _____

Child lives with:_____

This information is important because you will need to know whether there are other caregivers involved in the child's life. If the child has been adopted or has a unique family situation, such as a child who resides with grandparents or other relatives, you will need to know that information at this time. Later, in the last section of this form, you will be able to explore how the family constellation impacts on the everyday life of the family. For instance, a child of divorced parents may be in a shared custody arrangement that creates two different living environments. If so, this will need to be taken into consideration over the course of therapy. Different living environments mean different expectations, different routines, and more frequent transitions, all of which are particularly difficult for a child with this disability.

Section II of the form involves determining the source of this referral, the reasons for it, and how behaviors have been dealt with thus far.

II. REFERRAL INFORMATION

Referral source:_____

Reason for referral: _____

Behavioral concerns: From the list below, please indicate those behaviors you find most concerning.

Area of Concern	Level of Concern		
	Mild	Moderate	High
Difficulty with peer relations			
Monopolizes conversations			
Difficulty reading facial expressions			
Unusual interest in a singular topic			
High reliance on set routines			
Unusual mannerisms or movements			

Appears stubborn/unwilling to compromise			
Unusual or a lack of hygiene practices			
History of wandering			
Other odd or unexpected behaviors			

Approaches to troublesome behaviors: From the list below, please check off techniques most often used when dealing with your child's troublesome behaviors. Indicate the caregiver who uses them.

Approach	Caregiver 1	Caregiver 2
Distracting from the problem		
Diffusing the situation		
Talking things through		
Time-out		
Removing privileges		
Spanking		
Other form of physical touch		
Stressing the consequences		

Not every child will have a professional referral source. Some may be referred by insurance or by another client. Unfortunately, when this happens, you will have to work a little harder to get all of the background information you need. When the referral source is an agency, such as the school or a pediatrician, you will need to have the parent/guardian fill out a release of information form, giving you permission to consult. We recommend that you have a consent form ready to be signed at this point in the interview process. In addition to the specific referral source, if any, the parents/guardians may mention other providers who could also be good sources of pertinent information.

Be aware that asking to consult with other professionals may trigger questions or concerns on the part of the parents/guardians regarding the content of the consultation. These parents may well have experienced difficulties with previous professional relationships, leading them to feel a need to be overly protective of personal information. If you detect some concern here, the situation may warrant probing for further information, or it could be better to leave this discussion for another time.

The Behavioral Concerns section addresses the unique distribution of features for this child and those areas that have prompted the parents/guardians to seek treatment. In this section you will note that the parents/guardians have been asked to rate their level of concern in areas that are most typically affected in this population. For some, it is the lack of socialization that will be highlighted, and for others it will be the difficulty of living with a child who is rigid and perseverative. Still others will be most concerned with the oddity of their child's presentation. Regardless of what constellation of characteristics is reported as most troublesome, this section is going to be particularly difficult for the parents/guardians to discuss. In our experience, there is often embarrassment and shame associated with disclosing the particulars of their child's disability. The caregivers may even feel guilty or inadequate around events that, unbeknownst to them, are disability related. For example, wandering and elopement in the ASD population has been an area of study recently documented by the National Autism Association. They quote harsh statistics and serious concerns regarding the safety of these children (McIlwain & Fournier, 2012). As detailed in Chapter 2, many of the characteristics of this disability have a more "public face" and are obvious to others. The end result is often social rejection. By association, the family also experiences this harsh judgment from others.

At other times, the parents/guardians have experienced the attempts of others to normalize their child's unusual behaviors or to attribute them to a typical development stage. While this may be well intentioned and thought to be either kind or helpful, it has an opposite effect on the parents/guardians. Remember that it is difficult enough for the parents/guardians to acknowledge these behaviors. We have been told by numerous parents that they do not need or want to have their child's eccentricities dismissed or minimized. For you to unintentionally do that would be countertherapeutic to the process. It will be helpful for you to periodically review the information in Chapter 2 in order to familiarize yourself with the contrast between neurotypical children and those on the autism spectrum.

In looking at the section describing approaches to troublesome behaviors, you will be better able to understand differences in parents/guardians' approaches to the child's concerning behaviors. This will give you insight into parenting styles and disciplinary practices in the home. For a child on the spectrum, consistency in these areas is crucial for optimal developmental growth and emotional stability. Parents/guardians who differ sharply in their disciplinary practices create and intensify anxiety for the child. As we have said before, anxiety is a key factor in contributing to the difficult behaviors that these children exhibit. When predictability and consistency are absent, anxiety increases in ASD children. In this disability there is a sense of bewilderment and resulting confusion around ordinary expectations and social interactions.

Spectrum children who "misbehave" do not always recognize that they are violating a social norm or otherwise acting in ways that others will perceive as inappropriate. You will be working with the caregivers to understand that not all of their child's unexpected behaviors will be rooted in "naughtiness." Most will be due to a lack of awareness of what is expected in a given situation. For example, one young mother reported that her 5-year-old son had developed a habit of urinating on the fence in their backyard. The behavior continued despite having been told to stop and being given a time-out. Being a child on the spectrum, he was unable to see a direct connection between a behavior (urinating on the fence) and a consequence (a time-out sitting by himself) that was seemingly unrelated. It was not until his mother came up with a consequence that was more connected to the action that the behavior changed. Instead of a time-out, the child was required to come into the house hourly (upon being called) and try to use the bathroom. It was explained to him that he needed to only use the bathroom in the house. Because he was missing playtime by coming in the house hourly, he was then able to see the direct connection between the consequence and the behavior.

In your future course of treatment of ASD children, you will need to evaluate parenting practices. It is recommended that you elicit as many examples of behavioral concern and conflict as possible. This will allow you to tie them to more effective and consistent disciplinary practices as you guide the parents/guardians. As you do this, you may want to develop a treatment goal around formulating more effective approaches to dealing with troublesome behaviors. Teaching parents to think from their child's unique perspective enables them to provide a more meaningful consequence so that the child is able to learn from the experience. It should also lessen conflict within the family unit when consequences are clear, consistent, and connected.

In the next section of the Family Profile Form, you have requested a list of diagnoses given by skilled professionals and a history of testing evaluations performed. Ideally, you will be provided with copies of these reports for your review as soon as possible.

III. DIAGNOSTIC INFORMATION

CHILD'S DIAGNOSES:

Diagnosis:	
Diagnosed by:	
Date of diagnosis:	

Diagnosis:	
Diagnosed by:	
Date of diagnosis:	

Diagnosis:	
Diagnosed by:	
Date of diagnosis:	

TESTING COMPLETED:

Type (school/other):	
Date:	
Examiner:	

Type (school/other):	
Date:	
Examiner:	

Type (school/other):	
Date:	
Examiner:	

You should not be surprised to see a number of previous diagnoses listed, as it is common for high-functioning children on the spectrum to have been misdiagnosed and/or to have comorbid diagnoses. In terms of comorbidity, the *Handbook of Autism and Pervasive Developmental Disorders* states that anxiety and depression are most often diagnosed as being secondary to ASD. In addition, Tourette syndrome, OCD, and bipolar disorder are also associated with the autism diagnosis (Klin, McPartland, & Volkmar, 2005).

If multiple diagnoses are not listed, we recommend that you probe for additional information about the child's history. This may tell you that a circuitous route was taken before getting to the diagnosis, and it will help you understand the family's journey thus far. High-functioning spectrum children are often not originally recognized as meeting the ASD criteria. There may well be a history fraught with failure and frustration as the parents have tried to pinpoint the exact nature of their child's disability. For this very reason, parents/guardians may be cautious in the way they present themselves to you. You will most likely need to develop the therapeutic relationship slowly.

Another area to explore as you discuss the child's diagnostic history is how, when, and *if* the diagnosis of the identified client was shared with the child. If so, you need to know the level of his or her understanding and acceptance. It is common with this diagnosis for parents/guardians to have difficulty explaining what ASD means to *their* child. They often need time to understand it themselves before addressing it.

In one instance, a young teenage girl had just been diagnosed with Asperger disorder and a speech and language therapist at school told her that she had autism before her parents had chosen to speak to her about it. Without having had a proper disclosure from her parents, acceptance of the diagnosis then became a major treatment goal for her in therapy. Be aware that understanding and acceptance of ASD in the affected child are likely to be a treatment goal, regardless of whether it has been initially communicated appropriately by the parents/guardians.

Reviewing the testing history completed by private clinicians or by the school will give you some insight as to how the child's diagnoses have been determined. Ideally, you will have had the opportunity to request testing reports for review prior to the first interview. As you examine these evaluations, first note the form of testing done as well as the instruments administered. If the testing is a neuropsychological battery, you can expect to find measures of executive functioning, information processing, memory, attention, and tests of perception. Most neuropsychological assessments will also include a section describing social-emotional functioning. Some will include behavioral measures in the form of checklists or observations, and others may be more projective in nature. Expect to find reference to levels of anxiety and depression, as these are often observed characteristics for children on the spectrum.

There are times when the child's profile will have fit the criteria for a specific learning disability. Having this diagnosis in a school can mean that the diagnostic exploration stopped there and no further attention nor intervention was given to the child's ASD characteristics. Be aware that in many states school psychologists are unable to make diagnoses beyond standard learning disabilities. Our point is that despite long-standing social failures and unusual behaviors, high-functioning ASD children can go years without an accurate diagnosis.

For this reason, you should look for tests of social perception as well as pragmatic language skills in the reports you are reviewing. If this has not been an area of investigation, it is likely that the ASD diagnosis was not being considered at the time of testing. As mentioned earlier, the route to the diagnosis is often frustrating for the family and is a major factor in exacerbating the child's anxiety. This is due to the misunderstandings and confusion that arise when multiple diagnoses have been considered. Therefore, in addition to paying particular attention to the testing measures themselves, make note of all diagnoses within the reports and the chronological order in which they have been given.

While up to this point our focus has been on the diagnostic features of testing, the tests themselves can never be the sole source of diagnosis. They provide important informational pieces that contribute to the complex and unique profile of each child. Historical and anecdotal information complete the picture. Knowing how the child perceives the world and how the world perceives the child are crucial to determining the goals of treatment.

In the Background section of this form, you are requesting information to understand the family constellation. Family dynamics are influential on parenting practices. Demographic information will be important to treatment planning, particularly as you involve family members over the course of time.

IV. BACKGROUND

Mother (or Guardian)

Name: _____

Street Address:_____

City/State/Zip: _____

Home/Cell Phone: _____

Work Phone _____

Race/Ethnicity _____

Date of Birth _____

Level of Education:_____

Occupation: _____

Employer: _____

Father (or Guardian)

Name: _____

Street Address:_____

City/State/Zip: _____

Home/Cell Phone: _____

Work Phone _____

Race/Ethnicity _____

Date of Birth _____

Level of Education:_____

Occupation: _____

Employer: _____

Members of Household:

Name: _____ Age: ____ Sex: ___ Relationship: _____

Name: _____ Age: ____ Sex: ___ Relationship: _____

Name: _____ Age: ____ Sex: ___ Relationship: _____

Name: _____ Age: ____ Sex: ___ Relationship: _____

Age, education, and cultural affiliations are factors in the comprehension and acceptance of the child's diagnosis and all that that entails. For some, it may affect parent/guardian willingness to participate in treatment and/or it may determine the parameters of treatment. As stated in Chapter 2, there are important cross-cultural differences that exist in the many views of the developing child. Perceptions of autistic behaviors vary within the context of what is expected and what is not at a given stage of child development in each country. In a multinational study examining cross-cultural differences in children ages 2 to 16 years, the researchers found that while there is a universal consistency in the diagnostic criteria defining ASD, and in the manifestation of behaviors associated with it, there are significant cultural differences in how ASD symptoms are reported (Matson et al., 2011).

The typicality of age-related behaviors determines what is socially acceptable and can vary across cultures. For this reason, it is important for you to learn as much as you can about a particular culture when treating a child with cultural differences. One source you may want to consult is Dr. Fred Volkmar's comprehensive article published in the *Handbook of Autism and Pervasive Developmental Disorders* (2005).

V. MEDICAL HISTORY (FAMILY)
(*Family information is requested but optional.*)

From the list below, please check those areas that apply.

Issue/Disability	Mother (or Guardian)	Father (or Guardian)	Sibling(s)
Severe headaches			
Seizures			
Other chronic pain			
Anxiety			
Depression			
Attention problems			

Other emotional diagnoses/issues			
Drug/alcohol dependence			

List current medications of parents/guardians.

_____   _____   _____

List previous hospitalizations of parents/guardians.

_____   _____   _____

_____   _____   _____

List present and previous counseling experiences. Please include dates of treatment and the names of the providers.

	Parent/Guardian	**Parent/Guardian**
Therapist	_____	_____
Dates	_____	_____

It may be necessary to clarify the reasons for requesting the family medical history. Its relevance may not be apparent to the parents/guardians and may trigger apprehension around the idea of sharing personal information. If this is an issue raised by them, you will need to address this and convey your understanding and respect for their concerns. While it would be helpful to have this information to better understand the family, this section is marked as optional on the Family Profile Form.

If you have obtained this information, you will find it useful in a number of ways. Understanding the physical, emotional, and behavioral health issues of family members contributes to your knowledge of other factors that affect family dynamics. It also provides you with an opportunity to explore how the family has addressed counseling issues, with whom, and for how long. If one of the siblings is in therapy, it is now that you might want to consider broaching the idea that future collaboration with that child's therapist may be beneficial to treatment.

It will be helpful to know whether there is another child or family member who carries an ASD diagnosis. According to the National Institute of Mental Health (NIMH), studies have shown that there may be some genetic link to the prevalence of ASD in families. This link may be more pronounced in families where more than one child carries this diagnosis (Lichtenstein, Carlstrom, Rastam, Gillberg, & Anckarsater, 2010). There is also evidence to support an environmental factor, which means that ASD may be inherited or environmentally triggered (Insel, 2012). Either way, it is important for you to know that there is some likelihood that one or more family members of the identified client may be exhibiting some ASD characteristics or carrying the diagnosis. This will enhance your awareness of family dynamics and the personalities within the family constellation. We caution that if there are additional ASD diagnoses of family members, this is not the time to discuss them.

The child's medical history section of the Family Profile Form is particularly important and will be reviewed next. The reason that you will need a full understanding of the child's medical history is, in part, to explore the possibility of diagnostic differences. There may not be agreement among the medical providers due to a lack of understanding of the ASD diagnosis. Or there may be a tendency for the pediatrician or other treaters to normalize the child's unusual behaviors. In our experience, parents have often been frustrated by the conflicting feedback that has been given to them. Sometimes these differing professional views prolong their full acceptance of the diagnosis.

VI. MEDICAL HISTORY (CHILD)

Health-related diagnoses/concerns: List significant non–mental health issues.

_____   _____   _____

_____   _____   _____

Last Annual Physical Exam:

Provider:	
Date:	
Results/Concerns:	

Last Dental Exam:

Provider:	
Date:	
Results/Concerns:	

Current Medications: List prescription and/or over-the-counter medications with dosages.

_____   _____   _____

_____   _____   _____

Allergies:

Type of Allergy		
Severity		
Reactions/Symptoms		

Type of Allergy		
Severity		
Reactions/Symptoms		

Does your child have a history of illegal drug use?

Drug Type	Dates of Use	How Often	Amount Used

Does your child have a history of medical and/or psychiatric hospitalizations?

Date of Hospitalization	Where	Why

History of counseling or other treatment:

Name of Therapist	Setting	Dates	Reason for Treatment

Being aware of health-related diagnoses and concerns allows you to open up a conversation about medical care. You may detect connections between health concerns and the child's ASD diagnosis. For instance, compromised breathing related to an asthma attack may exacerbate anxiety levels in the ASD child. Our point here is to remind you to fully explore any medical concerns, how they affect the child, and how they are handled by the parents/guardians.

You should also carefully seek information related to appointments scheduled with pediatricians and dentists. Resistance to obtaining routine care may be attributed to a lack of parental organization *or* it may be due to the child's refusal to comply. If the latter is true, do not be quick to believe that there is a weakness in parenting skills. With the child on the spectrum, noncompliance with typical expectations may be more about an inability to tolerate the anxiety created by the sensory and environmental demands of an office visit.

Consider this: One little guy, fondly referred to as "Metaphor Man" (so called because his preferred mode of communication in therapy was to use metaphorical examples of his own experiences), related the happenings of his dental visit this way.

The Pillsbury Doughboy had a terrible experience this week. He went to the DENTIST! When he got there, the dentist trapped him in a chair and had three people hold him down while the dentist shoved his hands down the Pillsbury Doughboy's throat. Then, he poured awful white stuff in his mouth. The Doughboy screamed for help, but nobody came. Mr. and Mrs. Butterworth just sat in the office outside.

As it turns out, this little boy had to have a dental mold made to prevent tooth-grinding in his sleep. His well-meaning parents had no idea what the procedure involved or how their son would perceive it. This type of experience is common to the families of ASD children and makes routine health care appointments difficult to endure.

As you review the information in the Family Profile Form, you are continually defining priorities and targeting treatment goals in collaboration with the parents/guardians. For this boy, dental care was a goal to be addressed. It required the involvement of an occupational therapist to address his sensory needs.

You will notice that in this section there are questions about illegal drug or alcohol use and psychiatric hospitalization. Drug use is of particular concern in dealing with the ASD population because often times the reasons for using or not using illegal substances involve a complicated thought process routed in rigid perceptions. For example, one set of parents believed themselves to be "home free" in this one area due to their son's rigid adherence to rules. He believed that drinking prior to the legal age was not an option. However, upon turning 21 he adopted a view that drinking was part of a mandatory passage into adulthood. Immediately after turning 21, he drank to the point of blacking out. He felt that his behaviors were his own personal business and were age appropriate. With individuals on the autism spectrum, even the positive nature of following rules can be distorted through a narrow perception of what is developmentally appropriate for their age.

Underage drug/alcohol use is always a concern with teenage clients, but the concern is exacerbated by the atypical interpretations often made by the ASD client. As in the previous example, rigid thinking may lead to unexpected outcomes. Consider this example: A 13-year-old was found with prescription drugs, a jar of vodka, and a package of cigarettes in his backpack. It was not that he had any intention of using them, but he believed that to be "cool" as a teenager he had to have possession of them. This boy's narrow focus prevented him from predicting further consequences of his actions. His behaviors could have had serious consequences, but his mother intercepted his backpack and removed the materials. Typical of the rigid thinking associated with ASD, this young man focused only on one possible outcome to his behavior: acceptance into the teenage world. He never considered that his behavior could have led to suspension from school or to an arrest for illegal possession of drugs and alcohol.

Now let's turn our attention to the history of psychiatric hospitalizations. You will need to confirm with the parents/guardians that your information is complete in this area. Due to the sensitivity surrounding the trauma and stigma of having a child psychiatrically hospitalized, all details may not initially be shared by the parents/guardians. Do not assume that any particular psychiatric history indicates a pattern of risk in the traditional sense. We are not minimizing the significance of a history of hospitalizations. What we are saying is that with these clients, risk factors take on new meanings and are tied closely to the autistic features of the individual. Sometimes crises can arise suddenly and pass just as quickly. The precipitants to hospitalizations for ASD children are often different than what you might expect. For these reasons, it will be important to clarify the details of circumstances surrounding hospitalizations. Knowing the age and developmental levels of the child's functioning at the time they occurred will further enhance your understanding of the child's history.

It is often cited in the literature that early developmental problems are linked to an ASD diagnosis. By looking at the developmental milestones outlined by psychologist Robert J. Havighurst (1971), you can more easily focus on those tasks known to be linked to early signs of autism.

VII. DEVELOPMENTAL HISTORY

When did your child meet the following developmental milestones?

Ages 0–6 years:	Early	On Time	Late
Crawling			
Walking			
Eating solid foods			
Toileting			
Talking			
Appreciating sex differences			
Learning sexual modesty			

What, if anything, was different about the way your child accomplished any of these tasks? For example, walking on toes or skipping the crawling stage.

_____

_____

_____

Ages 6–12 years:	Early	On Time	Late
Developing skills for playing games			
Getting along with age-mates			
Demonstrate a consistent understanding of gender roles			
Making friends			
Participating appropriately in social situations			
Developing a sense of right and wrong			
Acquiring independent daily living skills			

What, if anything was different about the way your child accomplished any of these tasks ? For example, playing according to very specific rules or having meltdowns when having to share toys or games.

_____

_____

Ages 12–18 years:	Early	On Time	Late
Engaging in more mature social relationships			
Engaging in romantic interests			
Achieving emotional independence from parents/other adults			

Demonstrating concern for another's well-being			
Showing interest in occupational choices			
Managing home and school responsibilities independently			
Accessing the community independently			

What, if anything was different about the way your child accomplished any of these tasks? For example, refusing to ride a train or bus, etc.

_____

_____

In this section you will be looking for developmental patterns of behavior over time. You will want to explore these patterns with parents/guardians and look for connections across behaviors. For example, the emergence of anxiety is apparent in the following situation. One young man has been continuously plagued by debilitating anxiety. It was present, but not recognized, in his earliest years. Despite exhibiting healthy eating choices, one little boy had to have his food served in separate bowls to ensure that the foods would not touch. When he "graduated" to using one dish with dividers for separating the foods, his anxiety increased. If the foods mixed in any way, he would refuse to eat it. In hindsight, his anxiety was greatly apparent as he cried inconsolably when these rigid practices were not followed.

The _quality_ of developmental accomplishments may be influenced by anxiety or by other issues, including sensory sensitivities. For example, a child who previously reacted negatively to crawling on certain textures or to eating particular foods may now be showing these same sensory issues in a different way. Knowing these details gives you an opportunity to make behavioral connections between the child's past and present that the parents/guardians may not have recognized. For instance, one young teen dresses oddly, wearing only soft textures with labels and seams exposed. This helps him to avoid sensory irritants. As a young child, this same teenager could not tolerate clothing and was allowed to roam the house in his underwear.

As another example, one child could only wear sandals. He even insisted on wearing them through winter snow. Still another child insisted on wearing the same shirt for picture day at school each year. While he was able to do this for the second year before completely outgrowing the shirt, his insistence carried over year after year. It became yet another area of perseveration leading to increased anxiety in this young boy.

Variations of these examples are plentiful, so you should be prepared to find that many unexpected needs can predominate over common sense for the ASD child/adolescent. Understanding how development has unfolded is an important issue and necessary for gaining insight into individual patterns of behavior over time. Making these behavioral connections with the parents/guardians is also important, but it is a sensitive topic. Such idiosyncrasies can be amusing to others, but for the caregivers these memories may feel too uncomfortable and discouraging to be taken light-heartedly.

On this section of the Family Profile Form, shown above, pay particular attention to the area outlining ages 6 through 12. It is here where the social communicative demands of childhood begin to increase dramatically. Without mastery of these skills, the next stage of development becomes nearly impossible. It is in the later elementary/early middle school years where the difficulties with navigating the pressures of peer interactions and academic expectations become more obvious, and failures in these areas more frustrating.

If you are seeing an older child, the issues related to the achievement of developmental tasks are more complicated. This youngster is at greater risk, as the expectations have risen and the gaps have widened. Behaviors perceived as immature and childish will now be less tolerable to those who expect more age-appropriate actions. For the child who is intellectually average or above, the disability itself may not be recognized as the source of unexpected social interactions. Motives may be questioned and intentionality of behaviors may be misjudged by family and others. Malice may be suspected where none is intended. For example, one young teenage boy was continually disciplined for asking sexually explicit questions during health class. Although the questions were on topic and were triggered by the material presented, the language he chose to use and the loud volume of his voice were viewed as bordering on sexual harassment in the classroom. And yet both his language usage and his problem with volume control were intricately related to his ASD diagnosis. In this case, the psychologist working with him understood the problem and was able to revise his educational plan to include private tutorials for health class. In this setting, they focused on key concepts without overstimulating the student's curiosity and increasing his anxiety. Collaboration with the school's speech and language therapist was also required in this instance as a way to incorporate interventions stressing the pragmatic and social uses of language.

VIII. SOCIAL/COMMUNICATIVE/BEHAVIORAL DEVELOPMENT

Now is the time for you to bring together the pieces of information accrued so far and focus on those features that most clearly define the child. Remembering that ASD has many faces, the unique profile you will develop through this section should reflect most of the major concerns and issues to be targeted for your treatment plan. Here you will again see how these characteristics are experienced by the family and by others in contact with the child on a regular basis. Some of the questions in this section are similar to those asked in section II. This has been done intentionally and will provide you with more detailed material around those areas noted to be of concern to the family.

The first portion of this section (replicated below) includes statements similar to diagnostic checklists commonly used to support the ASD diagnosis (Gilliam, 2006; Myles, Jones-Bock, & Simpson, 2001). This information will give you an overview of the predominant characteristics and features of your ASD client. Combining the information below will be useful in formulating the treatment plan.

	Observed	Not observed
Speaks in a studious or pedantic manner		
Repeats words or certain expressions		
Perseverates on a single topic without listener interest		
Has difficulty understanding subtle jokes/humor		

Has distinctive voice patterns		
Seems to expect special treatment		
Shows decreased eye contact		
Displays limited/unexpected facial expressions		
Has difficulty with transitions		
Limited ability to empathize with others		
Unintentionally invades personal space		
Has difficulty maintaining peer relationships		
Adheres to set routines or rituals		
Strongly resists unexpected changes		
Displays emotional volitility when routines are altered		
Reacts to textures, noise levels, or smells		
Flinches when touched or hugged		
Has "meltdowns" when expectations are not met		
Has difficulty with written assignments		
Opposes learning information deemed irrelevant		
Difficulty organizing tasks		
Precisely organizes environment		
Seems to lack good sense		
Engages in rocking behaviors		
Engages in spinning, hand-flicking, or twirling motions		
Flaps hands when becoming anxious or frustrated		

The next portion of this section (replicated below) requests further social/communicative information. This will indicate how specific information about the child's functioning is tied to concerns for the ASD child and his or her family.

These questions are based on the child's experiences in and outside of school. They will help you to focus on the ways that disability-related behaviors could be causing significant problems for the ASD child now or in the near future.

Further Social/Communicative Information:

	Observed	Not observed
Has been a victim of bullying outside of school		

If observed, where and when:_____

	Observed	Not observed
Preoccupation with one particular subject or interest		

If observed, list topics: _____

	Observed	Not observed
Appears to have a tendency toward social withdrawal		
Appears to lack interest in other people and their interests		
Appears to lack initiative for engaging in activities with others		
Often does not pick up on nonverbal cues (i.e., body language)		
Difficulty with taking turns talking		
Often verbalizes his/her own internal thoughts (self-talk)		
Has a history of echolalia (the repetition of phrases and words)		

School-Related Information:

Has your child been a victim of bullying in school? If so, please explain.

_____

	Yes	No	Sometimes
Participates in nonacademic school activities			

Explain:_____

	Yes	No	Sometimes
Engages socially with at least one schoolmate			

Explain:_____

	Yes	No	Sometimes
Adheres to school rules and regulations			

Explain:_____

	Yes	No	Sometimes
Receives special accommodations to his/her academic program			

Explain:_____

	Yes	No	Sometimes
Demonstrates grade-level achievements in major subject areas			

Explain:_____

Especially important are those questions asking about bullying both in and out of school. According to studies in Tony Attwood's book, *The Complete Guide to Asperger's Syndrome* (2012), children with a diagnosis of Asperger syndrome were found to be at least four times more likely to be bullied than their typical peers. Some studies point to the specific characteristics of the child on the spectrum as being triggers for various aspects of bullying. They may be targeted for being odd or perceived as weak and friendless. Alternatively, they may be perceived as pedantic, arrogant, or rude. These behaviors can make them a target for bullying or being perceived as a perpetrator of bullying. It might surprise you to find that the bullying label has been attributed to the child you are considering treating. Further investigation may reveal that what looked like bullying behaviors in your client was really a manifestation of symptoms related to ASD. A lack of impulse control, perseverative thoughts, a lack of social awareness, or a response to felt anxiety could all look like bullying behaviors. You will need to strike a fine balance in supporting the parents in understanding their child's disability-related behaviors and how they are perceived to be inappropriate by others. This becomes a crucial issue for families during the adolescent years and will be addressed further in Chapter 9.

Additional school-related information is requested in this section in order to assist with your formulation of a comprehensive profile of the child. Behaviors noted in this area will be reflected in some of the ASD child's school experiences. Communication and socialization are central to the school environment. How the school supports the development of these skills and recognizes the limitations of the ASD child in these areas will have a direct influence in your role as the therapist. You will need this information to determine what would be a reasonable level of involvement for you in working with the school. These guidelines will be incorporated into your Collaborative Agreement, discussed in Chapter 6.

Working with parents/guardians and supporting them in their interactions with the school and community will be an important aspect of treatment as you begin this venture. Equally important will be the work you to do that affects everyday family life. Turning to this next section of the form, we have listed for you those areas most frequently targeted as areas of concern at home.

IX. EVERYDAY LIFE

Briefly explain how your child's unusual behaviors affect your everyday life.

	Yes	No	Sometimes
Dressing, for example, wearing only certain clothes or unusual styles			

Explain:_____

	Yes	No	Sometimes
Eating, for example, eating only certain foods; needing specific arrangements of food on the plate; refusal to eat in the presence of others			

Explain:_____

	Yes	No	Sometimes
Hygiene, for example, avoiding teeth brushing, showering, bathing, hair washing.			

Explain:_____

	Yes	No	Sometimes
Care of possessions and surroundings, for example, color coding CD's, keeping things in a specific order, inability to share possessions			

Explain:_____

	Yes	No	Sometimes
Transitioning, for example, unable to transition easily from wake to sleep, difficulty with using certain forms of transportation, unable to follow varied routes to and from familiar places			

Explain:_____

	Yes	No	Sometimes
Safety, for example, not recognizing dangerous practices, wandering away, not able to problem solve in case of an emergency, showing a lack of awareness around strangers			

Explain:_____

	Yes	No	Sometimes
Other unusual habits or behaviors, for example, unusual daily rituals or routines			

Explain:_____

Behavioral Characteristics: Please share three positive things about your child that you observe every day.

1. _____

2. _____

3. _____

The demands of having a child with ASD affect the entire family and increase over time. What was cute or quirky in earlier years is neither "cute" nor "quirky" when the same behaviors are being exhibited by an older child. What was quirky becomes odd, and odd becomes different, and different leads to marginalization and isolation. Perhaps that is why parents/guardians cling to the beliefs like "She is bright," "He is interesting," "She is bored in class," "She is so much smarter than the other students," or "He is gifted." The heartbreak of acceptance comes slowly and is often paved with grief and loss. It is here in this section of Everyday Life that you will come to a fuller understanding of the difficulties and struggles involved in raising this child.

Once completed, the Family Profile Form will help you to initially prioritize areas of difficulty and give you a place to start. The ASDP will provide you with a more specific profile for treatment and will identify for you the extent of this disability's impact on family life (see Chapter 5). As you probe carefully when reviewing this form with the parents/guardians, you will have an opportunity to empathize with them and obtain a clearer sense of their need for treatment. Finally, at this point in the process, you will determine whether you are a good fit for building a therapeutic alliance with this family, if you have not decided already.

An added benefit to using the Family Profile Form is that with the information you garner, you can gauge the levels of stress these parent/guardians are experiencing on a daily basis (Lessenberry & Rehfeldt, 2004). With this knowledge, you will encourage them to tap into current sources of support and to identify additional help that may be available to them.

X. SUPPORT SYSTEMS

Family/Friends:

Name	Relationship	Level of Support (high, moderate, low)

School/Community:

Name	Relationship	Level of Support (high, moderate, low)

Organizations/Other Providers:

Name	Relationship	Level of Support (high, moderate, low)

Please add any further information you think may be helpful to the understanding of your child and your family life. Thank you.

_____

_____

In this final section of the Family Profile Form, you will be asking two things: for support information and for further information about your client. Identifying who the parents/guardians rely on and feel they can trust is essential to the well-being of the family as a whole. Understanding the specifics of who they are and how they are helpful to the family allows you to be able to encourage the family to take full advantage of all that these supports can reasonably offer. Beyond family and friends, connecting to agencies that can supply care and resources is crucial as the demands of the disability make themselves felt in family functioning. In considering treatment of this or any disability, you will need to have an awareness of the services that can be provided through the agencies and organizations in your state. Contacting national organizations (e.g., Autism Speaks; Easter Seals) for listings of affiliates and autism-related services will provide you with valuable information you can pass on to your client.

As you end the first interview and complete your review of the Family Profile Form with the parents/guardians, we have found it useful to ask for any further information that they think may be helpful. This may relate to past events in the child's life or to the clarification of current stresses for them and their ASD child. This additional information is important and may help you in the structuring of your first interview with the ASD child.

CHAPTER 4

Interviewing the Child

I F YOU HAVE never had a one-on-one conversation with a child who functions on the high end of the autism spectrum, you are in for a challenge and in for a treat. It will be different from working with other children, and you will need to begin the therapeutic process in a different way. Some therapists who work with children find that having the initial interview take place in an environment that is conducive to play will allow for a more relaxed and interactive exchange. Watching the child at play is diagnostic and can provide insights into the kinds of behaviors that relate to the initial referral question. Play interspersed with gentle questioning facilitates the dialogue and provides valuable information. Play is important to children, and it is a milieu in which they can function freely. This is why it is so often the structure chosen for the first interview.

Different from most interviews with children, you probably will not be able to rely on games or play-centered activities with the ASD child. While it is never wise to speak in general terms about children on the spectrum (each one uniquely qualifies for the diagnosis in his or her own way), most often the child on the spectrum will *not* be at ease with unstructured pretend play activities.

While the effectiveness of play therapy has been the subject of research for some time, studies show it to be an efficient tool for helping to resolve emotional issues for children across genders and ages (Bratton, Ray, & Rhine, 2005).

The problem with using traditional forms of play therapy as a way to facilitate an initial interaction with a child on the spectrum is that the ASD child has not developed play skills across the generally expected sequences of development (Hess, 2009). Recall Chapter 2 and the developmental aspects of play. The autistic child does not make use of representation or symbolic play strategies in the same way as the neurotypical child. The social sharing and social learning aspects of pretend play are not reflected in ASD. Predictable patterns of exploratory, relational, and symbolic play do not emerge in the same way. According to research, the child on the spectrum engages in exploratory play longer than his or her typically developing peers and spends less time engaging in pretend play (Hess, 2009).

For many ASD children pretend play can be a source of anxiety because they cannot impart meaning to it. They tend to think literally and concretely and, for them, imagining what is "not real" can be confusing. They are not generative in the sense that in play they do not produce imaginative pretense spontaneously. Interestingly, though, with structure and guidance they can be engaged in the process (Jarrold, Boucher, & Smith, 1996). Once engaged, it is possible for the child to use the vehicle of pretend play to clarify confusion and problem-solve around social frustrations. Yet this can only be done when the child is given direct instruction on how to proceed in the activity of pretend play. Using play therapy in this way is something that might be considered once a therapeutic relationship has been formed. The use of play will ultimately depend on the child's unique capacity to participate in those kinds of activities (Levine & Chedd, 2007).

Given that so many high-functioning children on the spectrum have been diagnosed as having well-developed language abilities, a direct interview approach will be more effective initially. This approach will involve a fair amount of definition of terms and explanation of questions in order to get a more clearly defined profile of your client. For this reason, you will need to pay close attention to the wording of your questions, and you may want to take the time to structure your interview along the suggested lines of the Child Interview Form provided in Appendix D. Using the Form as it fits your needs and knowledge of the child will help you to acquire the kind of initial information you are going to require for treatment.

You will notice that the wording in the Child Interview Form is straightforward and specific. Any questions you may want to add will also need to be worded in this direct and specific format. Traditionally, as therapists working with children, we are instructed to ask open-ended questions, so as to provide the child with a platform on which to make safe offerings of pertinent diagnostic material. Rather than direct questions, we are urged to allow children choices as to how they want to respond, what they may want to emphasize, and what they may want to ignore. For example, in Susan Lukas's book *Where to Start and What to Ask*, the therapist is told to use specific diagnostic techniques. One of these strategies is a well-known means of acquiring important insights into the child's psyche. Lukas says, "Ask her: If you were going on a rocket ship to the moon and there was one seat for you and one seat for someone else, whom would you take with you?" (Lukas, 1993, p. 72).

With the neurotypical child, the therapist gains insights into the child's emotional level of functioning by using free play and by asking open-ended questions. With the ASD child, free play is anxiety provoking and the open-ended question is ineffectual. For this child, the question will be interpreted literally and without insight. For example, the question "Tell me how you think your mother might be feeling when you . . . . ?" might get the response, "I don't know. I am not my mother." That is not meant to be sarcastic; it is a direct answer. This "honesty" is based on having compromised Theory of Mind abilities. The child is unable to see how he or she is coming across due to the inability to take another person's perspective.

As pointed out by Susan Lukas (1993), the physical aspects of your meeting place are important. She describes the most conducive atmosphere for therapy with neurotypical children. In preparation for your first meeting with the ASD child, we too recommend that you consider the environment of your office, but in a different way. While it may be "child friendly," too many toys can be over-stimulating to a sensory-sensitive child. Other sensory considerations are important to keep in mind as well. For instance, the temperature and the lighting in the room may need to be moderated. The textures of the chairs or the walls, the scent of the perfume you wear, or even the coffee you are drinking may be disturbing to the child. You may not be able to control for some of these things, but it is important to note whether there are sensory issues you need to be aware of. From reviewing Section 8 of the Family Profile Form, you will already have had a conversation with the parents about sensory issues. Use this information in preparing your office environment as best you can.

We recommend that you start this initial interview session with the child by having the parents/guardians present as you explain what information will and will not be shared. The child needs to know that parental rights to particular information about him or her (i.e., safety concerns for self and others, etc.) is rule governed. Your plan for how to convey this information to the child should be formulated in advance of this first meeting. Keep in mind not only the child's age but also his or her level of functioning in making these decisions. For example, you may need to explain that the rules are governed by state laws. Children on the spectrum are unique in that despite their intellectual acuity, their comprehension is often compromised by a narrow and rigid perspective. This may impact on their understanding of the parameters of confidentiality.

As with all of your communications with your client, be precise, avoid ambiguity, and do not offer hypothetical situations to explain your point. For the ASD child these are triggers for engaging in the kind of perseveration that will ultimately distract from your main point. In this case, move on quickly. To stay with the subject is nonproductive and ultimately not helpful to your client.

As therapy progresses, siblings or other family members may need to be included in the treatment process. Through the use of the collaborative agreements found in Chapters 6 and 7, you will have a structure in place for this to occur without disrupting the therapeutic process. For the child on the spectrum, an unexpected break in a routine can cause a setback that will be out of proportion to the event. Therefore, you will need to anticipate the child's need for predictability in the way things will occur in therapy. The child needs to know how sessions will run, when and how sessions will terminate, and who will be privy to the information shared between the child and the therapist.

Let's begin with the first section of the Child Interview Form and talk about some of the information that you will be seeking. As you look at the questions from the Form (samples of which are provided throughout this chapter), you will get a sense of those that will be most helpful to you, given the age and circumstances of your client. Explore and probe where you can, remembering always that the answers you get will reflect the fact that the youngster before you has a distinctive view of the world and that view impacts his or her own life experiences.

I. BASIC INFORMATION

I will start with asking you some questions so that you can help me to get the information I need today. They will be questions like "What's your name? How old are you? Where do you live?" So let's begin . . .

What is your name?

How old are you?

When is your birthday? Do you know what year you were born?

Where do you live? Can you tell me your address?

What is your home phone number or your parent's cell phone number?

Where do you go to school?

What grade are you in?

Great! That was very helpful. I would like to ask a few more questions, just to get more information about your life at home and your life at school. Ready? It's time to begin . . .

In this section of the form, the standard questions are posed. You will note that the interview opens with a statement of purpose (i.e., *you can help me get the information I need today*) and brief examples of questions you will be asking. Because the order and the content of the actual interview questions in the Guide are not exactly the same as the examples given in the directions above them, you may find the child pointing out the differences. To avoid feeling confused in social circumstances, the ASD child tends to establish a rigid expectation of what will occur. When something different happens, the child is likely to mention it to you. For example, when you ask the third set of questions (i.e., the birthday questions), the child might say, "You are supposed to ask me where I live now. That is what you said you would be doing." This is not oppositional or controlling in intent. It is a characteristic typical of the disorder, and it reflects the rigidity of the child's thinking.

Inserting an unexpected question like the birthday question is a way to detect the level of the child's mental flexibility and his or her need for more preparation in terms of what to expect next. In the course of your interview we recommend you use this technique periodically to gather more information about your client's profile. For example, introducing a novel subject or activity into a therapy session is a way of assessing the level of your client's flexibility.

The inability to shift mental sets, to make transitions from one situation to the next, and to accept the unexpected are important features of the child's profile. Determining how these factors influence the child's daily functioning across all settings is a necessary component to treatment planning (see Chapter 5). The next section of the Child Interview Form (excerpt below) will elicit information about the child's home life.

II. HOME INFORMATION

Can you tell me who lives with you in your home?

Do you have brothers and sisters?

How old are they?

Are your parents married to each other? Do they both live with you?

When you are home, who helps you the most? In what ways does he/she help you?

In this section, you are trying to find out whether the child is living with biological parents or other guardians. In today's society having shared custody is common. If this is the case, it will be particularly important to understand the differences between the homes and how they affect the child. This is essential because the child on the autism spectrum has an increased need for consistency and predictability. While the rules in each home may be different, there has to be a consistent approach to issues of health, hygiene, safety, and discipline. As the therapist, you may have to consider the negotiation of consistency across domiciles as part of your treatment plan if the child is reacting negatively to differing expectations.

Asking straightforward questions about the child's view of home-life experiences is a good way to get information about his or her ability to function independently and effectively at home. Siblings are significant in all of this. As you will see in Chapter 8, some relationships may be more comfortable and less demanding for the ASD child, while other sibling relationships may have become parentified over the years. The neurotypical sibling may perceive himself or herself as a caretaker, even though appropriate providers are performing efficiently in their parental duties.

As your client describes his or her connections with siblings, you will learn that, while the child's perceptions are important to note, they may not be accurate. For example, it is common for the ASD child to have an excessive proprietary attitude toward possessions. There may be unwillingness to share and great anxiety at the prospect of being asked to do so. This can result in the development of fear around visits from friends or siblings due to a fear of someone touching, taking, or breaking a toy or cherished item belonging to the ASD child. As Tony Attwood (2007) describes, the visitation of friends is often viewed as a kind of "invasion" of personal space. You will notice the next portion of the form centers on questions designed to elicit more specific information about the child's home-life experiences.

Do you have your own room? (If the child shares a room, ask what that is like for him/her. Do the siblings argue over how to organize the room itself or sections of it?)

Tell me what your room looks like?

Do you like to keep your things a certain way? Can you explain that to me?

When you are in your room, is it important for you to have the window blinds opened or closed?

Sharing a room with a sibling or sharing in two households will also increase this type of anxiety in your client, as the ASD child has less control over his or her own space. This feeling of loss of control is tied to unpredictability and to a break in routine. This leads to exacerbation of ASD characteristics (i.e., further rigidity, perseveration, OCD-like behaviors) and to the deterioration of the sibling bond. Depending on the child, learning to coexist with siblings and other family members may become an important treatment goal.

You will notice that there are a number of questions on this guide that relate to the child's bedroom. This is because the bedroom is a "safe haven" for children on the spectrum. If it is shared with a sibling, areas are often distinguished with boundaries erected. The need to have segregated spaces is a reflection of the child's propensity to compartmentalize thoughts and experiences. It is a way for the ASD child to have control in a world that feels confusing and chaotic. Understanding the child's reasonable need for defined space is important for the entire family to accept and respect, and for you to validate in therapy.

Your alliance can be strengthened as you explore the details and descriptions of various aspects of the client's room. Be prepared to hear some things that may sound "quirky" or even paranoid. For example, one young teen insisted on keeping his window shades drawn during the daytime. He was not suspicious of others looking into his room; rather he felt that opening the shades compromised his private space. He felt a need to protect this area that was so important to him. It was a space that he cherished. It was here in his bedroom that he kept his most valued possessions and where he practiced his nighttime rituals.

For the ASD child, it is common to have rituals. That is why we suggest that you inquire about bedtime practices at this point in the interview. The information you are given may include references to unusual behaviors that have not been shared with parents/guardians. This may be one of those instances where you will have to determine whether certain behaviors represent a danger to the child or family members and will require disclosure. If it does, you must break confidence and share the information. We mention this because the ASD child is known to engage in practices that may appear bizarre but are not necessarily dangerous. Not all practices will require disclosure. However, some ritualistic behaviors can be extremely risky. Consider this example: Although not related to a bedtime ritual, one teenager disclosed his practice of using candles in his home. Through the process of exploration with his therapist, it was revealed that he was lighting candles while in the shower and placing them on a windowsill near a curtain. Had the therapist not probed deeply and rephrased her questions, this dangerous practice would not have been uncovered and reported to his parents.

Are there some parts of your home that you like better than others? Certain rooms? Or outside spaces? (Explore the child's preferences inside and outside of the home. Find out if there are or were particular areas of attraction, i.e., hiding in cabinets, playing under stairways or porches, etc. Probe for unusual practices.)

The set of questions above from the Home Information section is centered on varying aspects of the child's home and will elicit more information on the child's actions and choices as they relate to the broader aspects of home life. In addition to the bedroom, children on the spectrum will often create solitary spaces for themselves within and outside of their home. The need for escape and isolation is a mechanism for achieving a restored sense of balance. One little boy had a "special place" underneath his back porch, where he could soothe himself by engaging in a kind of rocking and swaying ritual that he did not want others to see. It is because of the social anxiety the ASD child faces each day that he or she needs the freedom to find spaces like this that will provide solace and safety. Although many caregivers, teachers included, see this behavior as unacceptable and will attempt to discourage it, we recommend that it be allowed within safe, reasonable parameters.

Clarifying how often and under what circumstances the child seeks separation in an isolated space is important. You will then be better able to help others understand that an acceptable provision for an "escape" is needed when the child is feeling overwhelmed. "Acceptable" refers to what is acceptable to the *child* (within reason) and not to the sole judgment of the caretaker. For the child on the spectrum, it is not always apparent or even logical what will work as a "safe space" at school or at home. It will take some creativity and patience to identify what works. This patience is also required when attempting to enforce the fulfillment of typical responsibilities with the ASD child. Understanding the way the child views his or her world is crucial in this area as well.

Do you have to help out around the house? I know some children have to sweep the floor or maybe do the dishes. Some others have to make their beds and clean up their own "stuff." How about you?

Additional activities that the child performs related to home life are important to discuss. For instance, it is essential to understand what chores are expected of the child and are adequately completed. While this is a common aspect of family life for everyone, and not one favored by most children, the level of resistance to participation is different with the ASD child. This is due to a number of factors, including a unique perception of fairness with chore distribution among siblings; a lack of recognition of the need for a chore to be done; or a rigid perception of how a chore should be done. Resistance can come from a lack of understanding of social cooperation among family members. For example, one young man could not understand why certain chores were assigned to his sister and others to him. How was washing the dishes comparable to taking out the trash? Because they were two different activities, he was "stuck" on how that decision was made and whether it was fair. Multiple attempts to switch various chores between him and his sibling never fully resolved his anxiety around his responsibilities and caused family conflict for years.

Another problem is that the child on the spectrum does not perceive a need for certain chores to be done at all. If the trash barrel is not completely full to capacity, there is no need to empty it. Or if the trash is able to be pushed down into the barrel to create a small amount of additional space, then why would it need to be emptied now? While these behaviors may be typical for many children who are just trying to get out of doing a task, for the child on the spectrum this thinking is disability related and demonstrates a singular view. This problem is so common across many areas of home life that you may need to tie certain practices (e.g., chores) into a treatment goal in working with the parents/guardians. Helping them to see things the way the child does before getting caught up in a fruitless argument will go a long way to alleviate tensions in the home. If a parent/guardian understands that reasons behind the child's resistance are tied to the disability, he or she is less likely to assume manipulative intent. This paves the way for more feasible negotiations with the child.

Parents/guardians will need your support in explaining to their other children how their ASD sibling perceives things and why it is sometimes important to accommodate his or her view. They will come to see that, with flexibility, life will run more smoothly for everyone involved. From the siblings' view, it may seem like it is "giving in" to the one child, but it is in their best interests to avoid conflict. Individualizing chores and customizing them to better fit the ASD child's strengths is strongly recommended. Assignment of a well-defined, individualized chore that is visually apparent upon completion leads to optimal success for the ASD child. For instance, putting away dishes, clearing a table, making a bed, and so on are preferable to vacuuming, dusting, or shaking rugs. The point here is that there are certain tasks that are more easily defined and more obviously completed. Concrete tasks have the advantage of giving immediate feedback regarding performance, and this clarity is what the child on the spectrum requires.

Our last topic for this section involves self-care. Prior to your interview with the child, be sure to review Section IX of the Family Profile Form (see Appendix C). This will give you a better sense of what to ask as you explore the child's perception of his or her functioning in this area. It is likely that the child will give a different account of his or her hygiene practices from those reported by the parents/guardians. One reason we see that hygiene issues abound in this population is that many individuals on the spectrum do not automatically recognize a need for particular hygiene practices. This is tied to the disability and occurs because thoughts and actions are compartmentalized. For instance, the child who is fastidious about his fingernails may not wash his hands regularly. Or the teenager who dresses impeccably may not use soap when bathing. For others it is not one specific thing; rather, general hygiene needs do not spontaneously register in their minds. As a result of not appreciating these needs, ensuring personal care and cleanliness is not seen as important.

How about things you do for yourself? Some kids are expected to get up and get dressed at a certain time and be ready for school. They are expected to use the bathroom, get washed up or showered, wash their hair, comb their hair, and brush their teeth each morning. And I know that not all kids like these things. It can be hard for them in the morning. What is it like for you?

As you can see from the questions above, eliciting details regarding self-care practices is best done through a conversational approach rather than a direct interview format. Remember that children, and especially adolescents, on the spectrum are often chided by parents/guardians and teased by peers for their lack of awareness regarding their appearances. Of course, the factors listed above are not ones that can be "solved" in a weekly therapy session. They are too complicated and these issues will need to be addressed in the home environment with your support. That is why it is best to work alone with the parents/guardians to help them find the best ways to educate their child in areas concerning hygiene.

While it does not always happen, further training can and should occur in the school. Some districts will provide home consultation depending on the child's level of need. There are also many good resources that you can recommend to the parents. For example, the book *Personal Hygiene? What's That Got To Do With Me?* by special educator and autism consultant Pat Crissey (2005) addresses personal care issues in the factual, straightforward manner that is most effective with high-functioning children on the spectrum. Books like this, as well as other referral sources, will help you to avoid the pitfall of taking on the role of "fixing" the problems yourself. It is a common misperception among parents/guardians that a 1-hour weekly session with a therapist is all it will take to change troublesome behaviors and teach practices that are currently lacking. With the child on the spectrum, it is particularly important to focus on parent training in your treatment planning and for the parents/guardians to invest in this process from the start. Their awareness of the need for this approach is key and will be explained further in the Collaborative Agreement Between Parents/ Guardians and Therapist (see Chapter 6 and Appendix I).

III. SOCIAL INFORMATION

At this point in your interview with the child, you should be about halfway through the time you have allotted. If the child is having difficulty sustaining interest in the interview, this might be a good time to take a short break. For instance, you can allow the child to talk about a preferred topic of interest. (Check Section II of the Family Profile Form ahead of time to be aware of special topics of interest to the child.) While it is ideal for you to complete the interview in one session, it may not be feasible. This is the nature of working with a child on the spectrum.

Coaxing or cajoling the ASD child to hurry through responses is likely to trigger anxiety. If you do this, you will see increased rigidity and insistence on telling you more than you need to know. This may feel like oppositional behavior, but it is more likely linked to ASD-related anxiety. One strategy for you to use in order to move the interview along (this tactic may also be used in your therapy sessions) is to explain to the child that you will keep a list of the things he or she wants to talk about to address at the next meeting. For instance, if the child wants to keep talking about the dog when you are reviewing the home life, take a pad of paper and show him or her that you have written down the dog's name on a list entitled "Next Meeting." When the child mentions the dog again, you can show him or her the list simply by pointing to it and then continuing on with the current topic.

The Social Information section begins with our recommendation to use specific statements to clarify the whole purpose of the interview for the child The child on the spectrum has difficulty with seeing connections and tends to "get stuck" on details. Bringing the pieces together and enlisting them to help you will facilitate the process and allow you to build rapport. The ASD child likes to be praised for competence. Being recognized for providing the right information and being made to feel that his or her contributions are valuable are prime motivators for gaining the child's cooperation.

After you have transitioned to this second half of the interview and to a new line of questioning, you will ask about the child's friends. This is a sensitive area for both your client and his or her caregivers. For parents/guardians, they may still be in the process of understanding and accepting the implications of the child's disability and how it affects friendships. For the child, the realization and the experience of being socially isolated and rejected may be a great source of anxiety and will need to be approached carefully. Alternatively, do not be surprised if the child does not have any awareness of what friendship means.

Do you have a friend who lives near you? Is this a person the same age as you? What kinds of things do you like to do with your friend?

Do you have other friends? Do they live near you? Do you ever visit them in their houses? Do they come to visit you at your home?

Do kids in the neighborhood come to your door and ask you if you want to play/hang out? Do they call you or text you? How often?

Do you have friends who live farther away from you? Do you ever invite them to your house? Do you ever go to your friend's house to visit?

What about birthday parties? Do you invite kids to your birthday party? Do you go to their parties? What is that like for you?

Do you have any pets? Is it your pet or does it belong to your whole family? Is your pet a friend to you? What kinds of things do you and your pet do together? Tell me about your pet.

You will note that in this section we refer to pets as friends. This is because the concept of friendship is different for the ASD child. Just as their developmental play patterns differ from the neurotypical child's, so do their patterns of friendship formation. According to Tony Attwood (2007), the developmental stages in the concept of friendship for typical children differ from those with Asperger syndrome from the earliest stage (age 3 to 6 years). Friendships for children on the spectrum take on a different meaning. It is not the socialization that they seek but rather the opportunity to engage in an activity that is of high interest to them. Social interactions are frequently compromised by a number of issues: problems with Theory of Mind, a lack of social understanding, a lag in social development (despite average to above-average intellectual functioning), a literal interpretation of social language, and an adherence to honesty above consideration of feelings.

These issues lead to specific problems that affect the formation of friendships. Look for answers that lead to an understanding of the child's perception of friendships. The child on the spectrum will have a unique perspective that can be unintentionally self-sabotaging in its rigidity. For example, Tony Attwood (2012) reports the comment of one child who said, "He can't play with me one day and then other friends another day—that wouldn't be a true friend."

You may find that your client defines friendships according to shared interests and not shared social time together. For instance, the youngster who discovers a friend with a shared interest in anime but finds out that this "friend" does not like the exact genre of anime will then no longer pursue the friendship. Another example of unintentional friendship-defeating behavior is exemplified by the 10-year-old boy with ASD who invited his classmate over for a swim and then insisted on spending the time in his room reading his book on the US Presidents. He could not understand why the child wanted to go home because, in his view, this was a mutually enjoyable playdate.

Some of these points are reflected in the questions on the Child Interview Form. The reason for inquiring about the age of friends is that it is common for the ASD child to report a preference for friends outside of his or her age group. This may be a child who is several years younger or an adult neighbor with whom he or she visits every day, or it may even be a cherished grandparent. In the child's view, these people are peers. Tread lightly around questions dealing with perceived friendships. They tend to be highly valued and have probably been questioned by others as to whether they are appropriate "friends," thus leading to defensiveness in the child.

Also in this section you will get information that will give you some insight into the life of the parents/guardians who struggle to assist their ASD children in forming friendships. To foster reciprocity, some will go overboard in staging elaborate parties, inviting the entire class is some cases to birthday celebrations that are designed to entice children to befriend their child. Parents/guardians will encourage participation in age-appropriate social interactions by having the child join sports teams or girls/boys clubs of various kinds. At times, the parents/guardians themselves will participate in these activities in such ways as to support or facilitate the friendship-making process.

Ultimately your goal is to best understand how uniquely complex friendship formation is for your client, how it is typically manifested in his or her behavior and how it impacts his or her family. The ever-present anxiety elicited in the process of seeking social interaction can result in clinical manifestations. The child may experience social phobia, elective mutism, and even school refusal (Attwood, 2002). Sometimes, anxiety will take the form of aggression in ASD children. The frustration of trying to "map out" the social norms and to follow directions in the social world can make the child feel more like an alien rather than a resident of his or her own world (Attwood, 2007).

Hopefully the school will have an adequate plan to help the child address these issues. At this point you should have reviewed school records and prior testing (as discussed in Chapter 3) to know whether these limitations have led to a formal educational plan. The importance of the school in the life of the child on the spectrum cannot be underestimated. For high-functioning ASD children, you will find that their needs are often misunderstood and/or minimized by educators. Because of this, your work with the family will most likely involve working with the school. This may warrant a specific treatment goal (see examples in Chapter 5). Regardless of whether it rises to this level, parameters around school collaboration will need to be set. This subject is spelled out more clearly in the chapters describing the Collaborative Agreements.

IV. SCHOOL INFORMATION

You will have a sense of the parents/guardians' concerns around school issues from their report in Section VIII of the Family Profile Form. What might surprise you is that the child may view his or her school situation from a totally different perspective than the parents/guardians. Just as the understanding of friendship affects his or her perception of friends outside of school, it also applies to friendships among schoolmates. Because a peer may be solicitous or even polite to the ASD child in school, he or she might be identified as a "friend." Sometimes all one needs to be is a classmate to be termed a "friend" by the child on the spectrum.

The neurotypical child has relationships with peers in which they engage in mutual play in gym and at recess. They meet up before and after school, share private conversation, and sit together at lunch. These are some of the aspects of having a friend at school. The child on the spectrum will have friendships that look different and are typically more focused on shared interests. Friendships are usually confined to the pursuit of particular interests. Consider this example: One boy became actively involved in Boy Scouts and was encouraged by his mother to invite certain members of his troop out for various activities (i.e., movies, bowling, pizza, etc.). The boy would refuse to comply with her wishes, finally saying to her, "I see them at Boy Scouts on Thursday nights. Why would I see them other than that?"

Using this connection of shared special interests is a way to expand the quality of the child's social experiences leading to friendships. It can also be an important treatment goal and you will have to determine how to develop it. You will need to be creative and attempt to make connections from the specific perseverative or unusual interest to something broader and more appealing to others. One boy who compulsively collected sporting statistics agreed to join Boy Scouts to achieve a Sporting Badge. Another teen who had a special interest in Civil War Battles was persuaded to join a History Club. Parents/guardians will need to learn that their child will experience his or her own unique feelings of friendship through these connections. The goal is for the friendship to be satisfying to the child, although it may not necessarily meet the definition of friendship set by others. These social differences often negatively impact the ASD child's ability to make academic progress. Learning more about the child's perception of his or her school life at this time will deepen your understanding of the sources of potential anxiety the child experiences every day.

Is it hard for you to be in school sometimes? Do you ever worry when you are in school? Do you have a "safe person" to talk to when you have a problem? Do you have a "safe place" you can go to when you feel like you need to calm down? If not, what do you do?

Do you get any special help in school? Are some subjects harder than others for you? What is your favorite subject? What subject don't you like? Do you get a chance to do some of your homework at school? Is there someone to help you with that? What kinds of grades do you usually get in school?

Tell me about your school day. Are you in many different rooms during the day? What time do you get there, and leave? Are you early or late most days? Is it noisy in the corridors? Do you ever get in trouble at school? What happens when you are in trouble at school? Is the trouble usually about the same thing?

The ASD child needs consistency and predictability. A lack of these leads to confusion, frustration, and anxiety. The buildup of anxiety can be the result of an accumulation of specific events during the school day. Knowing what happens in school situations and how your client copes will inspire treatment interventions. One of our clients, a 6-year-old boy, had such anxiety around recess that he would hide under the schoolyard slide until recess was over. When this was discovered, the playground supervisor insisted that he come out and play with the other children. She was unprepared for the major meltdown that ensued. In this instance, the parents needed the therapist to guide them in understanding how this behavior was rooted in the boy's disability. They were then able to advocate for their child to have a more structured "free time" instead of recess.

This idea of providing a structured and predictable environment applies to the concept Carol Gray (Gray & Williams, 2006) has introduced in her book *No Fishing Allowed Bullying Prevention Program*: *"Reeling in Bullying."* Mapping the child's environment to identify places of vulnerability and guiding the child to "safe" locations within the school are important strategies for protecting the ASD child from bullying peers. Another related intervention used in some high schools is the assignment of a peer mentor. This student is deemed to be mature and reliable and will point out those areas to be avoided in or around the school building. Having a mentor who is also aware of potential bullying dangers for the child on the spectrum is an effective deterrent. With this in place, it is not solely up to the child to recognize and report bullying.

The fact is that disability-related characteristics make it difficult for the ASD child to do either of these things. For example, parents and teachers may have recognized episodes of bullying by a specific student, but the ASD child may see the "bully" as a "friend." One boy who looked forward to being included in playing Dodge Ball at recess did not realize his "friend" was setting him up to be an easy target while the other children laughed. For him (the ASD child), he was a participant and no different from the others. He never realized that the laughs were at his expense and that he was being bullied. This instance was finally reported to the teacher by another student, and the game was brought to a halt.

The opposite can be true as well. With today's emphasis on bullying in schools, the child on the spectrum can become hypersensitive to peers' comments. Current laws have resulted in ongoing discussions in which students are encouraged to report episodes of bullying. With the ASD child's propensity for literal interpretation, he or she may interpret even the slightest negative comment as an example of bullying. For instance, one young teen was insulted by a mentally challenged boy. He reported the boy to the principal and accused him of bullying practices. The principal attempted to explain that this was not bullying and that there were extenuating circumstances related to the boy's disability. Feeling dissatisfied by the principal's lack of agreement with his point of view, the ASD child then took the matter into his own hands and proceeded to bully the boy by berating him publicly. As Tony Attwood points out, the intent here was not related to a lack of empathy but was an effort to address the perceived injustice done to him. The retaliation was done "with the intent of inflicting equal discomfort" (Attwood, 2007, p. 103).

Bullying is an enormous problem with this population and is particularly complicated. According to the *Archives of Pediatrics and Adolescent Medicine* (2012), a decade-long study found that 46.3% of youngsters with ASD are victims of bullying, 14.8% are perpetrators, while 8.9% fall into both categories simultaneously (Sterzing, Shattuck, Narendorf, Wagner, & Cooper, 2012). Complications arise because of the lack of social awareness that is characteristic of the individual with ASD. Levels of social immaturity can be up to 20%–25% lower than the child's chronological age. This is a point many people, professionals included, do not understand. The child on the spectrum may think it necessary to say outrageous things to get attention from peers, attention he or she does not normally receive.

One 14-year-old boy with ASD was reprimanded for making comments about his peers' genital parts, using slang terms, every time he exited the boys' bathroom at school. This appeared to be done in an effort to shock the boys and girls in his classroom. After being told that his behavior was not acceptable and that his language was offensive to others, he focused on only one aspect of the reprimand: the use of slang terms. He continued the behavior, only now using anatomically correct descriptions of boys' genitalia. This rigidity of thought, typical of the way information can be processed by ASD children, had to be addressed very specifically. To extinguish this behavior, the boy was temporarily restricted to use of a private bathroom so as not to trigger the socially unaccepted behavior.

Difficulties with social communication affect every aspect of school life for these children. From standing at the bus stop to getting help after school, the ASD child experiences challenges that other children do not. These range from difficult social interactions to experiences with bullying. As you complete this section of the interview and continue to ask your client for school information, focus on patterns of perceptions that seem to be provoking the most anxiety. Consulting the parents/guardians for further details about this information is necessary for prioritizing treatment goals.

You will notice that up until this point, we have not discussed academic issues in depth. This is because social needs are at the forefront for this population. There may be academic needs, particularly in areas of comprehension and organization, or there may be a specific learning disability affecting the child's school performance. Regardless of whether there are academic skill deficits, there will be problems with academic progress in some form. This can be tied to a lack of work production in the classroom and/or with homework. In our experience, there a number of common factors that account for this:

1. The ASD child frequently makes a clear distinction between work at school and work at home.
2. There may be confusion around work expectations and specific assignments.
3. There can be a sincere intent to do work, but that intent simply gets lost. Remember that the ASD child compartmentalizes information and the intent exists separately from the plan to follow through.
4. There can be exhaustion during and at the end of the school day, leaving the child with depleted resources to perform optimally.

All of these points lead to increased anxiety. This has to take priority over academic work production. Unfortunately, this is a point that many school professionals do not understand.

V. CONCLUSION

In concluding the Child Interview, you will be thanking the child for his/her help in giving you the information you need. You will then go on to ask the last few clarifying questions. What you should note here is whether the child has referred to his or her ASD diagnosis during this interview process. If you have been informed that the child *has* been told of the diagnosis (further discussed in Chapter 3) but the child has not mentioned it up to this point, you might want to introduce this as one of the reasons that the child is seeing you today. If the child has not been told of the diagnosis, you will be able to use the information gathered today to support the parents/guardians in sharing the child's diagnosis with him or her. This may require a treatment goal or may be something the parents can do on their own.

When the interview with the child is over and the parents/guardians are back in your office, you can share your empathy for them in the struggles they face every day. It is here you can emphasize your desire to learn more about them and to assist them as they chart their course in treatment with you. Your next appointment will be with the parents/guardians alone so that you can use the information you have to begin to formulate a treatment plan. To do this, we recommend that you give them the ASDP (explained in Chapter 5) at this time for completion before the next appointment. In summary, your treatment goals will be created from a combination of the following: your personal impressions; the Family Profile Form; parent and child interviews; and the rating scale, which will produce a profile we have entitled the Autism Spectrum Descriptive Profile (ASDP).

VI. POST-INTERVIEW IMPRESSIONS

It has been our experience that parents/guardians of children on the autism spectrum are often viewed as being overprotective, demanding, restrictive, and perceiving fictitious deficits in their child. The children themselves have a history of being seen as spoiled, domineering, rude, and out of control. It is with this in mind that we recommend you think about your initial observations and reactions to the child and parent/guardian interactions. Did *you* feel any of these things? What did you think about their relationship? Did it seem to you that the child had too much control? Were the parents/guardians "jumping in" to head off a tangential ranting on the part of the child? Or alternatively, did they seem fearful that the child would become defensive or angry if they tried to join in the conversation spontaneously or if they were asked for input? Who had difficulty separating during transitions in the interview process? If any or all of these things were noted, we are not surprised. The dynamic between the child on the spectrum and the parent/guardian is complicated and different from what you might expect.

Unlike a child diagnosed with a disruptive behavior disorder, the behavior of the child on the spectrum is not driven by a need to disregard the directions of authority figures, despite the fact that it can appear that way. The child's propensity to dominate is related to the disability in that it reflects a narrow perspective on the experience of others and a constant need for affirmation in what he or she thinks, knows, and values. Their perceived "obnoxious" behaviors represent their attempts to socially interact. They want to share what they know and they desire recognition for the sharpness of their intellect. We are not minimizing the need for correction or containment of difficult behaviors. In fact, these are the reasons why this family has come to you for help. Your role will be to identify specific needs of the child and guide the parents/guardians in finding supports and strategies necessary to promote a better quality of individual and family life.

Initially, you may not be able to accurately identify those needs. Because the ASD child experiences intense anxiety around new and unknown people, your client may have presented in a different manner with you as compared to how he or she typically behaves in more familiar settings. What you will have seen in this first interview is the behavior that the child uses to negotiate unfamiliar social circumstances, and that is diagnostic. It is likely that you will also be observing the parents/guardians attempts to diffuse the child's buildup of anxiety. As your therapeutic relationship builds, anxiety lessens and the needs of the child emerge more clearly.

We have learned that controlling the anxiety associated with ASD means controlling the "triggers" (or antecedents) that produce it. Doing this is more effective in reducing anxiety than is focusing on consequences. You may have witnessed this in the child's interactions with his or her parents/guardians. The following example occurred in one initial interview. The therapist was starting to explain confidentiality. The parent interrupted her to rephrase every sentence concretely to ensure that the point was being made in language that she knew her son would understand. This may have looked like a controlling parent, but in fact, it was a parent controlling a "trigger" that she knew would have induced anxiety in her child. These parents/guardians know what their children need to maintain a state of emotional stability. This may take the form of a particular verbal interpretation, as described above, or it may be allowing the child to make prolonged use of a transitional object.

For the ASD child, this object is frequently unusual and unexpected, not necessarily soft and cuddly. This could be a wooden truck (valued for the spinning of the wheels), an item associated with a perseverative interest (like a watch), or, as one 8-year-old boy held onto, a good-sized, rusty, broken sprinkler that had belonged to his grandmother. For this last child, while the transitional object was connected to a person, it was an unexpected choice. Like neurotypical children, these favored items accompany them everywhere. Make note if your client has one of these uncommon attachment objects and imagine how it is for the parents as their little 8-year-old lugs a rusty, broken sprinkler into restaurants, stores, and appointments.

In addition to being alert to family interactions and the need for transitional objects, we recommend that you make note of other behaviors referred to in Section IV of the Child Interview Form. If your client exhibits attention difficulties, heightened motor activity, unusual facial tics/hand movements, or other uncommon mannerisms, you may ultimately want to consider a referral to a neurologist or a psychiatrist for a medication evaluation.

As you consider the child's speech during the interview, you will want to focus on whether there are problems with volume, pitch, or tone that may be off-putting to others. If there is a perseverative quality to the discussion that distracts from the normal give-and-take of conversation, these would be reasons to start thinking about the involvement of a speech and language therapist.

Lastly, if the parents/guardians have reported that there are sensory issues that affect the child's behaviors, you will want to think about whether they were apparent during the interview. If not observed, make note to inquire further with the parents/guardians regarding these concerns and be sensitive to the presence of these factors in future sessions. Sensory issues may lead you to the recommendation for a referral to an occupational therapist. It is not unusual for the child with ASD to resist particular textures or have other sensory sensitivities. These may or may not rise to the level of requiring intervention.

The avoidance of sensory irritants can often be identified through the child's unusual style of dress, but there other reasons that may account for unusual appearances in the ASD child. One little boy decided that a particular Halloween costume, the draping robe of the Grim Reaper, had to be worn every year. He insisted on wearing it even after he had clearly outgrown it. The fact that the hood barely fit over his head and the sleeves ended at his elbows did not dissuade him from the belief that he could not go trick or treating without wearing this outfit. His mother resolved this dilemma by making a deal with him that he could wear the old costume under a new one that fit him properly. As you can see, therapists and parents/guardians will need to learn those social negotiation skills that will be most effective with each child. Recognizing and finding ways to help the child meet social expectations will likely become an area for consideration as a treatment goal.

In the next chapter, you will find an in-depth discussion, a rating scale, and a descriptive personality profile form for determining the extent, prevalence, and impact of unusual practices. This will help you set and prioritize appropriate treatment goals.

CHAPTER 5

Developing the Treatment Plan

AT THIS POINT you have committed to creating a therapeutic relationship with a child diagnosed with ASD and his or her family. Before developing the treatment plan, let's review what has been discussed so far and the corresponding steps you have taken.

1. You have completed the *Initial Contact Form* and made the preliminary decision to move forward in treatment with your client (Chapter 1).
2. You have familiarized yourself with the characteristics of this disability, in part, through your review of the *Developmental Guide* (Chapter 2).
3. You obtained further information by way of the *Family Profile Form* and continued to determine that this is a client and family you are able to treat (Chapter 3).
4. You met with the child and completed the *Child Interview Form* (Chapter 4).

Now that you have gathered information about the way this disability is manifested in your client and how it affects the whole family, you are ready to formulate the treatment plan. In this chapter you will be provided with guides to assist you in charting the course of treatment. The Autism Spectrum Descriptive Profile (ASDP) forms will support you in targeting problem areas and in identifying the intensity of needs for both the child and family. To select your treatment goals, you will use (a) prior diagnostic information that has been provided to you (e.g., school, clinical, or neuropsychological reports); (b) material resulting from steps 1-4 listed above; and (c) the completed ASDP forms presented in this chapter.

The information derived from the ASDP forms will assist you in determining the prevalent autistic features that are uniquely affecting your client and his or her family at this point in time. The forms will enable you to work with your client and the family to make the best decisions for setting treatment goals. These goals will "focus on improving social interaction and communication, addressing challenging behaviors, increasing educational engagement and achievement, treating commonly associated difficulties (e.g., anxiety), promoting independence, and improving quality of life" (Missouri Autism Guidelines Initiative, 2012). In addition, the information from the forms will create a narrative description of your client that can be used by you as well as by the parents/guardians to explain the child's needs to others. Although we will make reference to some therapeutic approaches that seem to be a good fit for this disability, reviewing the various treatment methods is not a focus of this book. Rather, it is our purpose to help you to understand how the structure of therapy differs when treating this population.

As you broaden your experiences in working with high-functioning children diagnosed with ASD, your therapeutic approach will likely be eclectic. Even if you tend to subscribe to a particular method of therapy, you will find that it may not always be effective with this population. As Karen Levine and Naomi Chedd (2013) point out in their book *Treatment Planning for Children With Autism Spectrum Disorders: An Individualized Problem-Solving Approach*, your therapeutic approach will need to be tailored to the child. In this book, problem-solving techniques that are effective in treating children and adolescents on the autism spectrum are explained. They go on to say that you will need to be creative in your selection of interventions and knowledgeable about ASD-related behaviors across a variety of domains. It is particularly important that your therapeutic approach be based on the measurable success of the interventions you have chosen.

You may select an approach to treat specific comorbid diagnoses or the symptoms thereof. Donoghue et al. (2011) reported that cognitive-behavioral therapy (CBT) is recognized as an effective intervention for anxiety, depression, and OCD in children and adolescents. They go on to say that little research has specifically singled out the effects of this treatment on individuals with an Asperger syndrome diagnosis. Yet, as we have been mentioned before, the symptoms associated with anxiety, depression, and OCD, or the diagnoses themselves, are frequently found in high-functioning children on the autism spectrum. For this reason, CBT is the basis for a number of therapeutic interventions successfully used with this population. For instance, CBT can be found in the work of speech and language therapists Elsa Abele and Michelle Garcia Winner (Abele, 2012; Garcia Winner & Crooke, 2004) The use of cognitive-behavioral therapy is also connected to Carol Gray's promotion of social stories in working with children (Gray & Williams, 2006).

In terms of treatment planning, we will start by discussing the role of the treatment team. In working with children diagnosed with mental health disorders, you are likely to have periodic contact with other professionals who are also treating your client. For instance, there may be times when you will have phone contact with the pediatrician, the psychiatrist, or the school counselor. You may even attend a special education team meeting to provide input regarding the needs of your client. While attending these meetings is commonly necessary when treating a child on the spectrum, the degree of your involvement with the school treatment team will likely be more extensive than with other disorders. Ideally, the treatment should take on an interdisciplinary approach to provide the particular type of consistency your client will need. The collaborative agreements in Chapters 6 and 7 will guide you in working with the child and parents/guardians for planning treatment team involvement.

The need for consistency across settings is greater for the child on the spectrum. These children do not spontaneously generalize from one situation to another, nor do they necessarily see similarities or make connections across situations as their typical peers do. They are more prone to perceiving mixed messages when conditions differ and when adults approach them differently. For example, consider the boy who engaged in unsafe cyberspace activities. This behavior was so serious that it was selected as a primary therapeutic goal in his private treatment. It was decided that computer privileges would be curtailed and supervised in the home. Additionally, the therapist was devoting time to discussing the potential dangers of cyberspace engagement with the boy. What was missing in this plan was the collaboration with the school. For this boy to generalize, he needed to have consistency with rules around computer access in school *and* at home. He also needed reinforcement regarding the dangers of Internet use by a designated school staff member. Because the treatment goal was not initially shared with the school, the boy did not generalize the learning and did not understand the importance of the computer restrictions in the home setting, refusing to abide by them. Speech and language therapists, school counselors, special educators, and teachers need to share in the implementation of goal-specific strategies in order to promote the kind of generalization needed for changing behaviors.

As you can see in this example, the young man did not gain insight into the depth, severity, and potential consequences of the situation. This lack of insight and inability to consider the possibility of personal risk is akin to what adolescent psychologists refer to as the Personal Fable (Alberts, Elkind, & Ginsberg, 2007). In this concept, egocentric thought processing allows the adolescent to see himself or herself as being invulnerable to harm. The typical adolescent moves beyond this type of thinking more quickly than the child diagnosed with ASD. It is exactly this thinking that puts individuals on the spectrum at risk for hurting or being hurt by others. And it is exactly this reasoning that makes sharing treatment planning with significant others such an important part of treating the child diagnosed with ASD.

While the process of formulating the actual treatment plan for a child with ASD is not different from standard procedures, the execution of the steps will be. You will state the problems and the goals. You will determine the method of intervention and decide upon probable outcomes within certain time frames. Yet the way you select the primary areas for treatment will differ. With the child on the spectrum, his or her perception is likely to be skewed and inconsistent. What this means is that your client's input regarding the major problems/issues affecting school and home life may differ significantly from the perceptions of others. This disparity will be beyond what you would typically expect in working with other children. Your client's report will often be based on the events of *that day* and will be seen from his or her unusual perspective. This unique view is different and is characteristic of the disorder. It is based on rigid thinking and an intensive focus on one aspect of the situation to the exclusion of all else. It is also affected by an inability to understand another person's perspective. While you still need to validate the child's feelings as they reflect his or her experience, keep in mind that you will need input from others to ensure the accuracy of what has been reported.

There will be times when you need to rely heavily on the observations and/or assessments of a trained professional in order to define a problem. This type of evaluation may assist you in identifying key factors in the environment that are contributing to the problems that the child is experiencing. It can also give you a clearer picture of how your client is responding in troublesome situations. There will be other times when you will need to recommend that parents/guardians request a formal evaluation from their school district. The resulting data from these sources can assist you in clarifying the issues affecting the child and family.

In formulating your treatment plan, the next step is goal setting. You will select your goals based on the problems you have targeted for treatment. With this population of children, the goals you select may not be understood or accepted by the child. Often children on the spectrum do not "buy into" the need to change their own behaviors. It seems more plausible to them that others would change their actions and perceptions in order to see things the child's way. For example, one child who insisted on lecturing peers and staff on recycling every item to save the environment failed to see how disruptive his behaviors were. When others were trying to move on from the topic and not discuss every piece of trash that went into the trash bin, he did not pick up on obvious cues to drop the subject, nor did he see how frustrating his behavior was to those around him. This is an instance where it may be necessary to negotiate a goal with your client because he or she does not recognize its relevance. You will need to include the parents/guardians in the formulation of the goal, particularly when the child's rigidity of mental set does not allow him or her to perceive things from a broader perspective.

As you move to choosing a therapeutic method for intervention, consideration of the impact of the child's diagnosis on his or her developmental levels of functioning is of paramount importance. For instance, the child who demonstrates academic excellence may have little appreciation or concern for personal hygiene. The point is that in order for your treatment to be effective, you will need to recognize that the developmental levels within the child may vary greatly. This is a unique aspect of the ASD diagnosis, and one that often baffles parents and educators alike. How could Timmy be so proficient in his knowledge of current world events but be more like a young child in terms of basic hygiene? With this population your role as a therapist will be to educate parents/guardians about developmental differences associated with ASD. Educating them should be part of each treatment goal and part of your overall intervention strategy. For instance, you might help Timmy's parents to understand that while he may be able to talk about the political changes in the Middle East, he may not automatically know to put toothpaste on his toothbrush. This does not mean that their child is not intelligent or that he is being "oppositional," it just means that he has unique needs for direct instruction in particular areas. Teaching and training the parents/guardians will provide them with the support they need in making necessary changes in the home and school. Successful outcomes for therapy will be closely tied to success in facilitating change in the parents/guardians' perceptions and approaches. This will lead to changes in the home environment and ultimately a positive change in the child.

Measuring outcomes will be different when working with the high-functioning child on the spectrum. Rather than focusing on the internal emotional states of the child and his or her perceptions, you will be measuring success resulting from external changes made to daily routines across all settings. These external changes are necessary to aid the child in his or her navigation of a confusing world. To achieve optimal outcomes, it is our view that *all* professionals working with children on the spectrum need to prioritize changes in three areas: changes in perceptions, changes in approaches, and changes in the environment. It is only through these changes, made by parents/guardians *and* professionals, that the child will best be able to interpret his or her surroundings.

Consider the outcome of the following case: The goal for private treatment was to promote self-advocacy. In this situation it was to assist a 6-year-old boy in asking to use the restroom. The boy, diagnosed with Asperger syndrome, rigidly interpreted the routine for bathroom breaks at designated times to mean that he could not access the facilities otherwise. Much to his embarrassment, he was very anxious around using the bathroom and was wetting his pants in class.

The teacher's perception of the problem was that it belonged solely to the child. She felt that he *simply* needed to change his behavior by raising his hand and asking to go to the bathroom. She did not understand that his behavior was based on a rigid way of thinking associated with his disability. The boy was confused by the bathroom break rules and was not able to call attention to himself by raising his hand. A change in the teacher's perception and a willingness to change the environment would have made this goal more quickly achievable for the child. In this case, the therapist had recommended that a visual cue card be placed on the boy's desk. The boy could simply turn the card over to indicate his need to use the bathroom. He could then leave the classroom to do so. After many weeks, the teacher relented and implemented this strategy, which was ultimately successful for the boy.

An extended outcome for using this strategy was that the boy came to understand that his needs could be met without calling attention to himself and causing himself needless anxiety. It is often the unintentional inflexibility of adult perceptions that trigger increased rigidity and anxiety in the ASD child. By creatively removing the source of the anxiety (i.e., the rigid interpretation of a practice) many problems can be solved before situations become unmanageable. In this case, the embarrassment of the child was quickly leading to school refusal and could have developed into school phobia.

Treatment outcomes depend on creating environments that will give the child clarity and predictability in daily life. Without clarity and predictability in the child's life, confusion and chaos can occur. Understanding the unique manifestation of the child's disability is the key to creating the kind of environment in which the child can thrive; therefore, it will be beneficial to have a current profile of the ASD child's strengths and weaknesses that can be used to target goals for treatment. That is why we have created the Autism Spectrum Descriptive Profile (ASDP). There are two parts to this profile form, both of which are explained below and provided in full in Appendices E and F. Part I is a measure for gathering information about the child's functioning across domains. Part II guides you through the process of using this information to create the child's profile and to assist in the development of your treatment plan.

In the Appendix of this book, you will find completed samples of the ASDP, Parts I and II, which are based on the presentation of a fictitious child, John, who is diagnosed with Asperger syndrome. Portions of the forms are included in this chapter. You will see how his parents rated him across four domains, yielding a sample narrative profile derived from these ratings. This narrative can be shared with other adults who work with John and have the ability to affect changes in his life. The intensity of the unique impact of John's disability is also measured in separate ratings on the forms. This was included to provide the therapist with another way to identify treatment goals. As explained in the beginning of this chapter, the ASDP should be used in conjunction with other sources of information in developing the treatment plan.

AUTISM SPECTRUM DESCRIPTIVE PROFILE (ASDP): PART I

I. SOCIAL DOMAIN

The first section of the Autism Spectrum Descriptive Profile (ASDP): Part I measures the child's current level of social functioning. We have divided the Social Domain into three sections: Social Relationships, Social Language, and Social Behaviors. These three areas are meant to represent the major aspects of social functioning affected in children who have been diagnosed with ASD. A sample item from each subdomain is replicated below.

A. Social Relationships:

My child **does not have** a same-aged **friend** that he/she has played with regularly over the past year.	Circle One
	agree
	somewhat agree
	neutral/no opinion
	somewhat disagree
	disagree

*This reflects a problem for my **child** in the following range (circle one):*

mild   moderate   severe   n/a

*This reflects a problem for my **family** in the following range (circle one):*

mild   moderate   severe   n/a

B. Social Language:

My child has great **difficulty with** participating in the give and take of **conversational exchanges**	Circle One
	agree
	somewhat agree
	neutral/no opinion
	somewhat disagree
	disagree

*This reflects a problem for my **child** in the following range (circle one):*

mild   moderate   severe   n/a

*This reflects a problem for my **family** in the following range (circle one):*

mild   moderate   severe   n/a

C. Social Behaviors:

My child **engages in** episodes of **non-purposeful behaviors** (e.g., walking in circles, copying numbers from the phonebook, or demonstrating more eccentric rituals).	Circle One
	agree
	somewhat agree
	neutral/no opinion
	somewhat disagree
	disagree

*This reflects a problem for my **child** in the following range (circle one):*

mild   moderate   severe   n/a

*This reflects a problem for my **family** in the following range (circle one):*

mild   moderate   severe   n/a

While there are overlapping social limitations across the subdomains of Social Relationships, Social Language, and Social Behaviors, there are important differences as well. In our experience, it is here in these three areas that the social profile of the child may be distinguished from that of another ASD child. Each person may be affected to some degree by the actions described in the items, but the degree to which they are affected will vary. These variations will result in a unique constellation of social functioning that will emerge as part of the individual's profile. This profile will change over time as the particular path of development unfolds for the ASD child. For this reason, filling out a profile form periodically helps to focus on the changes of skill and function over time.

As Lee Wilkinson points out in his book *A Best Practice Guide to Assessment and Intervention for Autism and Asperger Syndrome in Schools,* the "unique individual needs (of ASD children) present a challenge to the educators and other school professionals who are struggling to cope with the increasing numbers of students with ASD in the classroom" (2010, p. 16). Wilkinson goes on to say that, in general, students with social communication disabilities are placed in the regular education setting with teachers who have not been trained to work with them. The problem is that many professionals are not experienced in working with this population, resulting in a common misconception that all children on the spectrum share the same characteristics. Because of this, parents/guardians often have to invest unnecessary time and effort in explaining just how their child differs from the preconceived perception held by the professional. By dividing the social domain into three separate aspects of functioning, the areas of strength and weakness unique to each child are more clearly defined. This not only has the advantage of helping parents/guardians to understand their child better but also will assist them in explaining their child to others.

Another benefit of knowing how the child functions within these subdomains is that a more focused plan of treatment can be formulated. Therapists will be able to see where the problems lie and how they are impacting social functioning. Consider these examples: Billy's social behaviors cause him to be isolated by peers. He walks in circles when he is anxious; he sniffs his fingers for sensory input; and he exhibits unusual tic-like behaviors when he is unsure of an answer. Billy approaches peers and tries to engage in conversation with them. While the quality of the conversation is superficial, his attempts are real. His profile on the Social Domain would emphasize his need for change in social *behavior.*

Alternatively, Jenny's social profile is quite different from Billy's. She does not currently demonstrate significant difficulties in social behavior. Jenny does not engage in obvious nonpurposeful behaviors (e.g., walking in circles), nor does she exhibit a great need for sensory stimuli (e.g., sniffing fingers). She does not display notable unexpected behaviors (e.g., tics), but she, too, is isolated from typical peers. The reasons for her social struggles are quite different from Billy's and are largely based in her social language deficits. She tends to engage in repetitive speech, often quoting from movies (i.e., scripting), and has great difficulty in the give-and-take of normal conversation. For Jenny, her profile on the Social Domain would indicate a need for development of social *language.*

II. Learning Domain

The second section of the ASDP provides a rating of the child's functioning in relation to learning; again, much of the wording is taken from the *DSM-5* criteria for ASD. The Learning Domain is also divided into three sections: Response to Organizational Demands, Response to Emotional Demands, and Response to Environmental Demands. Below are examples from each of the Learning domains.

A. Response to Organizational Demands:

My child's learning is affected by an **excessive reliance on routines**.	Circle One
	agree
	somewhat agree
	neutral/no opinion
	somewhat disagree
	disagree

*This reflects a problem for my **child** in the following range (circle one):*

mild   moderate   severe   n/a

*This reflects a problem for my **family** in the following range (circle one):*

mild   moderate   severe   n/a

B. Response to Emotional Demands:

My child's learning is compromised by **inflexible patters of thought and expectations** resulting in anxiety (e.g., homework vs. schoolwork, fairness in group processes).	Circle One
	agree
	somewhat agree
	neutral/no opinion
	somewhat disagree
	disagree

*This reflects a problem for my **child** in the following range (circle one):*

mild   moderate   severe   n/a

*This reflects a problem for my **family** in the following range (circle one):*

mild   moderate   severe   n/a

C. Response to Environmental Demands:

My child's learning is impacted by his/her **excessive resistance to changes** in the environment (e.g., change of classroom, seating arrangement, lunch menu, etc).	Circle One
	agree
	somewhat agree
	neutral/no opinion
	somewhat disagree
	disagree

*This reflects a problem for my **child** in the following range (circle one):*

mild   moderate   severe   n/a

*This reflects a problem for my **family** in the following range (circle one):*

mild   moderate   severe   n/a

Now we are looking at how specific facets of ASD affect the ability to learn. Because most of this section refers to learning in the school, the parents/guardians should be advised to consult with a trusted teacher for input in completing the form. A familiar coach and/or a community leader are other sources that might be considered for feedback in filling out this section. Involving others in assessing the child's features in the learning environment is a good way to raise awareness of his or her struggles. It also allows the adults consulted to contribute to the profile that the ASDP is generating.

Much of the literature pertaining to high-functioning children on the spectrum focuses on social-communicative deficits. The specific effects on learning are not always considered. In our experience, teachers and others who work closely with these children often see their behaviors as being "behavioral issues" because they do not understand the root of the deficit. Often children on the spectrum are expected to act and react similarly to their neurotypical peers because they share similar overall cognitive and academic achievement profiles. As Goldstein, Naglieri, and Ozonoff (2009) point out, ASD children can have average or above-average global intelligence and academic achievement, but they have uneven cognitive skills. Some of these splinter skills serve to compensate for others in the bigger picture and can give a false impression. For example, they note that an 8-year-old may be able to decode at the level of a 10-year-old but may comprehend at the level of a 6-year-old. If one were to judge the child's skill on the broad reading score, reading ability would appear to be average. That is why it is so important for people working with this population to be cognizant of each child's various strengths and weaknesses as they are uniquely manifested in this disability.

The effects of these traits on the ASD child's ability to learn in a typical environment can go unrecognized. A typical environment is frequently unstructured and unpredictable. Even in highly structured classrooms with posted routines, disruptions occur. Classmates can act out, fire drills happen, poor weather cancels outdoor recess, unexpected assemblies take place, and loudspeaker announcements interrupt class. These are small changes for the neurotypical child for whom the learning process continues. They are major events for the child on the spectrum, and their impact is significant. Understanding how learning is compromised by some of the characteristics of a particular child will lead to solutions that minimize the recovery time it takes to return to learning. Having a current profile that focuses on how ASD features can impede learning in a particular child is a good start toward making the three changes that we previously discussed as priorities: changing perceptions, changing approaches, and changing the environment.

For example, once an educator or a coach understands that a child on the spectrum is not likely to learn in the same way as neurotypical peers, he or she can find ways to accommodate the needs of the child. A common and pervasive area of difficulty for the ASD child is the lack of ability to generalize learning across situations: What is learned in one class is not applied to another class or even to the same class the next day. This lack of generalization is a disability-related deficit. It is not due to limitations with memory or attention nor is it an act of defiance. It is a failure to automatically make a connection from one concept to another, from one situation to another, or even from one day to another. Each act of learning can be compartmentalized by the child. Consider this: Mary had learned about the Battle of Gettysburg in class with her regular teacher. The next day a substitute teacher unexpectedly arrived and continued the lesson, using the same materials. Mary was confused by having a different person instructing her and was unable to pay attention to the new information. When her teacher returned from her absence, she briefly reviewed the material presented by the substitute with Mary to assess her comprehension. In this case, the teacher determined that Mary would need additional individual instruction. Being familiar with this child's profile, her teacher was aware that a lack of generalization accounted for Mary's inability to learn from the substitute. This enabled her to change her perception of Mary's capacity to learn and her approach to working with her.

III. Independent Functioning Domain

The third section of the ASDP is designed to give information about how well the ASD child functions independently. As in the previous two domains, this area is divided into three sections: Self-Care Practices, Safety Practices, and Life Skills Practices. The wording of the items is not taken from the *DSM-5*, but rather reflects many of the practical skills that are affected by this disability. Expect variability across subdomains, as not all of these skills will be affected in each child/adolescent. For example, not every child on the spectrum has sensory issues, not every child has unusual eating habits, and not every child will have notable difficulty with chores and responsibilities. The information yielded from this domain will target very specific areas of functioning that are troublesome in the everyday life of the child and his or her family.

A. Self-Care Practices:

My child **does not demonstrate basic hygiene practices** expected for his/her age (i.e., wash hands, brush teeth, comb hair, wipe nose).	Circle One
	agree
	somewhat agree
	neutral/no opinion
	somewhat disagree
	disagree

This reflects a problem for my **child** in the following range (circle one):

mild   moderate   severe   n/a

This reflects a problem for my **family** in the following range (circle one):

mild   moderate   severe   n/a

B. Safety Practices:

My child **does not exhibit** age-appropriate **safe behaviors** when engaging **in cyberspace** activities, (ie., texting, Web surfing, game playing, social networking, e-mailing).	Circle One
	agree
	somewhat agree
	neutral/no opinion
	somewhat disagree
	disagree

This reflects a problem for my **child** in the following range (circle one):

mild   moderate   severe   n/a

This reflects a problem for my **family** in the following range (circle one):

mild   moderate   severe   n/a

C. Life Skills Practices:

My child **has not acquired** age-appropriate **money management skills** (i.e., understands the purpose of money, the value of coins and bills, the monetary value of material goods).	Circle One
	agree
	somewhat agree
	neutral/no opinion
	somewhat disagree
	disagree

This reflects a problem for my **child** in the following range (circle one):

mild   moderate   severe   n/a

This reflects a problem for my **family** in the following range (circle one):

mild   moderate   severe   n/a

An advantage of including the three areas listed above (Self-Care Practices, Safety Practices, and Life Skills Practices) is that it creates a broader description of how the child functions. You will be able to help parents/guardians identify specific self-care, safety, and life skill practices that can often be incorporated into the child's educational program as well as addressed at home. Coordinating efforts across environments to address these areas of need will strengthen learning, and hopefully prevent future failures. For example, a 9-year-old child may be open to instruction in more efficient bathing practices (e.g., visual aids at home or guidance by a school nurse). However, waiting until the child is 13 years old may mean that you have lost critical time for collaborating with others to teach this important life skill. At the age of 13, the child is likely to insist that this topic is off-limits for discussion, despite having developed a less than efficient approach to self-care.

If you are working with an older child, these areas of independent functioning are especially crucial to determine and define. Often times when the individual diagnosed with ASD graduates from high school, parents/guardians are largely unaware of how well their child will function without the structure of home and school. It is often the case that all of the services provided through Special Education programs (if any) are academically based and do not address the essential needs for functioning independently in the adult world. With the provisions dictated by IDEA (2004), it is mandatory to begin addressing special education students' transitional needs by the time the child turns 16 years of age. Commonly, the evaluations considered will address student interests, job-related knowledge, aptitudes, and vocational preferences. Those who are lower functioning are often provided with supported work environments and job coaches. It is often assumed by educators that for higher functioning adolescents on the spectrum, greater supports are not necessary and that their overall cognitive and academic abilities will carry them. Parents/guardians often find themselves surprised by how difficult the transition to college or postsecondary pursuits can be for the individual diagnosed with ASD.

As Temple Grandin points out, there are numerous people on the high-functioning end of the autism spectrum who are either unemployed or underemployed. She laments the fact that so many have valuable talents and strengths that have not been developed along the way. While many need mentors to teach them how to optimize strengths and identify obstacles, others will learn these things in the home (Grandin & Duffy, 2004). The reality is that basic skills of daily life have to be achieved in order to maximize talents and strengths needed for successful adult living. The achievement of these skills (as listed in the Independent Functioning domain) requires assessment/identification, individualized instruction in targeted areas, and ongoing monitoring in children and adolescents with ASD. Unlike their neurotypical peers who acquire such skills at a predictable developmental rate, the individual on the spectrum is not so predictable. His or her parents/guardians will need to have a clear picture of how their child functions independently in order to support the child in the transition from childhood to adulthood.

IV. Positive Attributes Domain

It is important for caregivers to recognize and appreciate the strengths of their ASD child. The attributes they possess can be invaluable when they are realized to their full potential. Tony Attwood points out that many qualities typical of children on the autism spectrum are traits that are valued in the home, school, and work environments. In his Attributes Activity, Attwood actually lists the ASD individual's positive qualities along with his or her difficulties. He recommends doing this as a way to assist in explaining the diagnosis to the child and family. Including the child's strengths is a way to refocus perceptions and create a clearer picture of the child's profile. Attwood states that this "is a way to introduce the benefits of having the characteristics of Asperger Syndrome" (2007, p. 332).

In this section we have included some of the positive characteristics suggested by Tony Attwood, and we have added many of our own that are often associated with people who carry an ASD diagnosis. Parents/guardians are asked to circle those that apply to their child and to generate some positive descriptors of their own. In doing this, we are incorporating a strength-based approach to working with parents/guardians of children on the spectrum (Mossman Steiner, 2010).

Positive Attributes Domain

Honest	Kind	Helpful	Reliable
Knowledgeable	Precise	Good memory	Humorous
Liked by adults	Observant	Persistent	Generous
Nonjudgmental	Confident in areas of expertise		Rule-follower

Other attributes:_____

By designating a separate section of the ASDP to positive traits, not only is the profile enhanced, but identified strengths can be used in the formulation of treatment goals. For example, if the goal is to increase the frequency of social interactions with peers, and your client has been described as helpful, the parent can share this attribute with the teacher. The teacher can then arrange periodic trips to the school office with a peer to deliver papers. This may be a way to foster a social relationship between the child and his or her classmate.

Teachers are usually receptive to reasonable suggestions for specific ways in which a child's strengths can be used to promote social and developmental growth. Parents/guardians may need to be creative, albeit reasonable, in helping teachers and other professionals understand what it takes for their child's attributes to be fully expressed. As the therapist, one of your functions will likely be to support them in forming and maintaining an effective relationship with teachers. This will include guiding them in what is an appropriate amount of communication and what are realistic expectations. When people are overwhelmed, their expectations can seem logical to them but may in fact appear as unreasonable to others involved. The work you do with parents/guardians in creating the collaborative agreements for treatment (see Chapters 6 and 7) will be helpful in encouraging parents/guardians to do something similar with teachers and other school professionals to avoid excessive communication and unrealistic expectations.

AUTISM SPECTRUM DESCRIPTIVE PROFILE (ASDP): PART II

In this section, we will discuss the second part of the ASDP. Referring back to our fictitious client John, we will review the formulation of his narrative profile and treatment goals by looking at portions of his completed ASDP, Part II below. (Reminder: A fully completed ASDP, Parts I and II, can be found in Appendices G and H.) The completion of Part II is a five-step process.

Step 1 identifies the areas of need that are unique to John. These areas are found in the bolded descriptors of the first three domains (Social, Learning, and Independent Functioning) rated by his parents as "agree" on the ASDP, Part I. They are listed below.

I. Social Domain

Relationships	Language	Behaviors
Prefers adults	*Difficulty with conversational exchanges*	*Doesn't relate to emotional experiences*
Bully or be bullied	*Gets stuck on a single interest*	*Exhibits unexpected behaviors*
Difficulty with perspective taking		*Unique perception of fairness*

Here you can see that John's social functioning reflects specific difficulties in each of the three aspects of the Social Domain. From the parents' ratings on the ASDP, Part I (see sample form in the Appendix) we know that John experiences other problems in his social world, but they are rated as being less problematic. These other issues may take on a greater importance in future treatment as John experiences developmental changes. At this time, the aspects listed above are most prevalent. Updating John's profile periodically is a way to assist you in determining whether there is a need for change in treatment goals.

II. Learning Domain

Organizational	Emotional	Environmental
Attention unpredictably captured	*Inflexible patterns of thoughts and expectations*	*Excessive resistance to change*
Memory overly focused on details	*Does not work well in groups*	*Absence of interest in others' opinions*
Difficulty with discussion-based learning	*Focuses on singular interests*	
Tendency to compartmentalize	*Mood can change unexpectedly/rapidly*	
Failure to generalize		

In the Learning Domain, John shows difficulties across the three subdomains. His excessive rigidity and lack of ability to make connections is interfering with his academic success. Additionally, his hyperfocus on his own areas of interest and apparent lack of appreciation for the views of others is precluding him from participating in group work with typical peers. This is leading to further social difficulty and will increasingly become more of a problem as he continues through adolescence.

III. Independent Functioning Domain

Self-Care	Safety	Life Skills
	Does not exhibit safe cyberspace behaviors	*Hasn't acquired money management skills*
		Hasn't acquired time management skills
		Doesn't complete home chores/responsibilities

Interestingly, in the Independent Functioning domain, John's parents do not rate his self-care practices as problem areas. This is unusual because hygiene issues with the ASD child are frequently a source of embarrassment and concern for caregivers. From the ratings it would appear that John does not stand out as being different from peers in the way he eats, drinks, or dresses. At home he exhibits safe behaviors in age-appropriate situations (e.g., answering the phone or door) and does not have safety issues in his use of potentially harmful tools (e.g., knives, scissors, etc.). Yet he *is* a safety risk in his use of cyberspace. Exploring John's risky online behaviors is crucial for the therapist in prioritizing treatment goals. Beyond the safety issues, the ASDP is showing that life skill issues are cited as troublesome. These are urgent areas to be addressed within the school's transition program and also at home.

Step 2 identifies John's areas of strength. These are found in the fourth domain, where a list of positive attributes has been created. This is included as an important reminder that remarkable strengths are a unique feature of this diagnosis. You will see on the actual form that we have allotted additional space in this section for parents/guardians to add their own positive descriptors, beyond the options we provided.

IV. Positive Attributes Domain

knowledgeable	*precise*	
good memory	*observant*	*persistent*
liked by adults	*confident in areas of expertise*	*polite to strangers*
enjoys being helpful in areas of interest	*takes pride in his work*	*works well one-on-one with adults*
works well independently in areas of high interest		

John's current strengths, as noted above, describe him as being someone who has areas of expertise that he enjoys sharing with others. The fact that he has strengths in working with adults (one on one) is useful in planning opportunities for instruction. Knowing that he can work independently in areas of high interest gives his teachers information they can use as contingencies for reinforcement when John is working in less preferred subject areas. Consider the following example: One young man diagnosed with Asperger syndrome had excellent computer skills and was able to participate in a work-study course requiring him to visit nursing homes and teach residents to play computer games. While this was not an effective way of promoting socialization with peers, it did tap into the development of a social awareness of the needs of others.

Step 3 combines the information from Steps 1 and 2 to generate a narrative profile for John. This profile has many uses and will support his parents' efforts to explain how their son is affected by his disability. It will also help to clarify for his parents where his strengths and weaknesses lie. Having this precise narrative will empower them in dealing with those who work with John.

John Jones is a 14-year-old, ninth-grade male who lives with his parents and younger sisters. He is diagnosed with Asperger syndrome, a social-communicative disorder. This uniquely affects his emotional and behavioral regulation across social, learning, and independent functioning areas of life.

*Socially, John is the type of child who **prefers the company of adults**. He is often ill at ease with peers because he has **difficulty understanding the perspective of others** and **participating in the give-and-take of conversational exchanges**. It is likely that John will **"get stuck" on a single topic of interest** without awareness of the listener's level of interest in that topic. Additionally, he will have **trouble relating to the emotional experiences of others**, and he may fail to understand their feelings. Because of John's sometimes unusual and **unexpected behaviors** (e.g., hand-flapping when he gets excited), his social presentation makes him a **target for bullying**. As part of his diagnosis, John may have a **unique perception of fairness** which can lead him to retaliate and exhibit **bullying-type behaviors**.*

*In terms of John's learning style, his **attention can be unpredictably captured** by something in the environment not normally of interest to others. He may also be distracted by a **his focus on a singular interest or in a particular topic**. John will not easily transition from one task to the* next and is **resistant to changes** he does not expect. Because his **memory is overly focused on details**, he can miss the main point of instruction. He learns best when essential facts are emphasized for him and tied to the larger picture. This method of instruction will compensate for his **tendency to compartmentalize and failure to generalize** across learning situations.

John has **difficulty with discussion-based learning**. He can become confused and anxious when presented with multiple opinions. Because he has **inflexible patterns of thought and expectations**, group work can be overwhelming for him and he can **appear to be uninterested in others' opinions**. In order to avoid the kind of frustration that can lead to **rapidly and unexpectedly changing moods**, John requires prior preparation and monitoring for any participation in group processes.

Functioning independently can be troublesome for individuals with this profile. Issues of safety commonly arise and more supervision is required. In John's case, he **does not engage in cyberspace activities safely**. Other areas of concern include his **lack of money management skills** which has been exploited by others. His **lack of time management** is also potentially unsafe and can lead to anxiety around issues of punctuality and the ability to meet deadlines. For John, a lack of maturity in social development and a rigid thought process also result in **difficulty with completing chores/responsibilities at home**. John does not see the communal need for participating in family-shared responsibilities.

It is important for the adults in John's life to be aware of his many strengths so that they can promote them to support his success. In fact, John is a young man who is **liked by adults. He is knowledgeable and enjoys helping others in his area of expertise.** He tends to be **observant, persistent, and precise** in executing tasks of high interest. He is **confident in what he can do**. John has a good memory and will **follow the rules** as he understands them. **He is generally polite** when out in public. John does his **best work alone** or in a one-on-one situation **with an adult**.

The full ASDP narrative profile describes John's behaviors across all domains: Social, Learning, Independent Functioning, and Positive Attributes. In part, it explains that he is a young man who will relate to the adults around him more than he will engage with peers. It states that he will not interact spontaneously with his age-mates and adds that John has difficulty with the pragmatics of language. This makes his social exchanges appear different from what would typically be expected of a boy his age. We also learn that John may exhibit unusual behaviors that could make him a target for bullying.

Using his reported strengths (positive attributes), his teachers will be able to tailor methods of instruction to promote John's success. Furthermore, this positive information can be used to enhance transitional planning (including vocational guidance) and future life choices.

Step 4 lists family and child concerns across the first three domains. It reflects only those areas rated (by the parents) as being a severe problem for either the family or for the child. As you see below, there are many examples in which John's parents do not rate him as experiencing their same high level of concern in the problem areas. In fact, there are only four areas (three in the Learning domain and one in the Independent Functioning domain) in which John's parents see him as being similarly impacted.

	Family concerns	Child concerns
I. Social Domain	Bully or be bullied	n/a
	Difficulty with Perspective taking	n/a
	Difficulty in normal conversation	n/a
	Gets stuck on a single interest	moderate
	Exhibits unexpected behaviors	n/a
	Unique perception of fairness	n/a
II. Learning Domain	Difficulty with discussion-based learning	moderate
	Memory overly focused on details	severe
	Tendency to compartmentalize	severe
	Tendency to generalize	severe

	Rigid pattern of thoughts and expectations	moderate
	Highly restricted/fixated interests	n/a
	Mood can change unexpectedly/rapidly	n/a
	Excessive resistance to change	mild
	Inability to inhibit behaviors and concerns for safety	n/a
III. Independent Functioning Domain	Does not exhibit safe behaviors engaging in cyberspace	n/a
	Not acquired money management skills	severe
	Not acquired time management skills	mild

Those areas rated as "severe" concerns for both the family and the child are areas that will need to be prioritized and addressed through a collaborative effort. The therapist will now be able to guide the parents on how best to involve other professionals in an interdisciplinary approach to intervene effectively. More specifically, there will be particular professionals at the school who can formulate plans to help John to manage money, that is, to expand his focus and to employ strategies for compartmentalizing and generalizing effectively. Special education teachers, speech and language therapists, and occupational therapists will be particularly helpful in introducing necessary accommodations and strategies for John. Most often this collaborative work will be between the parents and the school. In addition, John's therapist can use this impact list in formulating treatment goals.

Step 5 involves the creation of treatment goals. Note that the goals listed below were selected by the therapist, in conjunction with John's parents, as they reviewed the completed ASDP and other information. Together they decided upon the areas where therapy would be most effective at this point in time.

1. *John is exhibiting bully behaviors. This happens when he perceives that he has been unfairly treated by another child. The goal will be to work on developing skills in communicating his need for fairness. This work will involve training with the parents/guardians so that they can advocate for appropriate school supports.*

2. *John has a fixated interest in animé. This is disrupting his social and learning environments. The goal will be to create a plan with the client and his family to identify appropriate times for engaging in this pastime. Again, this work will involve parent training and the recommendation that they coordinate efforts with the school to create a related plan.*

3. *John does not exhibit safe behaviors when engaging in cyberspace. The goal will be to work with him to understand the dangers and to assist his family to set limits around computer use. The parents/guardians will need help* **with determining feasible parameters and training in how to coordinate a related plan with the school.**

In John's case, each of the three domains is reflected in his treatment goals. However, this will not always be true. For him, the risk for being bullied is increasing as his fixated interest in anime grows. He has a history of being bullied and is becoming more frustrated and likely to retaliate in response. Also, his interest in visiting chat rooms on the Internet and in writing blogs about his anime favorites put him at risk. Both the therapist and his parents are worried for John's safety. They will work with him on implementing strategies for safe cyberspace use both at home and at school.

Let's turn now to the next chapter, which focuses on the creation of a collaborative agreement for working with parents/guardians. This contract will define the expectations and boundaries of the therapeutic relationship.

CHAPTER 6

How and Why to Set Boundaries With Parents/Guardians

CONSIDER A DAY in the life of Ann Smith, a fictitious compilation of a number of clients we have known:

> Ann starts her day waking at 5 am to be sure that the heat gets turned up to exactly 68 degrees. She turns on five specific lights in the house and then goes to the kitchen to make a hamburger to be served on an English muffin, toasted twice with 2 tablespoons of ketchup underneath the burger (not on top). Ann pours two-thirds of a glass of blue Kool-Aid into a particular Star Wars cup with an attached straw. She then places the food on a placemat that sits at the far end of the table. As Ann's son is coming down the stairs for his breakfast, she rushes to the bathroom to put toothpaste on his toothbrush and lay it on the sink for him. This is just the first hour of Ann's day, and there is still much to be done before she drives her son to school at 7 am. Later, as he is getting ready to go out to the car, she will make sure he looks presentable, that he has his school supplies, and that his lunch is packed. It will be placed at the top of his backpack in a blue plastic lunch container that he uses every day. Ann's

son is 16 years old and in the 10th grade. He is a computer whiz and has an above-average IQ overall. He is diagnosed with Asperger syndrome.

"Originally identified as an emotional disorder caused by parental ambivalence and rejection, autism today is universally seen as a neurobiological difficulty, whose cause is organic and related to atypical brain development" (Mesibov, Adams, & Schopler, 2000, pp. 637–647). While parents are no longer viewed as the cause of this disorder, there are times when they are seen as contributing to it. In Ann's case in the vignette above, structuring the environment, anticipating needs, and providing preventative measures to maintain predictability for her child can all be perceived as inhibiting her son's growth and development. A therapist or teacher who becomes aware of her morning rituals might question how this adolescent will learn to become independent. He or she might perceive Ann's practices to be the basis of her son's rigidity and his need for routines to be rooted in her parenting choices. But Ann knows that this is not the case. She also knows that this *is* what people think. Therefore, she chooses to keep her home life very private. This means fewer friends, more restricted social interactions, and less participation in community events. Ann is also not comfortable allowing people into her home. Like so many parents/guardians of children with disabilities, Ann needs *more* support than parents of typically developing children, yet she gets less. What this parent needs is someone to talk to. She needs someone who will not judge her and who will understand the impact of having a child diagnosed with ASD. What she and others like her need is a therapeutic support that is clearly defined and consistently given.

To provide this it is crucial to establish an agreement of collaboration with the parents/guardians that delineates the extent of participation of the therapist. We recommend the use of this agreement in all therapeutic relationships with these caregivers. However, we find its use to be critical when dealing with parents/guardians who themselves exhibit ASD-like characteristics. Remember that these characteristics may stem from an ASD diagnosis, or they may be the result of years of engaging in compensatory strategies centered on understanding the world from their child's autistic point of view (Attwood, 2012).

The act of setting boundaries needs to be done in a straightforward, concrete, and nonthreatening way. Parents/guardians of ASD children appreciate clarity. They are already navigating a difficult path for themselves, their families, and for the ASD child. They should not have to spend time figuring out the specifics of your support. Additionally, this agreement serves the purpose of helping you to stay on track as you chart the course of treatment. This is especially necessary as time goes on and your empathy for the parents/guardians grows. It is our experience that having a set agreement from the start is necessary to establish a healthy, productive, and ongoing relationship. It has the advantage of preventing therapeutic "burnout" over time.

Determining prior limits on your time and involvement in each case will also prevent you from trying to compensate for the limitations of some parents/guardians. For example, some will have trouble collaborating effectively with an interdisciplinary team. Ineffective collaboration by the parents/guardians can result in slow progress for the ASD child and the family. This is one circumstance that can lead to overinvolvement on the part of the therapist in an attempt to move the process forward. Through the establishment of this collaborative agreement, you and your clients will be able to decide upon the best ways to work together. Spelling out the terms of your outside involvement in each case will prevent you from doing more than you should be doing.

There will be times when you will *want* to do more than your agreement stipulates. For example, you may waver in your decisions regarding phone calls. Or you might find yourself wanting to become more involved with the school to resolve certain difficulties. Often knowing that you are one of the few who understands the disability, particularly as it is affecting this family, is enough to make you want to cross the limits of your agreement. That is why we suggest that you revisit the collaborative agreement on a monthly basis to renew the understanding of what you and the parents/guardians have determined to be the best course of treatment. It will give you an opportunity to address with them your feelings of wanting to do more. It will serve as a reminder that your best work will be accomplished only within the agreed-upon bounds of your role as therapist.

To give you a better sense of what the parents/guardians are dealing with as they raise their ASD child, we will share with you some of the stressful factors described by Marcus, Kunce, and Schopler in the *Handbook of Autism and Pervasive Developmental Disorders* (2005). They report that "the parents and siblings of children with autism must cope with a unique and more intense pattern of stressors" (p. 1055). They list 10 factors they consider to be most stressful and which may influence the family's need for support. Those listed below, as cited from the *Handbook* are particularly relevant to parenting the higher functioning ASD child.

- *Diagnostic confusion.* "A sizable portion of parents, perhaps one-third to one-half, are told that there is no cause for concern or immediate action while others are referred to other professionals who may offer contradictory opinions or bury the autism diagnosis in terms such as 'developmental delays in social and language areas,' 'autistic tendencies,' and similar nonspecific labels" (DeGiacomo & Fombonne, 1998; Howlin & Moore, 1997; Smith et al., 1994). "Even when the autism diagnosis is given, all too often parents leave with a label but not with a clear and informative description of their child's problems and intervention needs" (Marcus, Kunce, & Schopler, 2005, p. 1056).

Considering the amount of ambiguity the parents/guardians have experienced up to this point in seeking a diagnosis and in getting clear professional advice, the clarity you are bringing to their situation now will be crucial for your work together. The structure of the collaborative agreement provides them with a sense of much needed security. The parents/guardians will know the extent of your commitment to them as together you clarify "diagnostic confusion" and, as stated above, provide them with an "informative description of their child's problems and intervention needs" (Marcus et al., 2005, p. 1056).

- *Uneven and unusual course of development.* While the course of development varies for each child with ASD, all children with this diagnosis present with inconsistencies across certain areas of skill. This is a prominent feature of ASD and is "confusing to parents, whose natural inclination is to expect normal development" (Marcus et al., 2005, p. 1056). Higher functioning children on the spectrum often exhibit particular skills in their earlier years that are viewed by the adults around them as being developmentally advanced. This makes it difficult for parents to figure out why the same child can have trouble with some simple tasks. "For example, when [the parents] see their child solve a complex puzzle or remember a route to a fast-food restaurant, they view these as evidence of healthy development and, understandably, overlook receptive language delays or weak imitation skills. Further, the child's uneven profile makes gauging appropriate expectations difficult and predicting future development challenging (Schunterman 2002)" (Marcus et al., 2005, p. 1056)

At this point, you should be aware of your client's individual profile, including areas of developmental strengths and weaknesses (see Chapter 2). The collaborative agreement provides assurances to the parents/guardians that you will assist them in setting realistic goals and expectations for their ASD child through the use of this knowledge.

- *The "can't versus won't dilemma."* "Children with autism frequently are inconsistent in their responses across settings, people and time" (Marcus et al., 2005, p. 1057). These inconsistencies lead parents/guardians to question whether their child is truly unable to comply and consistently perform certain actions (e.g., change their clothes, take out the trash, etc.) or whether he or she just won't. The reality is that the child's responses may be tied to a particular environmental cue rather than to the language of the request, causing a misunderstanding that can have a negative consequence. For example, the child is told that it is time to eat, but the dinner has not yet been served. The child might say, "I'm not coming" and refuse to come out of his or her room because the food was not yet on the table. This can be construed as being oppositional when, in fact, the environmental cue (food on the table) is what triggered the child's response (Dix, 1993).

When motives are misconstrued, power struggles ensue, tensions mount, and tempers rise. This is the life led by parents/guardians of ASD children as they attempt to resolve conflicts that are potentially explosive. It would not be unusual for them to contact you for help in such situations, particularly when they are explosive. Your Collaborative Agreement will direct them to address these issues themselves in the moment and then later with you, within the therapy session.

- *Behavior in public.* "Parents understandably may worry that others judge them as being unable to control what appears to be a physically normal child, while siblings may worry that peers may tease either their sibling or themselves. Thus, it is not surprising that some family members report feeling rejected or isolated (Avdi, Griffin, & Brough, 2000; Gray, 2002; Sharpley, Bitsika, & Ephrimidis, 1997)" (Marcus et al., 2005, p. 1058).

Time and time again parents of high-functioning children diagnosed with ASD report high levels of frustration and embarrassment around the public behavior of their children. Shonda Shilling says of her son (diagnosed with Asperger syndrome) who was having a tantrum in reaction to the noise of the baseball stadium: "All nearby heads turned in our direction. People had the most concerned looks on their faces, as if to say, 'What did you do to your kid, lady?' A few more 'I-wanna-gos' (sic) and the expression morphed into an indignant 'Jeez, why can't you get control of your kid?' " (Schilling & Shilling, 2011, p. 8). With your support, parents/guardians will be more prepared to deal with these situations, particularly as you process each incident with them during your parent-only sessions.

- *Professional relationships.* "Given the complexity of autism and its impact on multiple aspects of development, it is not surprising that effective intervention programs typically involve input from numerous professionals. The resulting need to manage relationships with those professionals creates multiple stressors for the families of children with autism" (Marcus et al., 2005, p. 1058).

Not all professionals are well versed in treating children on the spectrum, and some may propose the use of strategies and interventions that are inadequate or inappropriate for the ASD population. Therefore, your expertise will be needed and consultations will be requested by other professionals involved with your client. By establishing the terms and extent of your involvement with these other professionals in the collaborative agreement, parents/guardians will know the boundaries, while also feeling supported.

Next, let's look more closely at the Collaborative Agreement Between the Therapist and Parents/Guardians. We will examine the necessity and advantages of each section as it relates to the therapeutic process. (To review this form in its entirety, see Appendix I.)

COLLABORATIVE AGREEMENT BETWEEN THERAPIST AND PARENTS/GUARDIANS

Our collaborative form begins with the Statement of Purpose presented below. This is meant to succinctly explain the main reasons for recommending the formulation of an agreement between you and the parents/guardians. Based on your knowledge of the stressors in the family and the information in this chapter, you may choose to personalize and expand upon the wording of the Statement of Purpose as you introduce it to the parents/guardians.

STATEMENT OF PURPOSE: The course of treatment is not always predictable and clear. That is why it is best to begin this process with a written and signed statement of collaboration that can be referred to as the course of therapy unfolds. Defining mutual expectations from the outset is important. This will help to provide a level of comfort for the therapeutic process to flow more efficiently, effectively, and amicably.

After you have discussed the purpose of the agreement and feel assured of the parents/guardians' understanding, it will be time to move on to an explanation of the specific guidelines of your arrangement. On Section I of the form, entitled Sessions (see below), you will have predetermined the frequency and duration of your sessions based on your own availability and on the therapeutic needs of your client. You will have filled in parts A and B and will need to discuss scheduling appointments with the parents/guardians.

I. SESSIONS:

A. Frequency of sessions:	
B. Length of sessions:	
C. Consistent day & time:	

At this point it will be important for you to stress the need for consistency in choosing the day and time of your meetings. When working with this population, having predetermined meetings on a set day and at a set time can be crucial to the development of the therapeutic process. Children on the spectrum have a heightened need for predictability in order to manage their anxiety. Having a consistent therapy time as part of their scheduled routine benefits them, as well as their parents/guardians. It gives them all a sense of security to know that no matter how stressful their week has been, they will have a scheduled time with you to address their issues. Having this regularly scheduled appointment is likely to decrease the need for frequent calls to you when situations arise outside of the therapy session.

In keeping with the theme of maintaining structure and predictability when working with children diagnosed with ASD and their families, we recommend the following sequence for the therapy hour (see Section II below). You may follow this format, or you may choose a structure that fits your needs with this client. The point is, no matter what you choose, it should be spelled out in the agreement and adhered to as closely as possible for the benefit of all.

II. TYPICAL STRUCTURE OF SESSIONS:

A. Review of week with parent alone (10 minutes)

B. Review of week and discussion of current issues with child alone (30 minutes)

C. Summary work with child and parents/guardians (10 minutes)

While following a set course within the therapy session is always beneficial when working with children, it is especially anxiety reducing for children on the spectrum. Having the parents/guardians share their concerns alone at the beginning and then returning to join the child at the end of each session provides the therapist with a way of detecting commonalities of concerns. This format also helps to promote closure and increases the possibility of generalizing therapeutic learning through creating an environment of cooperative problem solving.

For example, one set of parents reported that their young teenager was having frequent meltdowns during a recent school vacation week. He was accusing his parents of being overprotective and not allowing him the same freedom as his cousins. His parents were angry and defensive about their son's accusations and were limiting his independent activities outside of the home for legitimate reasons. The teen had a history of wandering and then panicking when he got lost. After hearing this concern from the parents and then listening to the child in his individual time, the end of the session was devoted to problem solving around the situation with both parents and child present. The child *heard* that his parents' fears were well grounded and the parents *learned* that their son's need for independence was developmentally appropriate. The therapist then assisted the family in formulating a reasonable, short-term plan that allowed the child some additional freedom, while his parents felt assured of his safety. An added advantage of having structured the session this way is that it resulted in a solution rather than the continuation of family arguments around the issue. Children on the spectrum tend to perseverate on their concerns and have trouble negotiating with their parents. This is a common difficulty for ASD children.

In addition to these recommendations for the consistent structuring of your sessions, we also suggest implementing specific policies for further clarity and predictability in therapy. Those listed below represent the areas we have found to be most relevant when working with this population of children and families. You may want to choose some or all of them while adding your own policies to the list.

III. POLICIES:

A. *Parent–therapist sessions* will occur on a regular basis, taking the place of a typical session as described above. The frequency of these meetings will be scheduled by the therapist in conjunction with the parents/guardians. Any unscheduled parents/guardians' sessions must be planned in advance to allow adequate notice for the child.

Parents/guardians need to know that regular meetings without the child present will be scheduled so that sensitive information can be discussed openly. When the child is present for every meeting, parents/guardians often avoid bringing up provocative or sensitive topics in order to avoid confrontation with the child. Alternatively, out of frustration parents/guardians will bring up information with the child present that is evocative and counterproductive to the situation at hand. This can take the therapy in an unexpected direction, and it is less likely to occur when parents are given their own scheduled time. These parent–therapist sessions should occur at predetermined intervals that work best for all involved. It is important that the child understands this aspect of treatment from the start. It may be necessary to reiterate the terms of this part of the agreement to the child many times over. The child may need to be assured that you will be using these sessions to talk about important adult information, and you will not be disclosing your private conversations with him or her. This issue is best addressed openly and firmly without negotiation or lengthy discussion. It is simply a part of the process.

B. *Family sessions* **will occur as needed. These must be also planned in advance to allow adequate notice for the child.**

Family involvement is a necessary component to therapy and should be discussed with the parents/guardians. It will be important to explain that other family members need to participate periodically in order to understand the disorder. Familiarity with the best approaches for interacting productively with the ASD child begins with information shared in family sessions. As you will read in Chapter 8, siblings have a difficult role to play in the family of any child who has a disability, and particularly so in the family of the ASD child. Over time you will be able to determine how frequently you will need to involve certain family members.

As you consider the dynamics of the family and their needs, it may become apparent that some problems extend beyond the impact of the child's disability. There may be other issues in the family that need to be separated out from this therapy and be addressed elsewhere. If this is the case, you will need to insist that another therapist (e.g., a family therapist, couples counselor, or a separate individual therapist) becomes involved. Be sure that the person you recommend is open to consultation with you and has some awareness of the impact of ASD on a family. The sooner you recognize that unrelated issues exist, the better it will be for your own self-preservation and for the therapeutic path. We have found it helpful to remind ourselves that it is not possible to *treat* parents and to provide them with *guidance* in raising their ASD child at the same time. The total focus of your therapy has to be on treating the child within his or her family constellation. And yet, as we have so often emphasized, there are limits to what you can provide in terms of treating the child. For instance, you will find that contact outside of sessions is a frequent request and sometimes is needed for the ASD child. Having a plan that clearly defines the limits of your availability from the start is crucial to maintaining healthy therapeutic boundaries.

C. *Contact outside of sessions* will occur as follows:

1. The therapist's availability to attend school meetings will be:

_____

2. The therapist's availability to attend professional meetings will be:

_____

3. Compensation for attendance, including travel time: _____ per hour.

Setting boundaries is not always easy, and it is even more difficult if you wait until there is a need to establish them. Parents/guardians will appreciate knowing what to expect of your involvement outside of the therapy session and what compensation will be expected for it. It is imperative to make your clients aware that there are other demands on your time and that you will need to meet all of those demands within the structure of your workday. What we are emphasizing here is the need for you to be cognizant of how important your role can be to parents/guardians of ASD children, to the point that they will expect a lot of you. Remember that they, more so than other parents, have had past experiences of being dismissed, criticized, and judged by others. Developing a relationship with you may serve a long-held need for a compassionate and trusted confidant. Therefore, another boundary you will need to establish is your availability for phone consultations. Knowing the conditions under which you will consider providing support via the telephone serves as yet another reminder that you are there to work with them as a therapist, not as a friend.

4. Requests for therapist phone consultation with the parents/guardians and/or the child will be considered. Such requests should be made only when the situation is urgent and cannot wait until the next session. The caller will need to leave a brief summary of the situation and the reason for its urgency. The call will be returned by the therapist and handled accordingly.

Your clients will need to know that you will be checking your messages and will always return those of an urgent nature. Calls made by the child will be brought to the parents/guardians attention. They should also be informed that there may be a delay in returning nonurgent calls about situations that are best addressed within the therapy session. Parents/guardians need to know that excessive calls to you as the child's therapist can result in increased anxiety for the child. The collaboration being spelled out in this agreement has to take into consideration that the majority of the work will be done together, face to face. An overdeveloped alliance with parents/guardians via frequent outside contact can undermine the child's trust in the therapist and distort his or her view of the therapist's role. For these reasons, phone calls should be limited to urgent situations. The definition of what constitutes an emergency will need to be communicated directly upon presentation of this agreement according to your own practices. When urgent clinical issues arise at times when you are not available for an extended period (e.g., vacation), parents/guardians will need to know that you will be providing coverage for emergencies.

5. Professional coverage will be made available when the therapist is on vacation or otherwise away for an extended period of time. As previously discussed, this person should be contacted only for urgent matters. However when *safety* is a concern, care should be sought through the nearest hospital emergency room (i.e., call 911).

You may find that some parents/guardians will resist following your plan for emergency coverage. Their attachment to you and to the routines you have established together are integral to their concept of therapeutic support. Referring these clients to an unknown professional can cause increased anxiety for parents/guardians. It may also trigger explosive meltdowns on the part of the child. As you know, the ASD child needs sameness; changes in routines and schedules, and expected occurrences can precipitate behavioral difficulties. It may be helpful to the family for you to review potential flashpoints and preplan strategies to deal with these situations while you are away. For example, going to a favorite store or restaurant during the usual scheduled therapy time may serve as a way to diffuse and soothe anxiety.

6. Phone contact and consultation with school staff and other professionals will require a signed release form describing the parameters of the information to be shared. This will also be true in cases where hospitalization is required and the therapist is involved.

Your signed release of information form should be specific in stating when and how your advice will be needed. There will be some instances when parents/guardians want your involvement in school or other professional matters, and you will deem it unnecessary. In cases such as this, referring back to your personal release of information form and the collaborative agreement will provide the clarity parents/guardians need.

7. The need for nonurgent therapist consultation with the school and other professionals will be determined by the therapist in conjunction with the parents/guardians on a case-by-case basis.

Collaborating across disciplines is time consuming. This is why it is important to define your expectations around your involvement in consulting with school personnel. While you may need to change these expectations from time to time, it is good to have them explained generally and to adhere to them as much as possible. You may want to consider urging parents/guardians to hire an educational advocate in cases where the time commitment is beyond your limit and the interactions of the special education team warrant significant parental support. As in consultation with school personnel, your time and collaboration with a potential advocate would require set parameters to be spelled out within the collaborative agreement.

8. At this time, electronic forms of communication will not be used. The therapeutic relationship that is being formed depends upon personal exchanges.

We recommend curtailing any e-mail or text communication for at least the first month of therapy. By encouraging parents/guardians initially to participate solely in face-to-face discussions, you are building the therapeutic relationship as you discover the unique needs of the family. Unlike other disabilities, ASD is relatively new and continually being defined. Most recently, the *DSM-5* dropped older diagnoses, such as Asperger syndrome and pervasive developmental disorder, not otherwise specified, among others, and parents/guardians have legitimate concerns related to the outcomes of these changes. These are the same parents/guardians who have likely been navigating a confusing diagnostic path for many years, and now it is changing again. For this and other reasons already discussed, their anxiety levels are high and they live with constant stress. They may want to reach out to you in any way possible. Setting clear boundaries on communications right from the start is in the best interests of the therapeutic relationship. In our professional experience, not having these boundaries opens up the possibility of misunderstandings and misconceptions about your role as the therapist. With this population, it is hard to turn back and curtail the extent of communications and expectations. You may choose to loosen certain boundaries over time, but you must do it carefully. Your expectations around scheduled appointments will be the same as with your other clients. We have provided a recommendation for potential cancellations below.

D. *Cancellation of sessions* must be made a minimum of 24 hours in advance. Failure to do so will require a payment of_____ . Note that this fee will not be covered by insurance. You may not have the option of rescheduling the missed appointment. If the therapist determines that cancellations are occurring too frequently, in order to continue in treatment, a specific policy to address this issue will be formulated.

In working with ASD children and their families, we have found that some will never miss a scheduled appointment. In fact, the intensity of anticipation of meeting and the importance placed on it can exceed that of other clients. Conversely, if the family's life is chaotic, they may expect you to be overly flexible due to your understanding of the disability and their family circumstances. If you are dealing with family chaos, you may want to address that in a separate policy in the collaborative agreement.

E. *Other Policies:* _____

_____

Additional policies may address the need to separate ASD-related issues from other therapeutic needs of the family (see Part B of the Policies section above). Or they may involve further details regarding the way in which you will be involved in outside meetings. The point is that the family's particular needs can be addressed through these additional collaborative policies. These can be established at the start of your relationship or as the agreement is periodically reviewed. In addition, see the excerpt below taken from the last part of the Collaborative Agreement regarding confidentiality.

Note: This agreement is not meant to address the limits of confidentiality regarding your child. It is a contract between parents/guardians and therapist that may be modified periodically according to need.

As we conclude our discussion of the Collaborative Agreement Between Therapist and Parents/Guardians, we call your attention to the areas designated for making changes and modifications as needed. This agreement is meant to be a dynamic document that provides a therapeutic structure for the therapist and the parents/guardians. As you can see below, the agreement is meant to clearly define intent, and it requires the signatures of all involved. Through the signing of this written expression of collaborative effort, the focus of therapy is centered specifically on serving the best interests of the child.

This agreement represents the joint effort of the parents/guardians and the therapist to define those guidelines that will best serve the interests of the child.

Parent/Guardian: _____ Date: _____

Parent/Guardian: _____ Date: _____

Therapist: _____ Date: _____

FIRST REVIEW of the Collaborative Agreement

Parent/Guardian: _____   Date: _____

Parent/Guardian: _____   Date: _____

Therapist: _____   Date: _____

SECOND REVIEW of the Collaborative Agreement

Parent/Guardian: _____   Date: _____

Parent/Guardian: _____   Date: _____

Therapist: _____   Date: _____

MODIFICATIONS to the Collaborative Agreement

New Policy   *Date of Change   Initials*

_____

_____

_____

Our next chapter provides you with a separate collaborative agreement to be used between you and the child. The topics are similar but the words are different and meant to be more "child friendly." It is meant to establish an understanding with the child that is independent of parent/guardian involvement. In this way, conflict and misinterpretations around policies are minimized.

CHAPTER 7

How and Why to Set Boundaries With the Autistic Child

L*ET'S TALK ABOUT Amanda, a 13-year-old girl in middle school who lives with her parents and younger sister. It is Monday and a new school day is about to begin. As she lies in bed, she thinks again about the usual Monday schedule. She hates Mondays. It's gym day and she will have to change into shorts in the middle of the day. For the tenth time since waking up, she asks herself, "Why do I have to change into shorts? I can play in my school clothes." She will later ask her mother this question repeatedly and then go on to ask her classmates, and gym teacher, as she does every Monday. She will think about it all morning. She will also think about the food fight in the cafeteria two weeks ago. She is worried that it will happen again. She is so worried that she has refused to eat her lunch in there. She is afraid that another fight will break out.*

During the school day, Amanda concentrates on the clock because she does not want to be late for her next class. She is also worrying about getting caught in the chaos of the corridor. Amanda feels compelled to be the first student to arrive at her classes to ensure getting the same seat every time. Although seats are assigned in all classes, Amanda was not the first to arrive to a class a few months ago and someone had briefly sat in her seat. This was so worrisome to her that she now thinks about it every day. On top of these worries, Amanda struggles through her school day to understand what is expected of her both socially and academically.

By the time Amanda arrives home, she will be exhausted from worrying and will be overwhelmed by the demands of her day. She will not want to go to soccer practice, especially because her little sister is having a friend over to play. Amanda is concerned that they will go into her room and touch her "stuff." Throughout her school day as well as at home, Amanda has an all-consuming interest in Native American heritage. Sometimes when she is worrying about things, she makes herself think about her collections of books and Native American figurines. She makes lists of what she has and what she still needs to complete her collection. She even has a little village set up in her room.

Amanda is considered to be a "quirky kid" with unusual interests. But people outside of her immediate family do not understand the extent of her need for predictability and sameness. Nor do they understand the level of anxiety she experiences in all social situations. Amanda has been diagnosed with Asperger syndrome.

Individuals on the autism spectrum are notoriously misunderstood in terms of their strengths and weaknesses. Because Amanda is high functioning and demonstrates significant factual knowledge, teachers and others think that she should be advanced in all areas. They expect Amanda to be socially mature. Her social deficits, related to her disability, are often interpreted as intentionally arrogant or rude behaviors. Peers and adults tend to shy away from Amanda and feel uncomfortable in her presence. Most of the time, she simply gets ignored. She has been socially isolated at a time in her psychosocial development when friends become all important. Amanda *feels* different and will look to you, her therapist, to validate her strengths and recognize her struggles. As your bond with her grows, she will come to appreciate your honesty and value your respect.

Having a collaborative agreement for the child provides a way for him or her to know what to expect in therapy. It also makes your client feel like a respected participant in the process to have a separate collaborative agreement. Children on the spectrum need explanations and clarifications in ways that other children do not. That is why it is important for you to have a good sense of these children beforehand and a curiosity for learning more about them. In this chapter, we will provide information to help you better understand how individuals diagnosed with ASD perceive their world. We will identify examples of major stressors in their lives and provide you with case examples along the way. This knowledge will help you to understand why a collaborative agreement is important as you enter treatment with the child.

Formulating the collaborative agreement is a way to begin to chart the course for an effective therapeutic relationship. Being forthright in this way avoids the ambiguity that is likely to occur as therapy intensifies. In working with your client, you will find that direct communications are integral to the therapeutic process. Being specific with your language requires care. You will need to clarify with your client the exact nature of each issue and attempt to understand the details from his or her perspective. From there you will need to explain how others may have experienced the situation, while at the same time validating the child's feelings around it. Too often individuals on the spectrum do not get the concrete feedback they require in order to understand why their actions were not considered appropriate.

Despite their difficulty with interpreting social behavior, children on the spectrum are known to have an acute sense of other people. Perhaps it is because they are more attuned to details that they notice when a voice is strained or is too loud and intrusive (although surprisingly, they often do not recognize their own volume or pitch). Beyond what one would expect, individuals with ASD are also known to be able to observe insincerity in others' actions or the incongruities of what others have said when they contradict themselves in time. They often remember things that other people have forgotten, and in the interest of honesty will point out inconsistencies (Attwood, 2007).

For example, one teen diagnosed with Asperger syndrome had been hired as a salesman in a large department store. A knife demonstration was set up at a kiosk in the middle of the store and another salesperson was assigned to this area. As part of the knife sales pitch, the saleswoman was telling potential customers that this was their only opportunity to buy this knife at a discounted price. While working in the store, the teen heard her say that it was the "best deal of the day" and that it would only last an hour. He pointed out to her (and to all the potential customers standing around) that she was selling the same knife earlier that day, only for less money. This confused him and he truly was looking for clarification. He had no intent of embarrassing her in any way. She ignored him and he walked away without understanding what had just happened. Unfortunately, his behavior was reported, and he was eventually phased out of his job without any explanation. Had he been in therapy with someone trained to work with high-functioning individuals with Asperger syndrome, he could have processed this situation and avoided the confusion and anxiety that followed. Typical of this disability is a strong tendency for individuals, particularly adolescents, to discount the interpretations and perceptions of their parents/guardians, even when their relationship is a trusted one. They are more likely to accept feedback and direction from a therapist or counselor whom they trust.

As Richard Bromfield writes in his book, *Doing Therapy With Children and Adolescents With Asperger Syndrome*:

> I've found that children with Asperger's seem to enjoy the company of therapists with not just an honest but a solid, down-to-earth presence. These children are not ones for psychobabble or tentative hypothesizing. While lovers of concrete imagery and the metaphor, they respond best to direct and clear language, even if representative, that acutely captures experience. It is as if they are so fraught with their own anxiety and discomfort that they are relieved to be in the presence of another person who feels some measure of personal comfort and who appears not to be freaked or stressed by the child's being. These children do not routinely experience comfortable moments with other people. (2011a, p. 23)

It bears repeating that "these children do not routinely experience comfortable moments with other people." Like their parents, their lives are filled with stressors. In fact, the number of traumatic incidents experienced in the life of the child can be measured through the persistence and intensity of intrusive and repetitive thoughts. Tony Attwood likens this to posttraumatic stress disorder and states that "the person can have intrusive memories of the traumatic event that are difficult to 'block'" (2007, p. 129). One boy diagnosed with Asperger syndrome confided in his mother, after a stressful interaction with a classmate at school, "That is one more thing that I will have to think about tonight before I go to sleep." He went on to tell his surprised parent that he stayed awake each night in order to rank-order the negative, confusing things that had happened to him over the years. This latest, his being accidentally hit in the face by a ball in gym class, had to be added to the list and then compared to all the other negative occurrences.

The stressors confronting individuals with high-functioning ASD are numerous and ongoing. Consider these factors listed below that are often reported as being most stressful in the lives of children on the spectrum.

- *Loneliness and isolation from peers.* Perhaps one of the most poignant stories of the loneliness and isolation that children on the spectrum experience (and, truly, there are many stories like this) is the following. After several attempts to befriend a classmate, and deciding to share his love of dinosaurs with her, only to be completely ignored, John Robison, a respected businessman and author diagnosed with Asperger syndrome, says, "All my attempts to make a friend had failed. I was a failure. I began to cry. Alone in the corner of the playground, I sobbed and smashed (a) toy truck into the ground again and again and again, until my hands hurt too much to do it anymore" (2007, p. 10). John Robison was only in nursery school at the time.

Stories such as these abound among children diagnosed with ASD. They are stories linked to experiences of being social outcasts and to feelings of social shame. One young boy told his therapist, "I try so hard to fit in with other kids. I just don't know how. I try to laugh when they laugh and be serious when they are serious. When I really don't know what to do, I hide until the kids go home. Know what? They don't even know I am gone." This child's intense efforts to be like the other children never paid off. Figuring out how to act is important for many of these children. Their spontaneous choice of play may cause them to be excluded or ignored. One 10-year-old boy was told by his mother to "act like the other children at the bus stop." He had been walking in circles and acting very silly. His mother went on to advise him to *watch* the other children and act the way they do. He responded to this by saying, "I thought you told me that it was ok that I am not like everyone else." For these children and their parents, navigating everyday life is filled with obstacles. Being accepted by others without being judged is everything to them.

- *Pretending to be normal.* Pretending to be normal in order to fit in with peers is an exhausting activity that takes up much time and energy on a daily basis. For 15-year-old "Hannah," who wanted to be like other girls her age, wearing makeup, certain fashionable clothes, and having a particular hairstyle were important. She spent hours daily attempting to look "just right." Yet there were major flaws in her presentation that escaped her scrutiny. For instance, despite showering regularly, she did not wash her body or her hair properly as part of the practice. (This is a common area of difficulty for individuals on the spectrum.) Consequently, she routinely appeared to be dirty and had an off-putting body odor that she did not recognize. Her "carefully" applied makeup, her "special" hairstyle, and her version of stylish clothes came across as being overdone and ludicrous rather than attractive. Despite all this effort she was further shunned by peers. Although her mother and school counselor continuously tried to teach her the basics of expected hygiene, dress, and appearance, she was unable to take their feedback.

It is not easy for individuals on the spectrum to accurately perceive what is acceptable to others in terms of appearance and behavior. At times, their rigid mindset even prevents them from accepting direction from trusted advisors. The need to fit in is strong, but they often feel compelled to do things their own way, even when their pretense of normal is not producing the desired effects. In her book, *Pretending to Be Normal*, Liane Holliday Willey (1999) talks about the prevalence of this theme in her life. Luckily, as an adolescent, she had a strong support group of friends and she was spared the agony of "fitting in" experienced by others diagnosed with Asperger syndrome.

Many autistic children have anxiety-reducing routines and rituals that they follow in order to cope with the demands of their day. They keep these practices private, as they sense that they are not "normal." Some children will come home from school and immediately engage in the pursuit of their special interest. Attwood describes this as being "emotionally restorative" (2007, p. 164). It is likely that Amanda would spend hours focusing on her Native American village making everything "just so." That is why she is overcome with angst at the thought of someone coming into her room and touching her "stuff." Someone could casually move things around in her village and disrupt the precise order she has established.

Some children will engage in other repetitive behaviors to meet sensory needs. This could involve pacing in circles, jumping on a mini-trampoline, swinging on a swing, tree climbing, or incessantly tossing a ball. This might also include a fair amount of loud self-talk as a way of processing the events of the day. Some might simply prefer the safety of their own room. This allows them to release the pent-up energy that is the result of inhibiting the expression of unusual and different behaviors throughout the day.

There are still other children who need to sequester themselves in special hiding places (e.g., under the stairs, under the porch, or in the attic as a way of self-soothing). Temple Grandin, Ph.D., a famed scientist and author, invented her "squeeze machine" as a way to introduce deep pressure as a calming procedure. She states that "At various lecture meetings of parents of Autistic individuals, parents have reported various types of pressure-seeking of their offspring, such as wrapping arms and legs in elastic bandages, sleeping under many blankets even during warm weather, and getting under mattresses. In my case, I used to crawl under sofa cushions and have my sister sit on them" (Grandin, 1992, p. 1).

• *Understanding social language.* Imagine what it is like to go throughout your day never quite sure of what people are talking about. How sad it was to hear one young client report, "You know, half the time I don't have any idea of what people are saying to me. I just pretend." This was said in response to his mother's shock that he had not understood what seemed to be a simple conversational exchange between him and his teacher. His teacher had reprimanded him for having put his feet up on the chair in front of him. She said, "*We* don't put our feet up on chairs." He understood her to say that she and others *chose* not to do this. Therefore, he responded by saying, "I do." It was meant as a simple statement pointing out a difference between them. It was not meant to be a flippant response, but it came across that way. It further reinforced the teacher's belief that he was intentionally defying rules. He was angry, confused, and frustrated when his answer earned him a detention.

As Tony Attwood (2012) points out, children diagnosed with autism spectrum disorders are known to be brutally honest and literal. They do not "get" the meaning of sarcasm or ambiguous references in language. A good example of how social language is misinterpreted is found in the novel written by Mark

Haddon, *The Curious Incident of the Dog in the Night-time.* In this story of Christopher, an autistic boy turned self-made detective, an incident between him and a policeman results in his arrest. When Christopher is being questioned by the detective at the police station, the following exchange occurs:

> *Detective:* "Did you mean to hit the policeman?"
> *Christopher:* "Yes."
> At this point, the detective gets frustrated but changes his question.
> *Detective:* "But you didn't mean to hurt the policeman?"
> *Christopher:* "No." (2003, p. 17)

To the boy, these were two very different questions and both were answered honestly. As we have said before, concrete and literal interpretation of language is typical of individuals diagnosed with ASD. This is why we emphasize the need for all communications to be direct and forthright. That brings us to our next point, the importance of rules in the life of the ASD child.

- *Pros and cons of rules.*   Liane Holliday Willey explains for us the importance of rules in the life of someone diagnosed with Asperger syndrome. She says, "As long as things followed a set of rules, I could play along. Rules were—and are—great friends of mine. I like rules. They set the record straight and keep it that way. You know where you stand with rules and you know how to act with rules. Trouble is, rules change and if they do not, people break them" (1999, p. 43).

Rules are important because they bring order and predictability to the child diagnosed with ASD. With rules and the proper following of rules, the child experiences a sense of control in an otherwise unfamiliar social world. Rules serve to keep "feelings of anxiety at bay" (Tammet, 2006, p. 67). As so many experts in the field have noted, when rules change, or are not followed, the ASD child becomes stressed and ultimately anxious. Rules are often tied to routines and become a safety net for the autistic child. Yet they can also become stressors. Note the following examples:

> We wait for the bus at the corner, and we don't step into the street until the bus arrives.

We eat lunch at noon, and it is always a sandwich on white bread with no crusts.

We file into the school building in a straight line, staying to the right.

We say the Pledge of Allegiance immediately after the daily announcements are made.

A simple change can be devastating for the child who has a rigid need for rules. Once a rule gets incorporated into the expectation of the child, it cannot be dislodged easily. One change can cause stress and lead to increased levels of anxiety. When that happens, the need for rules works against the child on the spectrum.

As you can see from the vignette introducing this chapter, and in so many of the examples given throughout this book, anxiety is experienced in many ways for the individual with ASD. For instance, it can be somaticized and take the form of headaches or stomach aches that necessitate frequent visits to the nurse's office when the child is in school. For some, it will result in an increase in what are called stereotypical behaviors (e.g., hand-flapping, rocking, etc.). And, as Tony Attwood described in a recent talk, it can contribute to "depression attacks in individuals with ASD" (2012). These seemingly unexpected and unprovoked, brief periods of depression appear to start and end abruptly. He explained that these episodes should be taken seriously and are related to overwhelming anxiety.

Anxiety can also lead to perseverative thoughts and expressions. One young man was confronted with a school situation he could not grasp. He then repeatedly stated, "What difference does it make? What difference does it make?" as he paced in circles around the therapist's office. In this case, the boy had been reprimanded for being in the teachers' bathroom. While walking by, he happened to see that the paper towels were hanging raggedly out of their receptacle, and he went in to "fix" the situation. He was someone who needed to have everything "in the right order." His intent was to help, and he did not understand why his actions were not acceptable. He was not aware of the unwritten rule that students do not enter the teachers' bathroom. Understanding social rules is a problem for high-functioning individuals on the spectrum. When things go wrong due to a misperception, it is often viewed by others as being an intentional misbehavior. As we mentioned earlier, children and adolescents on the spectrum present as being knowledgeable and competent in many areas. As a result, it is expected that they would know the correct interpretation of both written *and* unwritten rules of social functioning.

- *Attention-drawing behaviors.* Shortly before the teacher's bathroom incident described above, this same young teen expressed a desire to act like what he perceived to be a "typical teenager." He told his therapist that he went on the Internet to learn about teenage behaviors. The teen then tried to make an impression on his peers by showing up at school with pornographic video clips on his cell phone. He then went around asking students if they wanted "to see something interesting." After showing several students the videos, school staff became aware of his activity and took action. The boy was upset because he felt unjustly punished when he was suspended from school for his behavior. He had only wanted to call attention to himself with peers and did not understand why this behavior was wrong if he could so easily access it on the Internet. Consistent with his Asperger diagnosis, the idea of what is socially acceptable is a concept that continually eludes this young man.

When the ASD child engages in a special interest, it may also result in drawing the attention of others. While the pursuit of these interests can be "emotionally restorative" for the individual, the fact is, engaging in them can be socially detrimental. For example, the child who keeps endless lists of baseball statistics, which he insists on sharing with others, will stand out as being odd and out of place even among fans.

Attention-drawing behaviors can also be noted in ASD individuals when a particular situation is envisioned by them as being anxiety provoking. In this case they may find a way to escape such situations altogether. One student deliberately refused to participate in a class he found to be loud and chaotic. He purposefully disrupted the class by doing silly things, earning himself the title of "class clown." The boy did this in order to get out of that class. His plan worked and he was removed from the setting. Unfortunately, it was a class required for the boy to progress into a work program that was much better suited to his needs. Not being able to understand social consequences spontaneously is a correlate of the ASD diagnosis. In this case, learning social consequence mapping or teaching the child diagnosed with ASD how to recognize the hidden rules of the social curriculum are just two of the many ways of helping these children resolve these problems more effectively (Hudson & Myles, 2007).

While a typical childhood is *sometimes* stressful, the stress is *ongoing* for the ASD child (Lopata, Volker, Putnam, Thomeer, & Nida, 2008). Making friends, playing with others, succeeding in school, and understanding social rules are demanding tasks for all children. However, as you can see from the factors listed above, they are experienced differently by children on the spectrum. For them, these tasks are draining and debilitating. They can affect mental health, school performance, and every other aspect of the child's life. Therefore, at this point, we think it is important to discuss the concept of stress in general and then as it relates to the ASD population. Understanding this concept will help you to appreciate the child's need for your support throughout treatment and as you involve the child in the formulation of this Collaborative Agreement.

"'Stress' has become so ubiquitous and so much a part of everyday life that, at first glance, there appears to be no need for a definition. Selye (1976), a pioneer of stress research, points out that 'stress is a scientific concept which has suffered from the mixed blessing of being too well known and too little understood'" (Linden, 2005, p. 1). Dr. Hans Selye was an experimental pathologist considered to be the "father of the field of stress research." His work on the effects of stress has been widely publicized. His concept of stress paved the way for treatment through the discovery that hormones participate in the development of many diseases, including high blood pressure, ulcers, and even cancer. He called these "diseases of adaptation," and his overall theory on the concept was entitled the "general adaptation syndrome." At present, much of the research extending from his work focuses on the body's stress resistance in dealing with personal, interpersonal, and group problems. And yet, as we investigated the topic of stress to provide you with a better framework with which to understand the ASD child, we came to an interesting realization regarding the generally accepted stages of stress. Those individuals predisposed to sensitivity in experiencing stress, by way of their disability, do not appear to experience the stages of stress in the same way that neurotypical individuals do.

If we look at the three stages of stress as defined in the general adaptation syndrome, we find that stress is first experienced through what is called the Alarm Reaction. In this stage, when an unexpected stressor is experienced, the body's hormonal systems create a "fight or flight reaction" and stress hormones are released into the body. One of the most pronounced hormones is cortisol. High levels of cortisol are produced in response to high levels of stress. This first stage is short, and is followed by the stage of Resistance, in which the body deals with the stressful situation in an attempt to return to normal hormonal levels. The third and final stage is that of Exhaustion, where the stress returns and depletes the body's ability to adapt any longer. According to Selye, it is because of this end stage that stress-related illnesses are likely to occur. These can be serious, as listed above, or they can be less serious (e.g., headaches, stomach aches, and insomnia). The important thing is that these illnesses are indicative of prolonged stress.

A number of researchers in the field have identified notable differences in the way that individuals diagnosed with ASD experience stress when compared to their neurotypical peers. After being exposed to unfamiliar and unpredictable events, significantly higher levels of cortisol were found in the ASD groups of children. Another finding indicated that cortisol levels were lower than would be expected in the morning and higher than expected at night (Corbett, Mendoza, Wegelin, Carmean, & Levine , 2008). It is our thought that the many challenges of the day contribute to heightened experiences of stress and resultant anxiety for the ASD population (indicated by high levels of cortisol at night). Also, it might be that lower than expected cortisol levels in the morning account for what has been observed as a slow morning arousal level for individuals with ASD.

Considering that ASD children experience a multitude of stressors in a day—fear of isolation, guessing at what is normal, deciphering social communications, clinging to sameness and rules, and the need for recognition and acceptance—it is no wonder that they are stressed and anxious when the day ends. It is likely that they do not fully resolve the second stage of the general adaptation syndrome and move on to the biological stage of Exhaustion described above. You will recall that this is not fatigue but a depletion of physiological and restorative resources. Consistent with this line of thinking, it not surprising that studies show a prolonged duration of high cortisol levels and resistance to recovery from stressors in children diagnosed with ASD (Spratt et al., 2012).

Life is complicated for the child you will be treating. Days are filled with confusion in attempts to overcome obstacles not apparent to others. As the therapist, you will have the opportunity to intervene in a way that is meaningful. As you create your own perceptions of how this disability uniquely affects your client, your approaches to treatment will lead you to guide others to make changes in the child's environment. This will help your ASD client to function optimally in the social world.

Similar to the last chapter, where we discussed the trials and tribulations of parents/guardians, you will note that we have tried here to give you further insight into the challenges and concerns of the children. Presenting the Collaborative Agreement using developmentally appropriate explanations will be key to its successful implementation. We remind you that high-functioning children and adolescents on the spectrum typically present as being a few years behind peers in social maturation, although they are generally of average or higher intelligence. It will be your challenge to determine how the characteristics of this disability are expressed in your client and, in light of this, how best to collaborate with them in presenting this agreement.

As Bromfield points out in *Embracing Asperger's,* "Strive to understand. It is easy to dismiss a child's words as nonsense or inadequate . . . Make an effort to meet the child where she is, to ascertain what she is trying to express and convey. Perhaps use her words or phrasing, even if not proper or correct, to show that you get it or are trying to approach the meaning she wants you to get" (2011b, p. 90). Following this advice, we recommend that you use the Collaborative Agreement Between Therapist and Child as a tool for establishing the initial trust you will want to build in this relationship. (To review a complete version of this form, see Appendix J.)

COLLABORATIVE AGREEMENT BETWEEN THERAPIST AND CHILD

As in the collaborative form for the therapist and parents/guardians, this agreement begins with a statement of purpose (see below). This is meant to be a clear explanation of what you are doing (creating a plan) and why (to solve problems and know what to expect). Based on your knowledge of the stress factors in the child's life and his or her level of functioning, you may choose to personalize and expand upon the wording we have recommended below.

PURPOSE: We are creating this plan so that we will know exactly what to expect as we work together. Using it will make it easier for us to solve problems. This will be our plan for now.

After you have discussed the purpose of the agreement and feel comfortable with the child's basic understanding of it, you will begin with a simple but direct summary of how your meetings will proceed. On Section I of the form, entitled Meetings (see below), you will have filled in parts A through D using the information agreed upon in your meeting with the parents/guardians. Part E is meant to give the child an opportunity to make additional suggestions, which you can discuss with him or her. This allows the child to collaborate with the process of formulating this agreement. For example, one boy insisted on always sitting in a certain chair and having the window curtains drawn three-quarters of the way. Another child, a 12-year-old girl, requested that her mother would wait for her outside the building rather than in the office waiting room.

I. MEETINGS:

A. How often will we meet?

B. How long will our meetings be?

C. What day and time will we meet?

D. Where will we meet?

E. Other meeting information:

Now is a good time to emphasize the need to have your meetings on the same day and the same time each week. Later on in the agreement you will be addressing the rules around the exceptions to this policy. For now it is important that the child knows the expectation is to come consistently to scheduled meetings and to participate in the process.

To maintain structure and predictability for the child, we recommend the following sequence for the therapy hour (see Section II below). You may choose to follow this format or one already decided upon by you and the parents/guardians. The child needs to understand that the format chosen is the one that will be followed in each meeting. However, if the child has a particular concern and there is a workable idea about how this structure can be modified, this can be added at the end under "Other meeting information." For example, one girl worried that her time alone with the therapist would run out before she was finished talking about her week. In this case, it was decided that any topics important to the child that were not covered in the meeting would be written down in a special notebook. They would then be referred to at the beginning of the next meeting with the child.

II. ORDER OF MEETINGS:

First, I will meet alone with your parents for about 10 minutes.

Second, I will meet alone with you for about 30 minutes.

Third, I will meet with both you and your parents for about 10 minutes.

Other meeting information: _____

It is worth saying again that following a set routine each week contributes to the process of therapy with this population. It provides predictability and consistency. It also promotes generalization and cooperation in solving problems within the family.

Structured meetings accompanied by concrete guidelines will allow the individual diagnosed with ASD to see the benefit of the process and consequently to invest in it. Tommy, an 11-year-old, did not initially buy into the format of having his therapist meet with his parents at the start and end of each session. Yet, through the use of this structure, he soon realized that including his parents this way helped his therapist to identify some of the issues he was experiencing. Together they worked with his parents to create solutions in order to make life at home less stressful.

Along with the structuring of sessions in a consistent and routine manner, we recommend that you introduce the following rules. This will prepare the child for possible variations to the meeting process. The rules listed below represent the areas that we have found to be most relevant when working with this population of children. You may choose to include additional, workable rules that you and your client decide upon.

III. RULES FOR OUR MEETINGS:

A. | Each time we meet, we will decide what to talk about to best help you.

B. | There will be weeks when I will meet with your parents alone for the whole meeting. I will let you know before this happens.

C. | There will be weeks when I will meet with you and your family together for the whole meeting. This may mean you and your parents, or it may include other family members. I will let you know before this happens.

D. | There will be times when you or I may need to cancel our meeting. I will work this out with your parents. Most of the time, we will follow our meeting schedule.

Other rules for our meetings: _____

_____

As you can see above, these rules largely explain exceptions to the routine. Importantly, two of the four introduce the idea of involvement of others. This is a hard concept for ASD children to understand because they have a tendency to focus on single entities and do not see the bigger picture. By explaining ahead of time why it is important for you to meet alone for periodic parent sessions and for them to sometimes be part of a larger family meeting, you are helping them to see that working with the family is a way to help them. By making the family interactions relevant to the child's well-being, you will assist them in viewing positive family relationships as a single entity. Guided by you, they will focus less on details of interactions that undermine family dynamics and more on the "bigger picture." For many, this means increased chances for family peace and harmony.

You will notice that we have made a distinction between rules for the meetings and rules to be adhered to outside of the meetings. We have done this to reduce the anxiety that the child is likely to feel when he or she learns that there will be communication and encounters with you outside of the office.

IV. RULES FOR OUTSIDE OF OUR MEETINGS:

A. | Once in a while, you may see me at your school when I come there for a meeting with your teachers. I will let you know before this happens.

B. | Once in a while, you may talk to me on the phone. This would only be for a serious situation and you will need to have your parents' permission before calling.

C. | There will be times when I will talk to people at your school or other people who work with you. I will be doing this to help you and cannot always tell you when this is going to happen.

D. | We will not be texting or using the computer to talk to each other.

Other rules for our meetings: _____

_____

The rules we recommend for outside of the therapy office involve seeing the child in other settings and phone conversations with the child, family, or others. Meetings outside of the office will typically involve the school. You will need to assure the child that advance notice will be given in the event of an outside meeting where you may see each other. This is yet another way of collaborating directly with your client. As you know, it is important to emphasize that therapists mostly work with clients within the structure of their scheduled meetings.

As you come to the end of the collaborative agreement, we recommend a final statement (see below) to summarize and reinforce your joint commitment to this plan and to the success of your work together. You will need to explain to the child the importance of signing the agreement. Signatures make documents official and show that you both agree. Once signed, the agreement should be copied and given to the child as well as the parents/guardians. You may want to instruct your client to keep the document in a special place at home. Explain to the child that this is private information, only to be shared with the parents/ guardians, or maybe a close family member.

We both agree to follow this plan as best we can for now. It will help us to understand what to do and what not to do as we work together.

Signed by: _____ **Date:** _____

Signed by: _____ **Date:** _____

The role of siblings is of special significance in the ASD family constellation and will be discussed in the next chapter. It is difficult for parents/guardians to meet the needs of their other children in addition to the demands of raising a child diagnosed with ASD. Even more challenging is instilling in the ASD child a true sense of their siblings' needs. Understanding the sibling experience will help you to work more effectively with the ASD child and will enable you to guide the parents/guardians in detecting the unmet needs of their other children.

CHAPTER 8

Working With Siblings

ASD IS A disorder that affects not only the individual with the diagnosis, but the entire family. Perhaps no one feels the impact more than the brothers and sisters of the child on the autism spectrum. The family, after all, is the first group and the delicate balance between members is sensitive to the interactions of each. It is this balance that defines the family system (Margolis, Dacey, & Kenny, 2007). And it is this balance that is so often disrupted in the lives of families that include a child diagnosed with ASD.

There are many factors that influence sibling relationships. Some of these factors are directly related to the family constellation, such as the number of adults and children in the family, the relationships of the children to the parents/guardians (i.e., biological, adopted, step, foster), the birth order, and the ages and spacing of children. Other factors include culture, ethnicity, race, socioeconomic status, religious beliefs, and family types/styles of parenting. All of these have an effect on how the family functions and defines its members.

Empirical investigations examining sibling relationships have revealed that children who have a positive relationship with a sibling show greater emotional understanding (Dunn, Brown, Slomkowski, Telsa, & Youngblade, 1991), greater cognitive abilities (Howe & Ross, 1990; Smith, 1993), greater social understanding (Bryant & Crockenberg, 1980; Dunn & Munn, 1986), greater moral sensibility (Dunn, Brown, & Maguire, 1995), and better psychological adjustment (Dunn, Brown, Slomkowski, Telsa, & Young-blade, 1994). In contrast, other studies have shown that a destructive relationship with a sibling may have detrimental effects for a child, such as disruptive and aggressive behaviors (Garcia, Shaw, Winslow, & Yaggi, 2000). (Milevsky & Levitt, 2005, p. 300)

Siblings are known to model each other's behaviors and form alliances within the family. Temperament or personality can influence the roles siblings play with one another. Other characteristics can have this influence as well. For example, birth studies describe the oldest child as the one who feels "in charge" of the younger siblings. These children have been noted by many to be high achievers and attain greater professional success (Nyman, 1995). It is not uncommon for the oldest child to get the reputation of being "bossy" and wanting to be in full charge of the younger siblings. In one family, the oldest child took it upon herself to select courses and give her younger sibling behavioral instruction on how to dress and what to say (and not say) to others as he entered high school. Another older child would often explain to her brother when he complained about her authority, "It's hard to be me, I was born first. It could have been you but it wasn't. It was me and you need to listen to me."

These are well-intentioned siblings whose behavior exemplifies a commitment and responsibility to the younger child in the family. There is also an assumption of having superior knowledge. Perhaps beyond the birth order influence, the need for control comes from a compelling need for compensation when the parents/guardians shift their attention away from the elder child and toward the younger. "In families of typically developing children, the relationship between children and their parents changes as parents cope with the needs and demands of a new baby (Stewart, 1990; Tetiet et al., 1996). Older siblings often experience a decrease in positive maternal attention and communication after the baby is born (Dunn and Kendrick, 1980)" (Stoneman, 2001, p. 134). For reasons cited above, behavioral changes can occur. There are times when the sibling of a newborn will show regression by acting in ways more appropriate to a much younger child. Some will engage in "acting-out" behaviors, doing anything and everything to capture parental attention. In all cases, the point is that the arrival of a new family member commonly triggers change, and that change can be difficult for the siblings to experience. This difficulty is greatly increased with the introduction of a child with a disability.

Thus far in the chapter, we have examined a number of influences that impact siblings in general as they define their roles in the family; now it is time to look more closely at the brothers and sisters of children with disabilities. Their circumstances are different and need to be understood by those adults involved with them. The extent and form of the disability impacts the family balance and raises the levels of anxiety within the family environment. The quality of life for family members as they influence each other is affected as the family system strives to meet the new demands (Brown & Brown, 2003; Turnbull, Brown, & Turnbull, 2004). The siblings define themselves over time in relation to each other, to their parents, and to their disabled brother or sister.

At one time, the experiences of living with a brother or sister who is cognitively, socially, or physically challenged were not considered. This absence of insight and concern for siblings of children with disabilities occurred all the way up until the 1970s and prompted one of the editors of the book cited below to refer to these individuals as the "Forgotten Children" (p. 33). In the book, *It Isn't Fair! Siblings of Children With Disabilities,* Dr. Meyer Schreiber is quoted as urging parents of disabled children "to provide help, direction, understanding and explanation to sisters and brothers" (Klein & Schleifer, 1993, p. 2).

In those years, services for disabled children were few and far between, and much of the care had fallen to the family. Prior to that time, children with disabilities were institutionalized and home care was not an option. It is no wonder that when the trend turned to caring for the disabled child at home, the effects on the typically developing siblings would be overlooked. Klein and Schleifer (1993) point out that it wasn't until the magazine *The Exceptional Parent* published an article on the topic that it became of interest to others. The article included excerpts from a discussion by four siblings of disabled individuals talking about their experiences living as brothers or sisters of a disabled person.

Today the research that focuses on these siblings unveils a multiplicity of views regarding their experiences. For some, they can be positive and enlightening. For others it can be a time filled with conflicting emotions (Moyson & Roeyers, 2012). Feelings associated with having a disabled brother or sister are powerful. Their impact on relationships, both in and out of the family, is profound.

In her book *The Normal One: Life With a Difficult or Damaged Sibling*, Dr. Jeanne Safer examines the effects of her experience. She points out, "No amount of psychic maneuvering can alter the fact that having siblings is one of the defining experiences of childhood, with lifelong reverberations" (2002, p. 39). That sentence brought to mind a moving account of a former client. He was the middle child of three boys close in age, two of whom had been diagnosed around the age of 7 as having Duchenne muscular dystrophy. This form of muscular dystrophy is sex-linked and generally affects males. It is a deadly disease of progressive muscle deterioration. It is first detected as excessive clumsiness observed in frequent falls. Over a short period of time, the child loses mobility and vital muscles weaken, affecting the ability to breathe or sustain cardiac stress. All major organs deteriorate and there is a continuous loss of functioning. Many of these children do not live beyond their late teens or early twenties.

The family of the client mentioned earlier placed great value on sports and expected their boys to excel in athletic activities. When the oldest boy began to lose his ability to stay on his feet while playing youth hockey, his father made him take extra practices on the ice. (Needless to say, this caused the father endless remorse once his son was diagnosed.) The middle boy who was not disabled was a youth hockey star by age 7. He soon went on to become the most valuable player in Little League baseball. His disabled brothers cheered him on, saying "Do it for us!" And he did, compensating as best he could for their losses. After both of his brothers had died an early death, the teen suffered what is called "survivor's guilt." Depressed and overwhelmed, he would often ask, "Why me? Why didn't I get MD? I should have been like my brothers." Truly, for him and many others, there are "lifelong reverberations."

Not all of the outcomes result in guilt. In *Growing Together* (2011), an informational publication of the Association for Children with Disability, many of the experiences of having a sibling with a disability are positive, with the brother or sister recounting a closeness and pride in the accomplishments of the disabled sibling. Among the positive aspects cited by some siblings is growing up feeling competent and assertive with healthy measures of self-esteem (Feiges & Weiss, 2004).

Some siblings report that their lives have been forever changed by their disabled sibling and that they have grown immeasurably from their experiences (Konidaris, 2005). Others report their difficulties and fears growing up with a child who was in some way "different" (Meyer, 2009). What most researchers report is that the experience of the sibling of a disabled child is tied to a number of factors, including family size, birth order, type of disability, level of psychosocial development of the typical sibling, level of cognitive ability of the typical sibling, and to the openness of family communications (Meyer & Vadasy, 1996; Marcus, Kunce, & Schopler, 2005). The consensus is that all of these factors need to be considered in order to understand the experience of the sibling who grows up with a disabled brother or sister.

In addition, "Family variables have also been documented to impact sibling relationships. VanRiper (2000) studied the impact of family variables on sibling relationships when one child has special needs. Results showed that families with lower levels of family demands, a higher number of resources, superior coping skills, and higher levels of affirmative problem-solving communication between parent and child experienced greater sibling well-being" (Sage & Jegatheesan, 2010, p. 195).

To this point we have examined many factors within the family as they relate to sibling relationships, and we have also highlighted some of the differing circumstances present in families with a disabled child. Now we will focus on the unique experiences of siblings who have a brother or sister who has been diagnosed with ASD. The impact of this particular diagnosis on siblings has been overlooked. We have referred to the diagnosis of autism spectrum disorder in high-functioning individuals as often being an "invisible" disability. The child can look and appear like any other child. In a conversation with adults, the disability is hardly recognizable. It is in the social realm of childhood that the aspects of ASD are painfully obvious. And when difficulties occur for the ASD child, siblings are greatly affected.

Siblings of high-functioning children on the spectrum have different challenges in their lives than do the siblings of children with more obvious disabilities. They find themselves in situations in which their typically presenting sibling may be behaving in a not-so-typical manner. They may be having meltdowns and drawing negative attention not just to themselves but to their families. Resultant anger, embarrassment, and shame are among the emotions they report (Feiges & Weiss, 2004).

Some siblings report getting tired of "walking on eggshells" and not being able to function spontaneously as other families do. In most families, even those who have a disabled child, family outings are a fun experience. Aspects of his or her disability are more apparent and needs can be anticipated. If the child is in a wheelchair, outings are planned accordingly. This is also true if the child has asthma or Down syndrome. For these children, going out to buy an ice cream from the ice cream man is not a major disruption in the day. One distraught young mother explained, "From the moment we hear the bell on the truck, I know there will be all hell to pay. Billy will not only want the same ice cream he always gets, but he will demand to know the precise time the truck is returning the next day. It is not beyond him to question the punctuality of today's arrival or, if God forbid, his favorite ice cream has sold out, he is likely to chastise the poor guy, demanding to know why." She went on to say that this was a terrible source of embarrassment for the boy's older sister. It also became a point of contention between the mother and her daughter. Because the situation was causing so much stress in the home, this mother decided to not allow either of the children to get ice cream from the truck and instead made a point of keeping her freezer well stocked with their favorite kinds of ice cream treats.

In cases like this, the siblings' embarrassment can lead to anger when situations are curtailed or entirely cut out of their childhood experiences. The siblings feel slighted and resentful because their lives are restricted by the often unpredictable demands (needs) of their siblings. When the embarrassment leads to resentment and anger, the sibling needs to have a way to work through the feelings with their parents/guardians without being judged or made to feel guilty. This will be an important part of your therapy, as you will need to help parents/guardians to understand these dynamics. At the end of this chapter, you will find a helpful guide to review with them the needs of their typically developing children.

"Sibling interactions are challenges that all families face on a daily basis. These interactions are significantly more difficult when one child has autism. With the apparent increase in diagnoses of autism, there are more families each year who are dealing with issues of relationships. Children learn, as part of the growing up experience, how to relate to their brothers and sisters. They also acquire future parenting styles by watching their own parents and how they relate to children with and without disabilities" (Ivey & Ward, 2010, p. 2). There are some who report that "The majority of brothers and sisters of children with ASDs function well as children, adolescents, and adults" (Ferraioli & Harris, 2009, p. 50). Others researchers have found that they pay a price. There are disappointments around a lack of emotional bonding with the ASD sibling, and there can be jealousy around the attention that the ASD child demands of the family (Feiges & Stern, 2004).

In an interview with the parents of two teenaged children, a 13-year-old neurotypical daughter and a 15-year-old son diagnosed with Asperger syndrome, the therapist was told, "Even though she is younger, our daughter is like a little mother to Josh. She directs and instructs him, even though she finds it disappointing that he doesn't seem to have the same amount of concern about her. Sometimes she just gets angry because it seems like all of the family attention focuses on Josh." Interestingly, Josh reported that he feels like his sister gets all the "respect" in the family. He tells his parents that they give the sister much more attention and freedom than he gets. He constantly reminds them, "You always let her do everything and she is younger!"

Consider this mini-interview: Here the siblings are in their twenties and the neurotypical daughter is the older of the two. Her younger brother has been diagnosed with Asperger syndrome. Interestingly, they have the same age difference as the teens mentioned earlier and are exactly a decade older. They were separately asked the same four questions. Note the differences as they recall their shared childhood and individually offer their perceptions of their sibling relationship.

Question #1 (to brother): *When you think about growing up with your sister, what good things do you remember about your relationship with her?*

"The great thing about having (my sister), or any older sibling, is that she looks out for me. She knew I had difficulties but wasn't sure why and she knew to help me anyway. Even now, if I have some social problem, she helps me. Sometimes she knows my problems aren't as big as I think they are and she listens anyway. I can text her anytime. She is closer to my age (vs. parents) and she has a better opinion because she is young. I bet that I will be 50 years old and still asking for her advice on things."

Question 1 (to sibling/sister): *When you think about growing up with your brother, what good things do you remember about your relationship with him?*

"My brother is more caring toward me than another 23-year-old young man would be. Growing up, he was always excited about things, even if it was to an extreme and he was fixated on some topic. It was enjoyable to see that and to participate in things with him. This was easier when he became interested in baseball. That is one sport that I really enjoy. When he was younger, he was fascinated by the solar system and the presidents of the United States. That made it harder for me to interact with him."

Question 2 (to brother): *When you think about growing up with your sister, what was difficult about your relationship with her?*

"The thing that is difficult when you grow up in a family where one kid has a disability, is that sometimes they take advantage of you. When I was younger, my sister would convince me to apologize for things that might not have been my fault because I trusted her so much. Now, I know better most of the time. She can be controlling and take advantage of me."

Question 2 (to sibling/sister): *When you think about growing up with your brother, what was difficult about your relationship with him?*

"Generally speaking, he required more of my mother's time because of his disability and I got less. Also, more so when I was younger, it was very frustrating for him to not "get things" socially. I didn't think it was fair that I had to "get things" but he didn't. Now I understand more. But, it still annoys me to this day that there are such different expectations of me, as compared to him. And sometimes, it still does not seem fair."

Question 3 (to brother): *When you think about growing up with your sister, did your parents treat you the same?*

"My parents definitely treated me the same. I got *some* extra help but not that much different at all. We both got the same amount of attention. Despite some small differences, I think we had a normal and healthy childhood."

Question 3 (to sibling/sister): *When you think about growing up with your brother, did your parents treat you the same?*

> "No. I do think we had the same rules but I think there were different expectations for us. For example, we had to do chores, do our school-work, and be respectful. But a lot more was expected of me. I had to help my brother a lot every day and so did my parents. "

Question 4 (to brother): *When you think about growing up with your sister, did you each have the same amount of freedom?*

> "To be honest, I think my sister had a little more freedom than me. She got to go on some trips out of the country and I didn't. Looking back, I can understand that I was not as mature, by a little bit, but at the time it really bothered me. Once we hit our late teens and early twenties, we are basically equal now."

Question 4 (to sibling/sister): *When you think about growing up with your brother, did you each have the same amount of freedom?*

> "I had less freedom because I felt an extreme need to be like his parent and take care of him. If he did not have a disability, I would not have felt that way. I will always feel like this, and it will always cause some conflict between us. It's better now but it will always be an issue."

When we look at the comments of the parents of the younger teens reported above, we detect some tensions, but there is also a clear caretaking role developing for the neurotypical sibling. It is not unlike the relationship evident in the decade older sibling pair quoted in the interview. What we note is that there appears to be an absence of the sibling rivalry so often reported in the literature about typical siblings. The older brother and sister have a very different view of their experiences. For her, there are some unresolved feelings of having to meet what she perceives as unfair expectations. For him, there were some differences but they are minimized, compartmentalized, and "put away." The experiences of growing up no longer affect his present. In contrast, his sister easily recounts her lack of freedom and the different parental expectations. For her, the past, the present, and the future are all connected and she envisions that her caretaking role and concerns for him will continue. Her brother views their relationship as "being equal" now. He does not understand the depth of her commitment nor the impact that her support has had on him over the years. Through his narrow focus, he can only acknowledge a need for her in very specific ways. For the sibling of a child on the spectrum, this can feel like a lack of appreciation and a failure to validate the real history of growing up together. That is why it will be important for parents/guardians to become aware of how profoundly their neurotypical children are affected.

It is generally accepted that over time, the sibling of the ASD child grows more accustomed to the limitations imposed by the disability. And, over time, the ASD child learns to accommodate the needs of the sibling. These changes result in greater acceptance between siblings. Developmental differences follow a unique pattern in sibling relationships in which one person is diagnosed with ASD. The closeness of that relationship during adolescence tends to continue at the same level into adulthood. This is different when compared to the relationships of typically developing siblings, in which there is a decrease in closeness during adolescence and increase in closeness in adulthood (Orsmond, Kuo, & Seltzer, 2009).

The effectiveness of parents in influencing the relationships of their children in a family where one has been diagnosed with ASD is supported in a number of studies.

"Parents play a role in the relationship developed among typical and affected children. In a study cited by Ross (2006), knowledge of the presence and condition of autism as well as open communication about the disorder and its manifestations had a significant impact on the well-being of the child who is not affected with autism. Another factor impacting the social adjustment of typically developing children and adolescents was that of the perception of fairness felt between the siblings. Those children that felt they received more negative treatment from their parents and were unjustly treated tended to have more behavioral and emotional ramifications (Orsmond & Seltzer, 2007)" (Ivey & Ward, 2010, p. 4).

There are concrete ways for parents to assist in deepening the connection among their neurotypical children and the disabled child:

Parents can be trained to elicit positive behaviors, such as cooperation, in their children (Strain & Danko, 1995). Mothers and sitters were taught to encourage typically developing siblings to engage in positive behavior and use certain social skills to benefit the child with autism. Their encouragement of positive interactions led to an increase in positive initiations and responses among siblings, and an increase in adult praise of children. This training also led to more spontaneous prompting of children at home. This research makes it clear that parents play a key role in nourishing sibling relationships, and that they can be trained to help sustain these sibling relationships. (Sage & Jegatheesan, 2010, p. 195)

Their role in doing this (i.e., nourishing sibling relationships) starts early on. Even in the first years of life, there is evidence that parental engagement in facilitating play with their autistic children has a positive effect.

"Research has documented that children with autism want to engage with their siblings. El-Ghoroury and Romanczyk (1999) observed nine families with children with autism in dyadic family interactions on home visits. Results indicated that although mothers and fathers exhibited more play behaviors with children with autism, children tried to initiate more play with their siblings through verbal requests. This study makes the important point that adults can enhance the sibling bond by creating opportunities for their children to play together. Kramer (2010) also suggested that adults should focus on nurturing cooperative relations amongst siblings by promoting social competence and minimizing conflicts between siblings" (Sage & Jegatheesan, 2010, p. 194).

In addition, there are other factors that affect the sibling relationships within the family constellation:

The impact of maternal influence in the sibling relationship of a child with autism has been documented by Jegatheesan and Witz (under review) in an ethnographic case study of a South Asian Muslim immigrant mother and her two sons: an 11-year-old typically developing son and a 6-year-old son with autism. The mother's positive interpretations of disability (e.g., child is a blessing from God; chosen parents to protect Allah's child) contributed to the mother being proactive in creating an advanced level of awareness in her typically developing son, which she firmly believed would enable him to support his brother with autism at all levels. The mother was also instrumental in teaching her typically developing son to be compassionate through the teachings of Islam. The authors found that the typically developing brother was extremely empathetic and protective of his brother and had a positive interpretation of disability (Sage & Jegatheesan, 2010, p. 196).

Enhancing the sibling relationship is an important component to the well-being of the ASD child and to that of his or her sibling. From early on and through the adult years, these parents/guardians will need to provide additional support for the continuation of the bonds among their children. One parent of a young adult confided that she still seeks out and promotes opportunities to encourage the camaraderie her ASD son feels when he is with his older brothers. She buys them tickets for sporting events she knows her ASD son can enjoy. She checks on the frequency of communications directed to the ASD son and arranges for "family time" that involves activities she knows he can tolerate. This same parent is aware that she does not do this with the two neurotypical brothers. With them, she does not feel responsible to be involved with promoting their connection to each other. She knows it is simply not her role in their adult world, but she is concerned about what will happen with their connection to her ASD son when she is gone.

Her children share this concern about the future. The uncertainty of caregiving responsibilities for siblings is surely a worry. The fact that their lives will be affected by obligations to the disabled sibling as parents age and/or die increasingly becomes a daunting realization. Siblings report that they are unclear on what their future responsibilities may be. Questions such as the following are common concerns: "How will this affect my life?" "Will I be able to move away if I choose to?" "What financial support will I have to provide?" The answers to questions such as these are more difficult to predict when considering the future needs of the high-functioning individual with ASD. Often times parents have provided a significant amount of support that has largely gone unnoticed by the neurotypical sibling(s). Parents/guardians tend to shield siblings from much of the parental caregiving actions, despite the siblings thinking otherwise. This shielding may be done in an attempt to protect the privacy of the disabled child and/or to maintain as much normalcy as possible for the neurotypical children. Whatever the reasons, and despite the likelihood of being well intentioned, being in the dark about the support provided to their disabled sibling does not appear to be in the best interest of anyone involved as the siblings near adulthood.

With emerging adulthood will come other concerns directly affecting siblings of individuals on the spectrum. Beyond those centered on additional family responsibilities, these thoughts are connected to more personal issues. Siblings report that it is a struggle to consider committing to a romantic relationship for fear of the ASD brother or sister being rejected by a potential partner. There is further worry about the possibility of having an ASD child themselves (Feiges & Weiss, 2004). These concerns are significant for this population. On an ongoing basis, the siblings of ASD children are faced with legitimate worries both big and small. It is important for you to take the time to clarify for parents/guardians some of the issues their children are facing as siblings of a child diagnosed with ASD.

For this chapter, we have created the document Thinking About Siblings: A Checklist (see Appendix K). We have done this in an effort to assist you and the parents/guardians with the process of considering siblings' needs. This document is based on our research and professional experiences. It will provide parents/guardians with a list of "things to do" and "things to be aware of" as they parent their neurotypical children. Ongoing communication about their unique family circumstances should begin early on between parents/guardians and their neurotypical children. There are many things to consider. For instance, they will have to monitor the extent of the caregiving responsibilities of the neurotypical children in the family. It will also be important to continuously attend to the quality of life of these siblings (e.g., Are they enjoying typical childhood experiences? How are their lives limited by the needs of the ASD sibling?). Furthermore, parents/guardians will need to be sensitive to behavioral changes in the siblings throughout childhood (e.g., regressive or acting-out behaviors). And, more generally, they will need to be aware of the feelings and fears engendered by having a brother or sister diagnosed with ASD. The guide associated with this chapter includes these issues and others. It will direct parents/guardians to think more concretely about the special needs of their neurotypical children and their responsibility to them.

CHAPTER 9

Dealing With Now While Preparing for the Future

U P TO THIS point, our focus has been on the need for you to understand the past and present of your client and his or her family. Now, as you chart the course of treatment, you will look toward the future. Because your client is a high-functioning child on the autism spectrum, planning treatment will involve unique challenges as you anticipate his or her future progress. With the neurotypical child, there are certain assumptions that can be made about the course of development over time. Behaviors change due to maturation, generalization, and socialization. These factors lead to a sense of predictability that will typically have a positive impact on the growth and development of the child. The 9-year-old who is in therapy because he is unable to regulate his behaviors and has angry outbursts can usually learn effective anger management strategies. Over time, he can come to appreciate the benefit of these techniques (maturation). His new behaviors will be reinforced in both school and home. Subsequently, he will recognize the connection of these approaches across situations and settings (generalization). Additionally, the change in his behaviors will result in greater social acceptance for him (socialization).

For the ASD child, these predictability factors are far less reliable. Despite having largely average to above-average intellectual abilities, their overall course of maturation and development will always lag behind their neurotypical peers. This lag is due to the inability of ASD children to generalize learning across situations and settings and to their lack of social skills acquisition. Given the above, your challenge will be to identify specific detrimental behaviors and practices before they become ingrained and habitual. You will also need to focus on helping parents/guardians to foster the growth of those skills that will not spontaneously emerge for the ASD child. The child's chances for future success depend on it.

Before exploring this topic further, let's review what we have covered thus far. Chapter 1 began by providing background information about ASD and general pointers for screening families seeking treatment. Chapter 2 presented the developmental differences you can expect to find between your client and the neurotypical child. This knowledge prepared you to assess the data collected from the Family Profile Form in Chapter 3. You were then able to determine the "goodness of fit" for you, your potential client, and the parents/guardians. Chapter 4 provided a tool for interviewing the client. It gave you some tips on things to consider. It introduced thoughts regarding the physical environment and other needs of the child.

Chapter 5 highlighted the key differences in treatment planning for these children, as well as the need for extensive involvement of their families. A tool entitled Autism Spectrum Descriptive Profile (ASDP) is included to assist you in the treatment process. The information derived from the ASDP forms will help you in determining the prevalent autistic features that are uniquely affecting your client and his or her family. The forms will also enable you to make the best decisions for setting treatment goals. In addition, information obtained from the ASDP will create a narrative description of your client that can be used by you as well as the parents/guardians to explain the child's needs to others.

The themes for Chapters 6 and 7 centered on the advantages of having formal and separate collaborative agreements with *both* the parents/guardians and the child. These guides are meant to help define the parameters of treatment. Because of the disability-related stress and anxiety experienced by the family and discussed at length in these chapters, these parents/guardians and their children tend to benefit from a more structured therapeutic approach. This added structure provides comfort and predictability in an otherwise chaotic family life.

Finally, in Chapter 8, we focused on the plight of the siblings. Unfortunately, their needs become secondary to the more pressing needs of the ASD child. In this chapter, a guide entitled Thinking About Siblings: A Checklist is provided to give parents/guardians direction on things to do and things to be aware of as they think about the experiences of their neurotypical children.

The intent of this final chapter is to connect *current* concerns to preparation for the *future* in terms of some specific deficits that the ASD child exhibits. Whether you are treating an 8-year-old or a 16-year-old, this information is important for you to know. As we have said, with the ASD child there are unusual practices that become ingrained, as well as limitations in skills that are apparent in earlier years. They will affect the futures of these children in unique ways. The ASD parents/guardians do not always understand the long-term significance of these unusual practices and deficits (Powell, 2002). It is often reported that they spend much of their time "just putting out fires" and they have to pick and choose their battles. Some parents/guardians are overwhelmed with the issues of the day and cannot think beyond the immediate present. Others hope that the practices and routines will automatically resolve over time. Then there are those whose shame and guilt about not being able to change these bizarre behaviors keep them from asking for help. There is also fear around the issues that prevent some from dealing with it at all. These parents/guardians do recognize that there are problems, but they do not even attempt to work them through with their child. For them, compartmentalizing becomes the coping mechanism. In summary, there are many reasons why parents/guardians need your support in identifying specific behaviors, practices, and skill deficits to target for optimal outcome.

As we see it, there are three areas of rising concern in childhood that are directly connected to future functioning as it leads to a productive adulthood for the high-functioning individual on the spectrum. In the specific areas of (1) safety, (2) health and hygiene, and (3) increasing autonomy, any significant lack of progress will become a major issue for the child as he or she gets older. So, in order to prepare for the future and address these areas, parents/guardians need to be *continually* aware of the following

- The defining details of the child's level of functioning in relation to safety, health, and hygiene and increasing autonomy

- The need for a plan to build skills and extinguish behaviors while carefully measuring progress in these areas
- The fact that there *are* ramifications related to the child's current deficits that will uniquely limit his or her future functioning if not emphasized and addressed adequately in the present

It is imperative for parents/guardians to seek help or guidance in a timely way as unusual practices and limitations emerge in the areas of safety, health, and hygiene and in the need for increasing autonomy. To not do this is to lay the foundation unintentionally for an ever-widening gap in the development of necessary life skills. Behaviors and practices become deeply imbedded and are more difficult to change as time progresses. For parents/guardians, years of increasing tolerance for bizarre behaviors and practices, and the absence of self-reliance make it difficult to recognize the extent of the ASD child's problems and potential impact on his or her future. As time goes on, they tend to lose their perspective on what is considered "normal and acceptable." They focus less on comparing their ASD child to neurotypical peers and focus more on small and often unessential gains. Capabilities are not assessed, capacities are not sufficiently challenged, and consequently expectations are lowered.

Another point to understand is that parents/guardians feel uncomfortable talking about these matters. For instance, issues around personal hygiene or rigid ritualistic behaviors are hard to admit. Embarrassment keeps them from disclosing concerns even to those closest to them. As we have stated, it also prevents them from asking for much needed help. It is quite possible that, in their experience, reaching out has resulted in criticism and negative judgment centered on their parenting skills and on their child as a person. This is the root of their secrecy and shame. This criticism and judgment occur because "outsiders" do not understand that the child or adolescent on the autism spectrum does not have the advantage of being able to learn incidentally from others. They do not model behaviors, nor do they "automatically" know what others learn spontaneously over time. It is one thing when a child of 8 years cannot use eating utensils appropriately, but when an adolescent continues to be unable to use a knife or fork, it draws attention and frequently evokes critical comments from uninformed others. Not using utensils in an expected way may not seem to be a very big problem when the ASD child is young, but if not addressed specifically and methodically, it becomes a much more noticeable and embedded behavior later on. A circumstance such as this, seemingly minor at one point in time, can limit social opportunities and even vocational advances in the future.

For parents/guardians of neurotypical children, not accomplishing mundane developmental tasks is seldom a problem. They do not need to worry about their children being able to demonstrate basic skills and acceptable behaviors that will lay the foundation for a productive adulthood. For them, serious thoughts about future planning can begin sometime in the child's mid-teen years. This is because they can assume that their child will acquire the "basics" as well as adequate social-emotional skills and independent living capabilities. For these parents/guardians, questions around academic potential and vocational interests will arise and be explored. Professions will be researched and pathways leading to them will be defined. All the while, the expected outcome for the child's future involves a steady and fairly predictable progression as he or she continues to mature. Concerns about the future are generally manageable as the neurotypical child develops. It is a different scenario in the household of the ASD child. Parents/guardians need your help in identifying problems and strategies associated with areas of functioning in safety, health, and hygiene and the need for increasing autonomy.

We have developed a checklist entitled Skills and Behaviors: A Checklist for Therapists (see Appendix L), to help you focus on these three areas and to clearly define related issues. This tool will promote discussion around sensitive areas, and it is meant to be used only after you have established a therapeutic bond with the parents/guardians. Using this checklist, you will record whether a task has been accomplished. On the *current progress* lines of the form, you will note details of the specific accomplishments. You will then be able to return to the form periodically to measure subsequent progress. The information you obtain will expand upon the profile generated by the ASDP. Referring to the information from the Developmental Guide and the Family Profile Form might also be useful to you. This checklist outlines specific practices associated with safety, health, and hygiene, and the need for increasing autonomy. You will likely uncover important issues that have somehow gone unrecognized. For these reasons, particular care and sensitivity on your part will yield the best results.

The Skills and Behaviors checklist is designed to elicit discussions and detect themes around behaviors and limitations that have the potential to compromise future quality of life. In each of the three categories listed above, items are presented in a sequence that we consider to progress from least to most intrusive in the functioning of the ASD individual. This should facilitate a smoother process for questioning and aid in gathering more in-depth information. You will then be able to use the data as a way for supporting the idea of treatment outcome via the targeting of measurable goals.

The first part of the checklist, copied below, highlights areas of concern dealing with safety issues related to the ASD child. In recent literature it has come to light that those with the diagnosis of ASD do not automatically develop self-preservation and survival skills. For example, wandering from caretakers or from familiar areas has been identified as a significant problem for the child on the spectrum. In a recent article in a journal entitled *Pediatrics*, a research study involving 1,218 families with autistic children found that 49% of the children engaged in wandering or elopement behaviors after the age of 4 years (Anderson et al., 2012).

The Integrative Autism Network of the Kennedy Krieger Institute reports that this behavior of wandering and elopement in ASD children is only in the preliminary stages of study (McIlwain & Fournier, 2012). It is commonly reported that there are more incidents associated with lower functioning children on the spectrum. Yet the reasons for wandering reflect motivational factors that would also influence high-functioning ASD children. These factors include the enjoyment of running or exploring, seeking a place of enjoyment, or pursuing a perseverative interest. Despite the current lack of research in this area, particularly as it applies to high-functioning ASD children, clinical experience indicates that these behaviors are a concern. In addition, these motivational factors do appear relevant as precipitants to wandering and elopement for high-functioning children. They lead to serious and unsafe situations. Let's now turn to the checklist itself so we can further examine the skills and behaviors related to safety.

SKILLS AND BEHAVIORS:
A CHECKLIST FOR THERAPISTS

<u>Task Accomplished</u>

YES   NO

1. Safety Issues:

Awareness of directions around home & other familiar places   _____ _____

current progress: _____

_____

Safe and proper use of cell phone   _____ _____

current progress: _____

_____

Safe and proper use of internet & social networks   _____ _____

current progress: _____

_____

Safe around potentially dangerous objects & products   _____ _____

current progress: _____

_____

Care in taking risks at home   _____ _____

current progress: _____

_____

Care in taking risks in school & community   _____ _____

current progress: _____

_____

Safe behavior around water, woods, & outside areas   _____ _____

current progress: _____

_____

Navigates community & can safely seek help   _____ _____

current progress: _____

_____

In addition to these areas of concern for the child's safety, other practices can result in dangerous situations. For instance, ritualistic behaviors can become so circumscribed in the ASD child's repertoire that he or she gives no importance to the dangerousness of the practice. One 10-year-old boy had his "secret" hideaway situated under some fir trees in his backyard. There he ritually lit votive candles before circling the area while chanting his own secret language. (The language, his own creation, was derived from actual rules and blends of several modern languages.) This particular boy was well known for his acuity in mastering foreign languages. His teacher and parents/guardians considered him to be "brilliant." Yet the basic idea of safe practices around fire was not intuitively registering with him. This is yet another example of why the deficits of high-functioning ASD children are not accurately perceived or adequately supported.

Like this boy, the behaviors of other ASD individuals also can stem from practices that become a fascination brought to extremes. For some it can become a full-blown compulsion. There is no guarantee that an early intervention will necessarily prevent these things from happening. However, early recognition and action offer the chance to set limits on a particular interest or practice before it gets out of control and is more difficult to manage. In the case cited above, the boy's perseverative interest in languages became associated with a dangerous practice. The increasing tolerance of those around him enabled the boy to include a risky practice surreptitiously as part of his special interest. If risky behaviors are identified and observed to be part of a pattern over time, an early intervention offers the opportunity to prevent them from intensifying. As these children and adolescents move into their adult years, such practices can become more ingrained and dangerous and the tendency to take risks in general can increase.

We have to be concerned about the ASD child for more than just safety reasons. The quality of adult life for this population is also greatly affected by unusual behaviors and limitations in the areas of health and hygiene. It is commonly known that these characteristics emerge in younger years but are often "swept under the rug" and minimized. Parents/guardians tend to assume that the odd behaviors or lack of development will take care of itself over time. This paves the way for limitations to continue and behaviors to become imbedded. When this happens, it will certainly affect future opportunities.

The second part of the Skills and Behaviors checklist, shown below, addresses health and hygiene. As with the safety issues listed in the prior section, the items here are largely self-explanatory.

Task Accomplished

YES   NO

2. Health & Hygiene

Covers mouth when coughing/sneezing;
uses tissues appropriately   ____ ____

current progress: _____

_____

Recognizes & seeks treatment for medical concerns   ____ ____

current progress: _____

_____

Demonstrates daily dental care & willingness to visit dentist   ____ ____

current progress: _____

_____

Demonstrates bathing/showering practices; hand/face washing ____ ____

current progress: _____

_____

Females: proper use of makeup, toiletries, & feminine products ____ ____

current progress: _____

_____

Males: proper use of toiletries & shaving equipment ____ ____

current progress: _____

_____

This is probably the most difficult topic to explore. It is here that we have found parents/guardians to be least likely to disclose fully. Excessive adult intervention, unusual hygiene practices, and lack of cleanliness are aspects of raising the ASD child that have a strong potential to produce shame and guilt in the parents/guardians. Tony Attwood talks extensively about the effects of poor hygiene in individuals with Asperger syndrome (2012). Generally speaking, clothing and cleanliness are perceived to reflect the time, care, and concern that parents/guardians invest in their children. When ASD children have issues in these areas, their caretakers take it personally and see it as something to hide.

One mother of a young teen boy with ASD explained her guilt this way. "I will always remember the day some relatives we had not seen for quite a while stopped by for an unannounced visit. I urged my disheveled 14-year-old son to wash up and change his clothes, but he loudly refused. To avoid embarrassment, I bribed him to stay downstairs in the family room watching videos. I said I would let him know when he could come upstairs. I still struggle with that guilt years later, as my son remembers that he has not seen those relatives again." In therapy, this mother came to realize that she had inadvertently been a participant in limiting her son's experiences in the social world. Luckily, with this realization, she invoked the use of appropriate therapeutic interventions. She was able to work with her son to better prepare him for the adult world. It should be noted that her diligence paid off. By learning more about the characteristics of ASD and how present factors affect future chances for a "normal" life, she changed her parenting approach and sought help.

Health and hygiene deficits are contributing factors to social isolation. As you can see in the above example, initial appearance can be off-putting and result in the ASD person being excluded from social interactions. A child who presents as unkempt or who does not adequately wash or clean himself in terms of bathing or toileting *will not* be accepted by peers and *will be* a target for bullying. Parents/guardians try to address these odd behaviors and limitations, frequently through excessive interventions. For example, one set of parents maintained the practice of wiping a very high-functioning 10-year-old boy after toileting. The parents kept this a secret for many years and subsequently confessed to the therapist that they simply hoped he would start doing this task on his own. Another mother shamefully confessed that because her 17-year-old son would not flush the toilet, she found out that he was no longer using toilet paper as he did when he was younger. She did not want to embarrass him and did not address it directly. Instead, when she saw him heading for the bathroom, she quickly made a tear in the last hanging sheet of the toilet paper in an effort to monitor whether he was using it or not. She, too, hoped that he would "grow out of it." Unfortunately, at age 25, his hygiene is worse than ever. Current attempts at interventions violate his privacy as an adult and are unsuccessful.

Along with bizarre toileting practices, there are hygiene issues around bathing, showering, washing, and other aspects of personal care. One of the most difficult for parents/guardians to address is the proper use of feminine products with ASD females. Often there is not only an aversion to the experience of bleeding but a resistance to using sanitary pads. For some mothers, the idea of teaching their ASD daughters to use tampons would not be feasible. Unlike with neurotypical girls, this is not a skill acquired independently, nor is it accepted as a rite of passage. Because the girl with ASD does not generally have girlfriends who can share in this experience, she feels alone in the process. Because she simply does not accept the idea, she does not plan ahead and take necessary precautions. For these parents/guardians, this is another sensitive and difficult topic that troubles them as they envision their daughter's future.

Lastly, there are disability-related issues around bathing and showering. What can initially be avoidance based on sensory sensitivities can turn into avoidance for a different reason. Sohn and Grayson state, "Sensory issues may have been a larger concern when the child was younger. Many Asperger children experience a reduction in their severity as they grow older. A behavioral issue that may have initially been sensory may now be maintained due to habit or rigidity" (2005, p. 38). For this reason it is important that the parents/guardians be guided in finding ways to address sensory needs early on. Involving an occupational therapist to determine the extent of the sensory impact and a behavior specialist to design a program to fade the intensity of the adversity are two recommendations you can make. The best route to follow will depend on the age of the child and how ingrained the avoidance/refusal behavior is. It is imperative that some plan of action is developed before the child becomes an adolescent. If the person you are treating is an older teen with these problems, it will be harder to make progress and will require a more creative approach. Nonetheless, it needs to be addressed. Openly talking about health and hygiene will encourage the parents/guardians to further disclose difficult information and seek appropriate help. An added advantage is that this can result in empowering the parents/guardians and decreasing their feelings of shame and guilt.

Acquiring skills of daily living is one thing; getting the child on the spectrum to implement them *independently* is still another. As we turn to examining factors aligned with developing autonomy, we will again find that there are major obstacles for the ASD child to overcome.

	Task Accomplished	
	YES	NO

3. Autonomy

Completes household chores; takes care of possessions _____ _____

current progress: _____

_____

Independently chooses acceptable clothing _____ _____

current progress: _____

_____

Understands concept of time & adheres
to schedules independently _____ _____

current progress: _____

_____

Awareness and management of money   _____ _____

current progress: _____

_____

Completes homework and school projects independently   _____ _____

current progress: _____

_____

Ability to be alone in: the home; neighborhood & community   _____ _____

current progress: _____

_____

Independent execution of hygiene practices & toileting needs   _____ _____

current progress: _____

_____

Age-appropriate understanding of sexuality   _____ _____

current progress: _____

_____

Developing independent living skills occurs sequentially, gradually, and over a fairly predictable period of time for the neurotypical child. As each developmental milestone is accomplished, parents/guardians feel increasingly assured of their child's growing competence in navigating the world independently. They take it for granted that they will be able to send their children on errands, drop them off at a mall, and give them directions on how to use public transportation. They expect them to be safe or appropriate when left alone and to be able to deal with any unforeseen events. They also expect them to be able to manage money and time. As stated before, the independent development of skills is not consistently observed in children and adolescents with ASD.

This lack of consistency makes parenting even more difficult for those whose older children are neurotypical and have followed a predictable pathway. The lack of predictability that is characteristic of development in the high-functioning child on the spectrum adds to the confusion these parents/guardians experience in determining an effective parenting approach. Discovering a "tried and true" approach with the ASD child is not an easy task because most parenting guidelines and suggestions will not work. Yet the path to independence requires moving through childhood into adolescence, all the while building a complicated skill base that will support them in their adult lives.

Increasing autonomy first requires parents/guardians to understand exactly what their child *can do* independently. It is commonly reported by these caretakers that they do not know what their child is capable of because they have never trusted him or her enough to test the boundaries. While this is completely understandable, it is not in the best interest of the child. Parents/guardians will need to find ways for assessing present capabilities in their ASD child. Again, it may take some creativity, but they need to be able to encourage their child to take reasonable and safe risks toward learning to function independently.

You will be discussing with parents/guardians their child's increasing need for autonomy in order to attain future success. This may be the first time that they are concretely determining what their child can do. The Skills and Behaviors checklist is a good place to start identifying areas to target for growth and development. You can expect resistance when introducing these ideas. This was the case when one 13-year-old girl with ASD complained to her therapist that she felt "like a baby" because she couldn't go out into her neighborhood alone. In fact, she was still not allowed to leave her yard. Her parents felt the need to protect her and to restrict any potentially perilous circumstance. She had never been trained to cross a street independently or to negotiate her own way around the neighborhood. When the therapist suggested that her client's capacity for independence needed to be defined and safely challenged, the parents balked at the idea. This is not uncommon, and it will be your challenge to discover how receptive parents/guardians are to discussing these topics and considering ways to promote their child's autonomy while guiding them through the process.

At this point, we want to remind you again that in order to achieve optimal outcomes, it is our view that all professionals working with children on the spectrum need to prioritize changes in perceptions and approaches, as well as changes in the environment. It is only through these changes that the child will best be able to interpret his or her surroundings. This means recognizing that behaviors appearing to be intentionally hostile or unusual are generally related to social confusion and anxiety. They should be *planned for* by the adults in their lives rather than *reacted to* in a disciplinary manner. An approach that addresses behaviors and limitations through anticipation and preparation will require making changes in the child's environment. Taking these steps will minimize anxiety and confusion, resulting in creating an atmosphere more conducive to learning those skills necessary for the ASD child to experience the potential for success now and in the future.

In conclusion, there have been many issues discussed in this guide for you to consider as you chart the course for treating your ASD client and his or her family. Yet the most important point of all is for you to remain ever compassionate and patient as you guide them through the course of treatment.

Appendices

Appendix A

Please note that all appendix forms can be found on the accompanying CD.

INITIAL CONTACT FORM

I. GENERAL INFORMATION

Name of caller: _____

Date of call: _____

Relationship to child: parent _____ guardian _____

Insurance information: _____

Name of company: _____

Type of policy: _____

Alternative payment method: _____

Additional Notes: _____

_____

_____

II. BACKGROUND INFORMATION

Mailing address: _____

Contact phone number: _____

Second parent/guardian name and contact information
(if applicable):_____

CHILD'S DIAGNOSES:

Diagnosis:	
Diagnosed by:	
Date of diagnosis:	

Diagnosis:	
Diagnosed by:	
Date of diagnosis:	

Diagnosis:	
Diagnosed by:	
Date of diagnosis:	

Current medical providers:

Name	
Specialty	
Prescribed medications	

Name	
Specialty	
Prescribed medications	

Current mental health provider:

Provider	
Dates	
Reason for treatment	

Current non–mental health therapists
(i.e., speech, occupational, physical):

Name of Therapist	Setting (school, home, etc.)	Dates	Reason for Treatment

Past counseling or other treatment:

Name of Therapist	Setting	Dates	Reason for Treatment

Source of this referral: _____

Additional Notes: _____

_____

III. CURRENT CIRCUMSTANCES

What precipitated the call for treatment? **Ask about a specific event or incident that triggered this call.**

_____

_____

Obtain a <u>brief</u> explanation of how the child is functioning in the following areas:

School: _____

_____

_____

Home: _____

_____

_____

Extended Family Relationships: _____

_____

_____

Peer Relationships:_____

_____

_____

Legal Problems (if any): _____

_____

_____

Additional Notes: _____

_____

_____

_____

Last: *Discuss the need for further information to be obtained via the Family Profile Form (see Chapter 3).*

IV. REFLECTIONS ON THE CALL

Length of phone call:_____

Tone of the conversation (disorganized, methodical, angry, anxious, frustrated, etc.): _____

_____

Quality of reciprocity in the conversation (interruptions, one-sided, talking over, perseverative, etc.): _____

_____

Clarity of responses (on topic, direct answers, ability to listen and comprehend, logical presentation, etc.):_____

_____

_____

Final impressions after call (Was the caller a sympathetic person? Did the story make sense?):_____

_____

Appendix B

DEVELOPMENTAL GUIDE

AGE	PHYSICAL DEVELOPMENT	SOCIAL-EMOTIONAL	COMMUNICATIVE DOMAIN
Birth–2 yrs	crawling*	matching/imitating/copying facial expressions and various movements of others*	imitating expressions*
	walking*	establishing attachment with primary caregivers*	cooing
	sleeping routines*	seeking and accepting comfort when distressed*	babbling
	eating (using a spoon, etc.)*	establishing joint attention with primary caregivers*	sustaining eye contact*
	toileting*	social referencing (engaging others through touching, showing, pointing, or otherwise seeking information)*	spontaneous social smiling*
	complies with hygiene practices (face washing, bathing, tooth brushing)*		prodeclarative pointing*
	fine motor (playing with puzzles, unzipping clothing, pointing, pinching, stacking)*	seeks adult company when left alone*	sharing eye gaze*
		discriminates familiar and unfamiliar adults*	one-two spoken words*
		recognizing distress in others—beginning of empathy*	
		emotionally attached to toys or objects for security*	
		engages in functional play that involves reciprocity (turn-taking in games and other interactions)*	

*Potential areas of concern in ASD

AGE	PHYSICAL DEVELOPMENT	SOCIAL-EMOTIONAL	COMMUNICATIVE DOMAIN
Birth–2 yrs		playing activity shifts from solitary to parallel play with others*	
		engages in turn-taking baby games (peekaboo)*	
		shows enjoyment of "baby games" (patty cake, etc.)*	
2–4 yrs	walking smoothly and in a straight line	facial expressions reflect an emotional range*	use of pronouns "I" and "me"*
	hopping on 2 feet, jumping*	beginning to offer comfort to others*	2–3 word sentences
	pedaling a tricycle*	resists major changes in routine*	uses words in a way that make sense (Baby sleepy, take nap.")*
	throwing and kicking a ball*	peaking of temper tantrums*	has approximately 2–300 word vocabulary (by age 2)
	feeding self (using a fork, holding a cup)*	beginning to share possessions and understand turn taking*	has approximately 1000 word vocabulary (by age 3)
	using toilet semi-independently*	beginning of cooperative play*	mastery of elements of adult-like speech (by age 4)
	hand and face washing independently, brushing teeth (unassisted), compliance with bathing practices*	appropriate functional use of toys*	answers "what," "who" and "where" questions*
		use of representational play (pretend and imitative)*	increasingly engages in reciprocal conversation

*Potential areas of concern in ASD

AGE	PHYSICAL DEVELOPMENT	SOCIAL-EMOTIONAL	COMMUNICATIVE DOMAIN
2–4 yrs	dressing (chooses clothing, removes clothes, puts on shoes and socks, knows front and back)*	beginning to understand negotiations of conflict*	
		often cannot distinguish between fantasy and reality*	
	fine motor (using scissors, copying shapes, zippering, some buckling, coloring)*	exhibits empathy for people in situations generalized from own experiences*	
4–6 yrs	hopping on 1 foot, skipping*	engaging in mutual friendships*	competent reciprocal conversational skills
	pumping self on a swing*	participating in sharing toys and taking turns in play*	recognizes meanings of emotional expressions*
	riding a bicycle with training wheels*	participating in rule-governed games*	sensitive to body languages and gestures*
	using a knife for spreading*	more likely to follow rules*	enjoys jokes and riddles*
	establishing specific food preferences*	initiates social interactions (cooperative play: visiting with friends, neighbors, etc.)*	learning 5 to 10 words per day
	adhering to mealtime routine (schedules and practices)*	able to distinguish fantasy from reality*	vocabulary of approximately 10,000-14,000 words
	daytime toileting achieved (some nightime bedwetting), adheres to toileting hygiene practices*	exploration of social roles*	functional use of language (within appropriate social context)*
		beginning to identify with story characters*	

*Potential areas of concern in ASD

AGE	PHYSICAL DEVELOPMENT	SOCIAL-EMOTIONAL	COMMUNICATIVE DOMAIN
4–6 yrs	exhibiting a desire for independent bathing, but still needing assistance*	exhibits empathy for experiences of others beyond their own personal experience*	
	dresses and undresses independently, may still need help with buckles, buttons and shoelaces*		
	printing first name with proper pencil grasp*		
6-12 yrs	Integration and coordination of movement (participating in sports, dance, and other activities requiring coordination of motor skills)*	strengthening and expanding mutual friendships*	uses concrete language
		moving toward peers for social support*	understanding of sarcasm*
	riding a bicycle*	developing a need to confide in friends*	understanding of expressions of speech, (colloquialisms)*
	using kitchen utensils appropriately*	conforming to peer expectations*	
	preparing snacks and small meals*	actively participating in team sports and related outside activities*	
	achieved bowel and bladder control*	increasing the understanding of unwritten social rules of behavior*	
	chooses appropriate clothing*	demonstrating an expressed need for rules*	

*Potential areas of concern in ASD

AGE	PHYSICAL DEVELOPMENT	SOCIAL-EMOTIONAL	COMMUNICATIVE DOMAIN
6-12 yrs	mastering basic motor skills (writing, cutting, painting, pasting, etc.)*	increasingly responsible for unsupervised behavior and time*	
		exhibiting gender-specific social behaviors*	
	jumping rope*	increasing awareness of physical appearances*	
		achieving personal, academic, and functional skills for everyday living*	
		internalizing moral values*	
		developing a sense of social responsibility and conscience*	
		empathy generalized to broader social circumstances and to the plight of others*	
12-18 yrs	acclimating to body changes	emphasis is on identifying with peers*	use of abstract language*
	experimentation with body, hair, and other physical expressions (dieting, shaving, piercing, tattooing, makeup, etc.)*	consideration of experimenting with drugs and alcohol*	understanding of metaphorical expression*
		expressed loyalty to peer groups*	
		need for privacy*	developing an understanding of abstract concepts*
		sensitivity to perceptions of others*	communicating one's thoughts about abstract ideas*

*Potential areas of concern in ASD

AGE	PHYSICAL DEVELOPMENT	SOCIAL-EMOTIONAL	COMMUNICATIVE DOMAIN
12-18 yrs		preoccupation and concern about personal differences compared to peers*	
		need for peer acceptance and validation*	
		achieving more mature relations with peers of both sexes (including budding romances, intimate friendships)*	
		achieving emotional independence from parents and adults*	
		preparing future goals*	
		anticipating independence in living (with excitement)*	
		exploring ethical and moral beliefs*	
		experiencing guilt and hopelessness in the face of social injustice*	

*Potential areas of concern in ASD

Appendix C

FAMILY PROFILE FORM

I. GENERAL INFORMATION

Name of Child:_____

Name of Parent(s)/Guardian(s):_____

Child is yours by: birth ___ adoption ___ stepchild ___ other
_____

Parent(s)/Guardian(s) are: married ___unmarried___divorced ___other _____

Child lives with:_____

II. REFERRAL INFORMATION

Referral source:_____

Reason for referral: _____

Behavioral concerns: From the list below, please indicate those behaviors you find most concerning.

Area of Concern	Level of Concern		
	Mild	Moderate	High
Difficulty with peer relations			
Monopolizes conversations			
Difficulty reading facial expressions			
Unusual interest in a singular topic			
High reliance on set routines			

Unusual mannerisms or movements			
Appears stubborn/unwilling to compromise			
Unusual or a lack of hygiene practices			
History of wandering			
Other odd or unexpected behaviors			

Approaches to troublesome behaviors: From the list below, please check off techniques most often used when dealing with your child's troublesome behaviors. Indicate the caregiver who uses them.

Approach	Caregiver 1	Caregiver 2
Distracting from the problem		
Diffusing the situation		
Talking things through		
Time-out		
Removing privileges		
Spanking		
Other form of physical touch		
Stressing the consequences		

II. REFERRAL INFORMATION

Mother (or Guardian)   **Father (or Guardian)**

Name:_____   Name: _____

Street Address:_____   Street Address:_____

City/State/Zip: _____   City/State/Zip: _____

Home/Cell Phone: _____   Home/Cell Phone: _____

Work Phone _____   Work Phone _____

Race/Ethnicity _____   Race/Ethnicity _____

Date of Birth _____   Date of Birth _____

Level of Education:_____   Level of Education:_____

Occupation: _____   Occupation: _____

Employer: _____   Employer: _____

Members of Household:

Name: _____ Age: ____Sex: ___ Relationship: _____

Name: _____ Age: ____Sex: ___ Relationship: _____

Name: _____ Age: ____Sex: ___ Relationship: _____

Name: _____ Age: ____Sex: ___ Relationship: _____

V. MEDICAL HISTORY (FAMILY)

(*Family information is requested but optional.)

From the list below, please check those areas that apply.

Issue/Disability	Mother (or Guardian)	Father (or Guardian)	Sibling(s)
Severe headaches			
Seizures			
Other chronic pain			
Anxiety			
Depression			
Attention problems			
Other emotional diagnoses/issues			
Drug/alcohol dependence			

List current medications of parents/guardians.

_____   _____   _____

List previous hospitalizations of parents/guardians.

_____   _____   _____

_____   _____   _____

List present and previous counseling experiences. Please include dates of treatment and the names of the providers.

	Parent/Guardian	Parent/Guardian
Therapist	_____	_____
Dates	_____	_____

VI. MEDICAL HISTORY (CHILD)

Health-related diagnoses/concerns: List significant non–mental health issues.

_____   _____   _____

_____   _____   _____

Last Annual Physical Exam:

Provider:	
Date:	
Results/Concerns:	

Last Dental Exam:

Provider:	
Date:	
Results/Concerns:	

Current Medications: List prescription and/or over-the-counter medications with dosages.

_____   _____   _____

_____   _____   _____

Allergies:

Type of Allergy		
Severity		
Reactions/Symptoms		

Type of Allergy		
Severity		
Reactions/Symptoms		

Does your child have a history of illegal drug use?

Drug Type	Dates of Use	How Often	Amount Used

Does your child have a history of medical and/or psychiatric hospitalizations?

Date of Hospitalization	Where	Why

History of counseling or other treatment:

Name of Therapist	Setting	Dates	Reason for Treatment

VII. DEVELOPMENTAL HISTORY

When did your child meet the following developmental milestones?

Ages 0-6 years:	Early	On Time	Late
Crawling			
Walking			
Eating solid foods			
Toileting			
Talking			
Appreciating sex differences			
Learning sexual modesty			

What, if anything, was different about the way your child accomplished any of these tasks? For example, walking on toes or skipping the crawling stage.

_____

_____

_____

Ages 6–12 years:	Early	On Time	Late
Developing skills for playing games			
Getting along with age-mates			
Demonstrates a consistant understanding of gender roles			
Making friends			
Participating appropriately in social situations			
Developing a sense of right and wrong			
Acquiring independent daily living skills			

Ages 12–18 years:	Early	On Time	Late
Engaging in more mature social relationships			
Engaging in romantic interests			
Achieving emotional independence from parents/other adults			
Demonstrating concern for another's well-being			
Showing interest in occupational choices			
Managing home and school responsibilities independently			
Accessing the community independently			

What, if anything was different about the way your child accomplished any of these tasks ? For example, playing according to very specific rules or having meltdowns when having to share toys or games.

_____

_____

_____

VIII. SOCIAL/ COMMUNICATIVE/ BEHAVIORAL DEVELOPMENT

Please rate your child as having been observed or not observed to exhibit these behaviors.

	Observed	Not observed
Speaks in a studious or pedantic manner		
Repeats words or certain expressions		
Perseverates on a single topic without listener interest		
Has difficulty understanding subtle jokes/ humor		
Has distinctive voice patterns		
Seems to expect special treatment		
Shows decreased eye contact		
Displays limited/unexpected facial expressions		
Has difficulty with transitions		
Limited ability to empathize with others		
Unintentionally invades personal space		
Has difficulty maintaining peer relationships		
Adheres to set routines or rituals		
Strongly resists unexpected changes		

Displays emotional volitility when routines are altered		
Reacts to textures, noise levels, or smells		
Flinches when touched or hugged		
Has "meltdowns" when expectations are not met		
Has difficulty with written assignments		
Opposes learning information deemed irrelevant		
Difficulty organizing tasks		
Precisly organizes environment		
Seems to lack good sense		
Engages in rocking behaviors		
Engages in spinning, hand-flicking, or twirling motions		
Flaps hands when becoming anxious or frustrated		

Further Social/Communicative Information:

	Observed	Not observed
Has been a victim of bullying outside of school		

If observed, where and when:_____

	Observed	Not observed
Preoccupation with one particular subject or interest		

If observed, list topics: _____

	Observed	Not observed
Appears to have a tendency toward social withdrawal		
Appears to lack interest in other people and their interests		
Appears to lack initiative for engaging in activities with others		
Often does not pick up on nonverbal cues (i.e., body language)		
Difficulty with taking turns talking		
Often verbalizes his/her own internal thoughts (self-talk)		
Has a history of echolalia (the repetition of phrases and words)		

School-Related Information:

Has your child been a victim of bullying in school? If so, please explain.

_____

	Yes	No	Sometimes
Participates in nonacademic school activities			

Explain:_____

	Yes	No	Sometimes
Engages socially with at least one schoolmate			

Explain:_____

	Yes	No	Sometimes
Adheres to school rules and regulations			

Explain:_____

	Yes	No	Sometimes
Receives special accommodations to his/her academic program			

Explain:_____

	Yes	No	Sometimes
Demonstrates grade-level achievements in major subject areas			

Explain:_____

IX. EVERYDAY LIFE

Briefly explain how your child's unusual behaviors affect your everyday life.

	Yes	No	Sometimes
Dressing, for example, wearing only certain clothes or unusual styles			

Explain:_____

	Yes	No	Sometimes
Eating, for example, eating only certain foods; needing specific arrangements of food on the plate; refusal to eat in the presence of others			

Explain:_____

	Yes	No	Sometimes
Hygiene, for example, avoiding teeth brushing, showering, bathing, hair washing.			

Explain:_____

	Yes	No	Sometimes
Care of possessions and surroundings, for example, color coding CD's, keeping things in a specific order, inability to share possessions			

Explain:_____

	Yes	No	Sometimes
Transitioning, for example, unable to transition easily from wake to sleep, difficulty with using certain forms of transportation, unable to follow varied routes to and from familiar places			

Explain:_____

	Yes	No	Sometimes
Safety, for example, not recognizing dangerous practices, wandering away, not able to problem solve in case of an emergency, showing a lack of awareness around strangers			

Explain:_____

	Yes	No	Sometimes
Other unusual habits or behaviors, for example, unusual daily rituals or routines			

Explain:_____

Behavioral Characteristics: Please share three positive things about your child that you observe every day.

1. _____

2. _____

3. _____

X. SUPPORT SYSTEMS

Family/Friends:

Name	Relationship	Level of Support (high, moderate, low)

School/Community:

Name	Relationship	Level of Support (high, moderate, low)

Organizations/Other Providers:

Name	Relationship	Level of Support (high, moderate, low)

Please add any further information you think may be helpful to the understanding of your child and your family life. Thank you.

_____

_____

_____

_____

_____

_____

_____

_____

_____

_____

_____

_____

_____

Appendix D

CHILD INTERVIEW FORM

I. BASIC INFORMATION

I will start with asking you some questions so that you can help me to get the information I need today. They will be questions like "What's your name? How old are you? Where do you live?" So let's begin . . .

What is your name?
How old are you?
When is your birthday? Do you know what year you were born?
Where do you live? Can you tell me your address?
What is your home phone number or your parent's cell phone number?
Where do you go to school?
What grade are you in?

Great! That was very helpful. I would like to ask a few more questions, just to get more information about your life at home and your life at school. Ready? It's time to begin . . .

II. HOME INFORMATION

Can you tell me who lives with you in your home?
Do you have brothers and sisters?
How old are they?
Are your parents married to each other? Do they both live with you?
When you are home, who helps you the most? In what ways does he/she help you?

(If the child has two homes, ask . . .)

How often do you visit your mother/father in his/her home?

Are there are other children living at that house?

How old are they?

Are there other adults living there?

Who helps you the most in that home? How do they help you?

Now I need to find out a little more about what it is like for you living at the home where you spend most of your time. Let's start by talking about your bedroom . . .

Do you have your own room? (If the child shares a room, ask what that is like for him/her. Do the siblings argue over how to organize the room itself or sections of it?)

Tell me what your room looks like.

Do you like to keep your things a certain way? Can you explain that to me?

When you are in your room, is it important for you to have the window blinds opened or closed?

Do you have a closet in your room? Do you share it with others?

Tell me what your closet looks like.

Do you like to have the closet door opened or closed? Do you ever like to go in there?

Do you have your own bed? Do you sleep in it every night?

Do you stay in it all night?

Is your bed comfortable for you?

What does your bed look like? (Ask about textures, blankets, sheets, and pillows. Be sure to probe if you are given any indication of unusual practices.)

What is it like for you when others go into your room? Do others touch the things in your room? Do they use your things without asking you? Do you get upset when this happens? What do you do when you are upset in this way?

Do you like to spend time alone in your room? Are you in there at a certain time each day or just when you are sleeping? Do you ever go in there just to calm down? Do you ever get sent to your room as a punishment?

Let's talk about the rest of your home . . .

Are there some parts of your home that you like better than others? Certain rooms? Or outside spaces? (Explore the child's preferences inside and outside of the home. Find out if there are or were particular areas of attraction, i.e., hiding in cabinets, playing under stairways or porches, etc. Probe for unusual practices.)

Okay. Now I want to find about the kinds of things you have to do when you are at home. Some of them may be chores like taking out the trash, and some of them may be things you do for yourself like brushing your teeth.

Do you have to help out around the house? I know some children have to sweep the floor or maybe do the dishes. Some others have to make their beds and clean up their own "stuff." How about you?

How about things you do for yourself? Some kids are expected to get up and get dressed at a certain time and be ready for school. They are expected to use the bathroom, get washed up or showered, wash their hair, comb their hair, and brush their teeth each morning. And I know that not all kids like these things. It can be hard for them in the morning. What is it like for you?

III. SOCIAL INFORMATION

Wow! So many questions! I feel like this is really helping me so I can understand what life is like for you. First we talked about your life inside your home, and now I am wondering about what it is like for you outside your home. Can you help me to understand what it is like in your neighborhood?

Do you have a friend who lives near you? Is this a person the same age as you? What kinds of things do you like to do with your friend?

Do you have other friends? Do they live near you? Do you ever visit them in their houses? Do they come to visit you at your home?

Do kids in the neighborhood come to your door and ask you if you want to play/hang out? Do they call you or text you? How often?

Do you have friends who live farther away from you? Do you ever invite them to your house? Do you ever go to your friend's house to visit?

What about birthday parties? Do you invite kids to your birthday party? Do you go to their parties? What is that like for you?

Do you have any pets? Is it your pet or does it belong to your whole family? Is your pet a friend to you? What kinds of things do you and your pet do together? Tell me about your pet.

What kinds of other things do you do outside of your home? Do you like to go to the library? Sometimes there are activities at the library. Do you ever go to things like this?

Do you go to church or any classes at the church? Do you take any lessons like karate, music, or dance lessons?

Do you belong to Girl/Boy Scouts? Do you play any sports? (If yes) Where do you do that? Is that fun for you? Do you like to watch sports? Which ones do you like?

Now let's talk about what school is like for you . . .

IV. SCHOOL INFORMATION

Do you have friends at school? What kinds of things do you do with your school friends? Are you in the same classes? Do you see them at recess? Tell me what happens for you each day at recess.

Let's talk about gym class. Do you like going to gym? Do you have friends in gym class? What games do you play? Do you like them? Do you have a favorite one? What do you do in that game?

Now I will ask you some questions about lunch at school. Who do you sit with at lunch? Are they your friends? Where in the cafeteria do you sit? Do you like to talk during lunch? Who is your favorite person to have lunch with? Why do you like that person?

What is it like for you when other kids are eating? Does the way they eat bother you? Is your cafeteria noisy? Is there a lot of talking and yelling in the cafeteria? Do you eat the school lunch or do you bring your own? What do you usually bring for lunch? Do you usually finish everything?

Do you use the school bathroom? What is that like? Is it loud? Do you or the other kids fool around a lot in the restrooms? Do you go in the bathroom when there are other kids in there?

Is it hard for you to be in school sometimes? Do you ever worry when you are in school? Do you have a "safe person" to talk to when you have a problem? Do you have a "safe place" you can go to when you feel like you need to calm down? If not, what do you do?

Do you get any special help in school? Are some subjects harder than others for you? What is your favorite subject? What subject don't you like? Do you get a chance to do some of your homework at school? Is there someone to help you with that? What kinds of grades do you usually get in school?

Tell me about your school day. Are you in many different rooms during the day? What time do you get there, and leave? Are you early or late most days? Is it noisy in the corridors? Do you ever get in trouble at school? What happens when you are in trouble at school? Is the trouble usually about the same thing?

Do you ever stay after school for extra help? Do you belong to any after-school groups or clubs?

V. CONCLUSION

Thank you for giving me all of this information. You've done very well today. Now let me ask you the last of the questions . . .

Why do you think your parents/guardians brought you here today?

How do you think I can help you and your family?

Do you have any questions?

VI. POST-INTERVIEW IMPRESSIONS

1. When initially meeting with the child and the parents/guardians, who dominated and directed the flow of conversation (parent or child)?

_____

_____

2. Was the child able to transition away from the parents/guardians when they left the office?

_____

_____

3. Did the child bring any unusual items to the interview? If so, how did the child hold them or use them during the interview?

_____

_____

4. Behavioral observations:
   a. attention (focused or not)
   b. motor activity (heightened or not)
   c. mannerisms and/or tics

Describe:_____

_____

   d. voice (loud or soft); (unusual tone or pitch)

Describe:_____

_____

   e. speech (pedantic or conversational)

Describe:_____

_____

f. conversation (on or off topic)

Describe: _____

_____

g. use of conversation (comments on aspects of the environment; the examiner)

Describe: _____

h. conversation control (used to return on high-interest, perspective topic; used to monopolize)

Describe: _____

_____

i. physical presentation (neat or not) (age appropriate or not) (clean or not)

Describe: _____

_____

j. personal space (awareness of personal space)

Describe: _____

_____

k. willingness to be touched

Describe: _____

_____

Appendix E

AUTISM SPECTRUM DESCRIPTIVE PROFILE (ASDP) FORM, PART I BLANK

I. <u>SOCIAL DOMAIN</u>: This section measures your child's current level of social functioning.

A. Social Relationships: This section measures your child's current level of social functioning.

My child **does not have** a same-aged **friend** that he/she has played with regularly over the past year.	**Circle One**	This reflects a problem for my **child** in the following range (circle one):
	agree	mild moderate severe n/a
	somewhat agree	
	neutral/no opinion	This reflects a problem for my **family** in the following range (circle one):
	somewhat disagree	
	disagree	mild moderate severe n/a

My child **does not play/socialize agreeably** with peers.	**Circle One**	This reflects a problem for my **child** in the following range (circle one):
	agree	mild moderate severe n/a
	somewhat agree	
	neutral/no opinion	This reflects a problem for my **family** in the following range (circle one):
	somewhat disagree	
	disagree	mild moderate severe n/a

My child often **prefers** the company of **adults** to the exclusion of engaging with peers.	**Circle One**	This reflects a problem for my **child** in the following range (circle one):
	agree	mild moderate severe n/a
	somewhat agree	
	neutral/no opinion	This reflects a problem for my **family** in the following range (circle one):
	somewhat disagree	
	disagree	mild moderate severe n/a

My child's social limitations lead him/her to **bully _or_ be bullied**.	**Circle One**	This reflects a problem for my **child** in the following range (circle one):
	agree	mild moderate severe n/a
	somewhat agree	
	neutral/no opinion	This reflects a problem for my **family** in the following range (circle one):
	somewhat disagree	
	disagree	mild moderate severe n/a

My child has **difficulty with perspective-taking** (seeing things from another person's point of view).	**Circle One**
	agree
	somewhat agree
	neutral/no opinion
	somewhat disagree
	disagree

*This reflects a problem for my **child** in the following range (circle one):*

mild   moderate   severe   n/a

*This reflects a problem for my **family** in the following range (circle one):*

mild   moderate   severe   n/a

B. Social Language:

My child has great **difficulty with** participating in the give and take of **conversational exchanges**.	**Circle One**
	agree
	somewhat agree
	neutral/no opinion
	somewhat disagree
	disagree

*This reflects a problem for my **child** in the following range (circle one):*

mild   moderate   severe   n/a

*This reflects a problem for my **family** in the following range (circle one):*

mild   moderate   severe   n/a

My child consistently **engages in repetitive speech** (e.g., movie quotes) or repetitive questions (e.g., "Who, what, where, why, when . . . ?")	**Circle One**
	agree
	somewhat agree
	neutral/no opinion
	somewhat disagree
	disagree

*This reflects a problem for my **child** in the following range (circle one):*

mild   moderate   severe   n/a

*This reflects a problem for my **family** in the following range (circle one):*

mild   moderate   severe   n/a

My child "**gets stuck**" **on** a **single** focus of **interest**.	**Circle One**
	agree
	somewhat agree
	neutral/no opinion
	somewhat disagree
	disagree

*This reflects a problem for my **child** in the following range (circle one):*

mild   moderate   severe   n/a

*This reflects a problem for my **family** in the following range (circle one):*

mild   moderate   severe   n/a

My child has great **difficulty interpreting nonverbal** social **cues** (e.g., reading facial signals and body gestures of others).	**Circle One**
	agree
	somewhat agree
	neutral/no opinion
	somewhat disagree
	disagree

*This reflects a problem for my **child** in the following range (circle one):*

mild   moderate   severe   n/a

*This reflects a problem for my **family** in the following range (circle one):*

mild   moderate   severe   n/a

My child **relies on literal interpretations of** social language and misses the point of ambiguous communications (e.g., sarcasm, teasing, joke-telling, vagueness of directions).	**Circle One**
	agree
	somewhat agree
	neutral/no opinion
	somewhat disagree
	disagree

This reflects a problem for my **child** in the following range (circle one):

mild   moderate   severe   n/a

This reflects a problem for my **family** in the following range (circle one):

mild   moderate   severe   n/a

C. Social Behaviors:

My child **does not** fully **relate to** in the **emotional experiences** of others. (May understand the plight of another but not recognize the other's feelings.)	**Circle One**
	agree
	somewhat agree
	neutral/no opinion
	somewhat disagree
	disagree

This reflects a problem for my **child** in the following range (circle one):

mild   moderate   severe   n/a

This reflects a problem for my **family** in the following range (circle one):

mild   moderate   severe   n/a

My child **engages in** episodes of **nonpurposeful behaviors** (e.g., walking in circles, copying numbers from the phonebook, or demonstrating more eccentric rituals).	**Circle One**
	agree
	somewhat agree
	neutral/no opinion
	somewhat disagree
	disagree

This reflects a problem for my **child** in the following range (circle one):

mild   moderate   severe   n/a

This reflects a problem for my **family** in the following range (circle one):

mild   moderate   severe   n/a

My child's **reactions to sensory stimuli** in the environment result in an inability to engage socially, (e.g., light, sound, smells or textures).	**Circle One**
	agree
	somewhat agree
	neutral/no opinion
	somewhat disagree
	disagree

This reflects a problem for my **child** in the following range (circle one):

mild   moderate   severe   n/a

This reflects a problem for my **family** in the following range (circle one):

mild   moderate   severe   n/a

My child **exhibits unexpected behaviors** when feeling anxious in social situations (e.g., explosive, aggressive, or unusual behaviors).	**Circle One**
	agree
	somewhat agree
	neutral/no opinion
	somewhat disagree
	disagree

This reflects a problem for my **child** in the following range (circle one):

mild   moderate   severe   n/a

This reflects a problem for my **family** in the following range (circle one):

mild   moderate   severe   n/a

My child's **unique perceptions of fairness** can lead to difficult behaviors (e.g., work refusal, unkind behaviors in retaliation for a perceived injustice).	Circle One
	agree
	somewhat agree
	neutral/no opinion
	somewhat disagree
	disagree

*This reflects a problem for my **child** in the following range (circle one):*

mild   moderate   severe   n/a

*This reflects a problem for my **family** in the following range (circle one):*

mild   moderate   severe   n/a

II. LEARNING DOMAIN: This section measures your child's current level of functioning with learning.

A. Response to Organizational Demands:

My child's learning is affected by an **excessive reliance on routines**.	Circle One
	agree
	somewhat agree
	neutral/no opinion
	somewhat disagree
	disagree

*This reflects a problem for my **child** in the following range (circle one):*

mild   moderate   severe   n/a

*This reflects a problem for my **family** in the following range (circle one):*

mild   moderate   severe   n/a

My child's **attention can be unpredictably captured** by objects, resulting in a preoccupation that undermines learning-at-hand.	Circle One
	agree
	somewhat agree
	neutral/no opinion
	somewhat disagree
	disagree

*This reflects a problem for my **child** in the following range (circle one):*

mild   moderate   severe   n/a

*This reflects a problem for my **family** in the following range (circle one):*

mild   moderate   severe   n/a

My child has **difficulty with** the give-and-take of **discussion-based learning**.	Circle One
	agree
	somewhat agree
	neutral/no opinion
	somewhat disagree
	disagree

*This reflects a problem for my **child** in the following range (circle one):*

mild   moderate   severe   n/a

*This reflects a problem for my **family** in the following range (circle one):*

mild   moderate   severe   n/a

	Circle One	
My child's **memory** for learning may be **overly focused on details** to the exclusion of the main concept and/or on what he/she <u>perceives</u> to be relevant.	agree	*This reflects a problem for my **child** in the following range (circle one):* **mild moderate severe n/a** *This reflects a problem for my **family** in the following range (circle one):* **mild moderate severe n/a**
	somewhat agree	
	neutral/no opinion	
	somewhat disagree	
	disagree	

	Circle One	
My child's learning is affected by his/her **tendency to compartmentalize and a failure to generalize** across situations (e.g., the English teacher should not teach History, the need to have an agenda book signed by both teacher and parent is not understood).	agree	*This reflects a problem for my **child** in the following range (circle one):* **mild moderate severe n/a** *This reflects a problem for my **family** in the following range (circle one):* **mild moderate severe n/a**
	somewhat agree	
	neutral/no opinion	
	somewhat disagree	
	disagree	

B. Response to Emotional Demands:

	Circle One	
My child's learning is compromised by **inflexible patterns of thought and expectations** resulting in anxiety (e.g., homework vs. schoolwork, fairness in group processes).	agree	*This reflects a problem for my **child** in the following range (circle one):* **mild moderate severe n/a** *This reflects a problem for my **family** in the following range (circle one):* **mild moderate severe n/a**
	somewhat agree	
	neutral/no opinion	
	somewhat disagree	
	disagree	

	Circle One	
My child's **learning** is **impacted by ambiguity** (e.g., maybe vs. yes/no answers, expectations that are not well defined or concrete).	agree	*This reflects a problem for my **child** in the following range (circle one):* **mild moderate severe n/a** *This reflects a problem for my **family** in the following range (circle one):* **mild moderate severe n/a**
	somewhat agree	
	neutral/no opinion	
	somewhat disagree	
	disagree	

	Circle One	
My child **does not work well** in cooperative learning **groups**.	agree	*This reflects a problem for my **child** in the following range (circle one):* **mild moderate severe n/a** *This reflects a problem for my **family** in the following range (circle one):* **mild moderate severe n/a**
	somewhat agree	
	neutral/no opinion	
	somewhat disagree	
	disagree	

My child **focuses on singular interests** with such severity as to negatively impact his/her learning.	Circle One
	agree
	somewhat agree
	neutral/no opinion
	somewhat disagree
	disagree

*This reflects a problem for my **child** in the following range (circle one):*

mild   moderate   severe   n/a

*This reflects a problem for my **family** in the following range (circle one):*

mild   moderate   severe   n/a

My child's **mood can change unexpectedly and rapidly** with heightened emotions followed by periods of calm.	Circle One
	agree
	somewhat agree
	neutral/no opinion
	somewhat disagree
	disagree

*This reflects a problem for my **child** in the following range (circle one):*

mild   moderate   severe   n/a

*This reflects a problem for my **family** in the following range (circle one):*

mild   moderate   severe   n/a

C. Response to Environmental Demands:

My child's learning is impacted by his/her **excessive resistance to changes** in the environment (e.g., change of classroom, seating arrangement, lunch menu, etc).	Circle One
	agree
	somewhat agree
	neutral/no opinion
	somewhat disagree
	disagree

*This reflects a problem for my **child** in the following range (circle one):*

mild   moderate   severe   n/a

*This reflects a problem for my **family** in the following range (circle one):*

mild   moderate   severe   n/a

My child's apparent **absence of interest in others' opinions** creates challenges in the learning environment.	Circle One
	agree
	somewhat agree
	neutral/no opinion
	somewhat disagree
	disagree

*This reflects a problem for my **child** in the following range (circle one):*

mild   moderate   severe   n/a

*This reflects a problem for my **family** in the following range (circle one):*

mild   moderate   severe   n/a

My child's apparent **absence of interest in others' views** creates challenges in the learning environment.	Circle One
	agree
	somewhat agree
	neutral/no opinion
	somewhat disagree
	disagree

*This reflects a problem for my **child** in the following range (circle one):*

mild   moderate   severe   n/a

*This reflects a problem for my **family** in the following range (circle one):*

mild   moderate   severe   n/a

	Circle One	This reflects a problem for my **child** in the following range (circle one):
My child's heightened sensitivity to **sensory stimulation can interfere with learning** (e.g., lighting, temperature, sound and pitch levels, smells, environmental activity, and textures).	agree	mild moderate severe n/a
	somewhat agree	
	neutral/no opinion	This reflects a problem for my **family** in the following range (circle one):
	somewhat disagree	
	disagree	mild moderate severe n/a

	Circle One	This reflects a problem for my **child** in the following range (circle one):
My child's learning potential is affected by a **need for sensory input**, (i.e., weighted vest) **or sensory breaks** (i.e., walking, jumping).	agree	mild moderate severe n/a
	somewhat agree	
	neutral/no opinion	This reflects a problem for my **family** in the following range (circle one):
	somewhat disagree	
	disagree	mild moderate severe n/a

III. INDEPENDENT FUNCTIONING DOMAIN: This section measures your child's current level of functioning with daily living practices.

A. Self-Care Practices:

	Circle One	This reflects a problem for my **child** in the following range (circle one):
My child **does not demonstrate basic hygiene practices** expected for his/her age (i.e., wash hands, brush teeth, comb hair, wipe nose).	agree	mild moderate severe n/a
	somewhat agree	
	neutral/no opinion	This reflects a problem for my **family** in the following range (circle one):
	somewhat disagree	
	disagree	mild moderate severe n/a

	Circle One	This reflects a problem for my **child** in the following range (circle one):
My child **does not demonstrate complex hygiene practices** expected for his/her age (i.e., bathing/showering, hair washing, toileting).	agree	mild moderate severe n/a
	somewhat agree	
	neutral/no opinion	This reflects a problem for my **family** in the following range (circle one):
	somewhat disagree	
	disagree	mild moderate severe n/a

My child's **dressing preferences** are **not similar** to those of his/her **peers** (i.e., wears clothes that are appropriate to season and style, demonstrates awareness of fit and cleanliness of clothing).	**Circle One**
	agree
	somewhat agree
	neutral/no opinion
	somewhat disagree
	disagree

This reflects a problem for my **child** in the following range (circle one):

mild   moderate   severe   n/a

This reflects a problem for my **family** in the following range (circle one):

mild   moderate   severe   n/a

My child's **eating and drinking habits** are **not similar** to those of his/her peers (e.g., he/she varies food/drink choices, consumes normal amount of food, uses utensils efficiently, exhibits age-appropriate table manners).	**Circle One**
	agree
	somewhat agree
	neutral/no opinion
	somewhat disagree
	disagree

This reflects a problem for my **child** in the following range (circle one):

mild   moderate   severe   n/a

This reflects a problem for my **family** in the following range (circle one):

mild   moderate   severe   n/a

My child's **food expectations** are **not typical of** his/her **age** (i.e., shows a tolerance for differences in meal preparation and presentation).	**Circle One**
	agree
	somewhat agree
	neutral/no opinion
	somewhat disagree
	disagree

This reflects a problem for my **child** in the following range (circle one):

mild   moderate   severe   n/a

This reflects a problem for my **family** in the following range (circle one):

mild   moderate   severe   n/a

B. Safety Practices:

My child **does not exhibit** age-appropriate **safe behaviors inside of** the home (e.g., can be trusted around hot surfaces, near open windows, with sharp objects, to answer the door or phone).	**Circle One**
	agree
	somewhat agree
	neutral/no opinion
	somewhat disagree
	disagree

This reflects a problem for my **child** in the following range (circle one):

mild   moderate   severe   n/a

This reflects a problem for my **family** in the following range (circle one):

mild   moderate   severe   n/a

My child **does not exhibit** age-appropriate **safe behaviors outside of** the home (e.g., can be trusted to stay within agreed-upon areas, to exercise care in navigating the environment, to demonstrate good judgment regarding strangers).	**Circle One**
	agree
	somewhat agree
	neutral/no opinion
	somewhat disagree
	disagree

*This reflects a problem for my **child** in the following range (circle one):*

mild   moderate   severe   n/a

*This reflects a problem for my **family** in the following range (circle one):*

mild   moderate   severe   n/a

My child **does not exhibit** age-appropriate **safe behaviors in school** (e.g., can navigate the school environment, can adhere to a schedule, resists risk-taking behaviors).	**Circle One**
	agree
	somewhat agree
	neutral/no opinion
	somewhat disagree
	disagree

*This reflects a problem for my **child** in the following range (circle one):*

mild   moderate   severe   n/a

*This reflects a problem for my **family** in the following range (circle one):*

mild   moderate   severe   n/a

My child **does not exhibit** age-appropriate **safe behaviors** when engaging **in cyberspace** activities, (ie., texting, Web surfing, game playing, social networking, e-mailing).	**Circle One**
	agree
	somewhat agree
	neutral/no opinion
	somewhat disagree
	disagree

*This reflects a problem for my **child** in the following range (circle one):*

mild   moderate   severe   n/a

*This reflects a problem for my **family** in the following range (circle one):*

mild   moderate   severe   n/a

My child **does not exhibit** age-appropriate **safe behaviors in advocating for him/herself** (e.g., understands when to ask for help, identifies safe/helpful people, communicates his/her own needs effectively).	**Circle One**
	agree
	somewhat agree
	neutral/no opinion
	somewhat disagree
	disagree

*This reflects a problem for my **child** in the following range (circle one):*

mild   moderate   severe   n/a

*This reflects a problem for my **family** in the following range (circle one):*

mild   moderate   severe   n/a

C. <u>Life Skills Practices:</u>

My child **has not acquired** age-appropriate **money management skills** (i.e., understands the purpose of money, the value of coins and bills, the monetary value of material goods).	Circle One
	agree
	somewhat agree
	neutral/no opinion
	somewhat disagree
	disagree

*This reflects a problem for my **<u>child</u>** in the following range (circle one):*

mild   moderate   severe   n/a

*This reflects a problem for my **<u>family</u>** in the following range (circle one):*

mild   moderate   severe   n/a

My child **has not acquired** age-appropriate **time management skills** (i.e., allocates time efficiently, meets timelines, and transitions in a timely way from one environment to another).	Circle One
	agree
	somewhat agree
	neutral/no opinion
	somewhat disagree
	disagree

*This reflects a problem for my **<u>child</u>** in the following range (circle one):*

mild   moderate   severe   n/a

*This reflects a problem for my **<u>family</u>** in the following range (circle one):*

mild   moderate   severe   n/a

My child **does not participate** as expected in age-appropriate **school/ community activities** (i.e., Boy/Girl Scouts, sports teams, afterschool clubs or other programs).	Circle One
	agree
	somewhat agree
	neutral/no opinion
	somewhat disagree
	disagree

*This reflects a problem for my **<u>child</u>** in the following range (circle one):*

mild   moderate   severe   n/a

*This reflects a problem for my **<u>family</u>** in the following range (circle one):*

mild   moderate   severe   n/a

My child **does not complete** age-appropriate **chores/ responsibilities at home** (i.e., household tasks, care of possessions or pets, spontaneously recognizes needs in the home and initiates appropriate actions).	Circle One
	agree
	somewhat agree
	neutral/no opinion
	somewhat disagree
	disagree

*This reflects a problem for my **<u>child</u>** in the following range (circle one):*

mild   moderate   severe   n/a

*This reflects a problem for my **<u>family</u>** in the following range (circle one):*

mild   moderate   severe   n/a

My child **does not complete** age-appropriate **chores/ responsibilities at school** (i.e., classroom tasks, care of school-related possessions, spontaneously recognizes needs in the school and initiates appropriate actions).	Circle One
	agree
	somewhat agree
	neutral/no opinion
	somewhat disagree
	disagree

*This reflects a problem for my **<u>child</u>** in the following range (circle one):*

mild   moderate   severe   n/a

*This reflects a problem for my **<u>family</u>** in the following range (circle one):*

mild   moderate   severe   n/a

IV. POSITIVE ATTRIBUTES DOMAIN: This section is designed to assist you in generating a list of positive characteristics that most often describe your child at this point in time.

Circle all that apply:

Positive Attributes Domain

Honest	Kind	Helpful	Reliable
Knowledgeable	Precise	Good memory	Humorous
Liked by adults	Observant	Persistent	Generous
Nonjudgmental	Confident in areas of expertise		Rule-follower

Other attributes:_____

_____

_____

Appendix F

AUTISM SPECTRUM DESCRIPTIVE PROFILE (ASDP) FORM, PART II   BLANK

STEP 1: Using the completed ASDP, Part I, list the bolded descriptors rated as "agree" for the domains below.

I. Social Domain

Relationships	Language	Behaviors
_____	_____	_____
_____	_____	_____
_____	_____	_____
_____	_____	_____

II. Learning Domain

Organizational	Emotional	Environmental
_____	_____	_____
_____	_____	_____
_____	_____	_____
_____	_____	_____

II. Independent Functioning Domain

Self-Care	Safety	Life Skills
_____	_____	_____
_____	_____	_____
_____	_____	_____
_____	_____	_____

STEP 2: Using the completed ASDP, Part I, list the entries in the Positive Attributes domain below.

IV. <u>Positive Attributes Domain</u>

_____   _____   _____

_____   _____   _____

_____   _____   _____

_____   _____   _____

STEP 3: Create your Autism Spectrum Descriptive Profile. Combine the information obtained in Steps 1 and 2.

STEP 4: Using the completed ASDP, Part I, list the areas in each domain that are rated as "severe" concerns for the child or family. Note the differences in the ratings of severity in child/family concerns.

	Family concerns	Child concerns
I. <u>Social Domain</u>	_____	_____
II. <u>Learning Domain</u>	_____	_____

III. <u>Independent Functioning Domain</u>

_____   _____

_____   _____

_____   _____

_____   _____

STEP 5: Create your Treatment Goals, in part, by reviewing the information obtained in Steps 3 and 4.

1. _____

_____

_____

2. _____

_____

_____

3. _____

_____

_____

Appendix G

AUTISM SPECTRUM DESCRIPTIVE PROFILE (ASDP) FORM, PART I   SAMPLE FORM

I. <u>SOCIAL DOMAIN</u>: This section measures your child's current level of social functioning.

A. Social Relationships: This section measures your child's current level of social functioning.

My child **does not** have a same-aged **friend** that he/she has played with regularly over the past year.	Circle One
	agree
	(somewhat agree)
	neutral/no opinion
	somewhat disagree
	disagree

This reflects a problem for my **_child_** in the following range (circle one):

mild   moderate   severe   (n/a)

This reflects a problem for my **_family_** in the following range (circle one):

(mild)   moderate   severe   n/a

My child **does not** play/**socialize agreeably** with peers.	Circle One
	agree
	(somewhat agree)
	neutral/no opinion
	somewhat disagree
	disagree

This reflects a problem for my **_child_** in the following range (circle one):

mild   moderate   severe   (n/a)

This reflects a problem for my **_family_** in the following range (circle one):

(mild)   moderate   severe   n/a

My child often **prefers** the company of **adults** to the exclusion of engaging with peers.	Circle One
	(agree)
	somewhat agree
	neutral/no opinion
	somewhat disagree
	disagree

This reflects a problem for my **_child_** in the following range (circle one):

mild   moderate   severe   (n/a)

This reflects a problem for my **_family_** in the following range (circle one):

mild   (moderate)   severe   n/a

My child's social limitations lead him/her to **bully *or* be bullied**.	**Circle One**
	(agree)
	somewhat agree
	neutral/no opinion
	somewhat disagree
	disagree

*This reflects a problem for my **child** in the following range (circle one):*

mild   moderate   severe   (n/a)

*This reflects a problem for my **family** in the following range (circle one):*

mild   moderate   (severe)   n/a

My child has **difficulty with perspective-taking** (seeing things from another person's point of view).	**Circle One**
	(agree)
	somewhat agree
	neutral/no opinion
	somewhat disagree
	disagree

*This reflects a problem for my **child** in the following range (circle one):*

mild   moderate   severe   (n/a)

*This reflects a problem for my **family** in the following range (circle one):*

mild   moderate   (severe)   n/a

B. Social Language:

My child has great **difficulty with** participating in the give and take of **conversational exchanges**.	**Circle One**
	(agree)
	somewhat agree
	neutral/no opinion
	somewhat disagree
	disagree

*This reflects a problem for my **child** in the following range (circle one):*

mild   moderate   severe   (n/a)

*This reflects a problem for my **family** in the following range (circle one):*

mild   moderate   (severe)   n/a

My child consistently **engages in repetitive speech** (e.g., movie quotes) or repetitive questions (e.g., "Who, what, where, why, when . . . ?")	**Circle One**
	agree
	somewhat agree
	neutral/no opinion
	(somewhat disagree)
	disagree

*This reflects a problem for my **child** in the following range (circle one):*

mild   moderate   severe   (n/a)

*This reflects a problem for my **family** in the following range (circle one):*

mild   moderate   severe   (n/a)

My child "**gets stuck**" on a **single** focus of **interest**.	**Circle One**
	(agree)
	somewhat agree
	neutral/no opinion
	somewhat disagree
	disagree

*This reflects a problem for my **child** in the following range (circle one):*

mild   (moderate)   severe   n/a

*This reflects a problem for my **family** in the following range (circle one):*

mild   moderate   (severe)   n/a

My child has great **difficulty interpreting nonverbal** social **cues** (e.g., reading facial signals and body gestures of others.)	**Circle One**
	agree
	somewhat agree
	(neutral/no opinion)
	somewhat disagree
	disagree

*This reflects a problem for my **child** in the following range (circle one):*

mild   moderate   severe   (n/a)

*This reflects a problem for my **family** in the following range (circle one):*

mild   moderate   severe   (n/a)

My child **relies on literal interpretations of** social **language** and misses the point of ambiguous communications (e.g., sarcasm, teasing, joke-telling, vagueness of directions).	**Circle One**
	agree
	somewhat agree
	(neutral/no opinion)
	somewhat disagree
	disagree

*This reflects a problem for my **child** in the following range (circle one):*

mild   moderate   severe   (n/a)

*This reflects a problem for my **family** in the following range (circle one):*

mild   moderate   severe   (n/a)

C. Social Behaviors:

My child **does not** fully **relate to** the **emotional experiences** of others. (May understand the plight of another but not recognize the other's feelings.)	**Circle One**
	(agree)
	somewhat agree
	neutral/no opinion
	somewhat disagree
	disagree

*This reflects a problem for my **child** in the following range (circle one):*

mild   moderate   severe   (n/a)

*This reflects a problem for my **family** in the following range (circle one):*

mild   (moderate)   severe   n/a

My child **engages in** episodes of **nonpurposeful behaviors** (e.g., walking in circles, copying numbers from the phonebook, or demonstrating more eccentric rituals).	**Circle One**
	agree
	(somewhat agree)
	neutral/no opinion
	somewhat disagree
	disagree

*This reflects a problem for my **child** in the following range (circle one):*

mild   moderate   severe   (n/a)

*This reflects a problem for my **family** in the following range (circle one):*

mild   moderate   severe   (n/a)

My child's **reactions to sensory stimuli** in the environment result in an inability to engage socially, (e.g., light, sound, smells or textures).	**Circle One**
	agree
	(somewhat agree)
	neutral/no opinion
	somewhat disagree
	disagree

*This reflects a problem for my **child** in the following range (circle one):*

(mild)   moderate   severe   n/a

*This reflects a problem for my **family** in the following range (circle one):*

(mild)   moderate   severe   n/a

My child **exhibits unexpected behaviors** when feeling anxious in social situations (e.g., explosive, aggressive, or unusual behaviors).	**Circle One**
	(agree)
	somewhat agree
	neutral/no opinion
	somewhat disagree
	disagree

*This reflects a problem for my **child** in the following range (circle one):*

mild   moderate   severe   (n/a)

*This reflects a problem for my **family** in the following range (circle one):*

mild   moderate   (severe)   n/a

My child's **unique perceptions of fairness** can lead to difficult behaviors (e.g., work refusal, unkind behaviors in retaliation for a perceived injustice).	**Circle One**
	(agree)
	somewhat agree
	neutral/no opinion
	somewhat disagree
	disagree

*This reflects a problem for my **child** in the following range (circle one):*

mild   moderate   severe   (n/a)

*This reflects a problem for my **family** in the following range (circle one):*

mild   moderate   (severe)   n/a

II. LEARNING DOMAIN: This section measures your child's current level of functioning with learning.

A. Response to Organizational Demands:

My child's learning is affected by an **excessive reliance on routines**.	**Circle One**
	agree
	(somewhat agree)
	neutral/no opinion
	somewhat disagree
	disagree

*This reflects a problem for my **child** in the following range (circle one):*

(mild)   moderate   severe   n/a

*This reflects a problem for my **family** in the following range (circle one):*

mild   (moderate)   severe   n/a

My child's **attention can be unpredictably captured** by objects, resulting in a preoccupation that undermines learning-at-hand.	**Circle One**
	(agree)
	somewhat agree
	neutral/no opinion
	somewhat disagree
	disagree

*This reflects a problem for my **child** in the following range (circle one):*

mild   (moderate)   severe   n/a

*This reflects a problem for my **family** in the following range (circle one):*

mild   (moderate)   severe   n/a

My child has **difficulty with** the give-and-take of **discussion-based learning**.	**Circle One**
	(agree)
	somewhat agree
	neutral/no opinion
	somewhat disagree
	disagree

*This reflects a problem for my **child** in the following range (circle one):*

mild   (moderate)   severe   n/a

*This reflects a problem for my **family** in the following range (circle one):*

mild   moderate   (severe)   n/a

My child's **memory** for learning may be **overly focused on details** to the exclusion of the main concept and/or on what he/she <u>perceives</u> to be relevant.	**Circle One**
	(agree)
	somewhat agree
	neutral/no opinion
	somewhat disagree
	disagree

*This reflects a problem for my **child** in the following range (circle one):*

mild   moderate   (severe)   n/a

*This reflects a problem for my **family** in the following range (circle one):*

mild   moderate   (severe)   n/a

My child's learning is affected by his/her **tendency to compartmentalize and a failure to generalize** across situations (e.g., the English teacher should not teach History, the need to have an agenda book signed by both teacher and parent is not understood).	**Circle One**
	(agree)
	somewhat agree
	neutral/no opinion
	somewhat disagree
	disagree

*This reflects a problem for my **child** in the following range (circle one):*

mild   moderate   (severe)   n/a

*This reflects a problem for my **family** in the following range (circle one):*

mild   moderate   (severe)   n/a

B. Response to Emotional Demands:

My child's learning is compromised by **inflexible patterns of thought and expectations** resulting in anxiety (e.g., homework vs. schoolwork, fairness in group processes).	**Circle One**
	(agree)
	somewhat agree
	neutral/no opinion
	somewhat disagree
	disagree

*This reflects a problem for my **child** in the following range (circle one):*

mild   (moderate)   severe   n/a

*This reflects a problem for my **family** in the following range (circle one):*

mild   moderate   (severe)   n/a

My child's **learning** is **impacted by ambiguity** (e.g., maybe vs. yes/no answers, expectations that are not well defined or concrete).	**Circle One**
	agree
	(somewhat agree)
	neutral/no opinion
	somewhat disagree
	disagree

*This reflects a problem for my **child** in the following range (circle one):*

(mild)   moderate   severe   n/a

*This reflects a problem for my **family** in the following range (circle one):*

mild   (moderate)   severe   n/a

My child **does not work well** in cooperative learning **groups**.	**Circle One**
	(agree)
	somewhat agree
	neutral/no opinion
	somewhat disagree
	disagree

*This reflects a problem for my **child** in the following range (circle one):*

mild   (moderate)   severe   n/a

*This reflects a problem for my **family** in the following range (circle one):*

mild   (moderate)   severe   n/a

My child **focuses on singular interests** with such intensity as to negatively impacts his/her learning.	**Circle One**
	(agree)
	somewhat agree
	neutral/no opinion
	somewhat disagree
	disagree

*This reflects a problem for my **child** in the following range (circle one):*

mild   moderate   severe   (n/a)

*This reflects a problem for my **family** in the following range (circle one):*

mild   moderate   (severe)   n/a

My child's **mood can change unexpectedly and rapidly** with heightened emotions followed by periods of calm.	**Circle One**
	(agree)
	somewhat agree
	neutral/no opinion
	somewhat disagree
	disagree

*This reflects a problem for my **child** in the following range (circle one):*

mild   moderate   severe   (n/a)

*This reflects a problem for my **family** in the following range (circle one):*

mild   moderate   (severe)   n/a

C. Response to Environmental Demands:

My child's learning is impacted by his/her **excessive resistance to changes** in the environment (e.g., change of bus route, classroom, seating arrangement, lunch menu, etc).	**Circle One**
	(agree)
	somewhat agree
	neutral/no opinion
	somewhat disagree
	disagree

*This reflects a problem for my **child** in the following range (circle one):*

(mild)   moderate   severe   n/a

*This reflects a problem for my **family** in the following range (circle one):*

mild   moderate   (severe)   n/a

My child's **inability to inhibit behaviors** in certain circumstances can lead to **concerns for his/her safety**, (e.g., wandering away, hiding, bolting, curiosity-seeking behaviors).	**Circle One**
	agree
	(somewhat agree)
	neutral/no opinion
	somewhat disagree
	disagree

*This reflects a problem for my **child** in the following range (circle one):*

mild   moderate   severe   (n/a)

*This reflects a problem for my **family** in the following range (circle one):*

mild   moderate   (severe)   n/a

My child's apparent **absence of interest in others'** opinions creates challenges in the learning environment.	**Circle One**
	(agree)
	somewhat agree
	neutral/no opinion
	somewhat disagree
	disagree

*This reflects a problem for my **child** in the following range (circle one):*

mild   moderate   severe   (n/a)

*This reflects a problem for my **family** in the following range (circle one):*

mild   (moderate)   severe   n/a

My child's heightened sensitivity to **sensory stimulation can interfere with learning** (e.g., lighting, temperature, sound and pitch levels, smells, environmental activity, and textures).	**Circle One**
	agree
	(somewhat agree)
	neutral/no opinion
	somewhat disagree
	disagree

This reflects a problem for my **child** in the following range (circle one):

mild (moderate) severe n/a

This reflects a problem for my **family** in the following range (circle one):

mild (moderate) severe n/a

My child's learning potential is affected by a **need for sensory input** (i.e., weighted vest) **or sensory breaks** (i.e., walking, jumping).	**Circle One**
	agree
	(somewhat agree)
	neutral/no opinion
	somewhat disagree
	disagree

This reflects a problem for my **child** in the following range (circle one):

(mild) moderate severe n/a

This reflects a problem for my **family** in the following range (circle one):

(mild) moderate severe n/a

III. INDEPENDENT FUNCTIONING DOMAIN: This section measures your child's current level of functioning with daily living practices.

A. Self-Care Practices:

My child **does not demonstrate basic hygiene practices** expected for his/her age (i.e., wash hands, brush teeth, comb hair, wipe nose).	**Circle One**
	agree
	somewhat agree
	neutral/no opinion
	somewhat disagree
	(disagree)

This reflects a problem for my **child** in the following range (circle one):

mild moderate severe (n/a)

This reflects a problem for my **family** in the following range (circle one):

mild moderate severe (n/a)

My child **does not demonstrate complex hygiene practices** expected for his/her age (i.e., bathing/showering, hair washing, toileting).	**Circle One**
	agree
	(somewhat agree)
	neutral/no opinion
	somewhat disagree
	disagree

This reflects a problem for my **child** in the following range (circle one):

mild moderate severe (n/a)

This reflects a problem for my **family** in the following range (circle one):

mild (moderate) severe (n/a)

My child's **dressing preferences** are **not similar** to those of his/her **peers** (i.e., wears clothes that are appropriate to season and style, demonstrates awareness of fit and cleanliness of clothing).	**Circle One**
	agree
	somewhat agree
	neutral/no opinion
	somewhat disagree
	(disagree)

This reflects a problem for my **_child_** in the following range (circle one):

mild   moderate   severe   (n/a)

This reflects a problem for my **_family_** in the following range (circle one):

mild   moderate   severe   (n/a)

My child's **eating and drinking habits** are **not similar** to those of his/her peers (e.g., he/she varies food/drink choices, consumes normal amount of food, uses utensils efficiently, exhibits age-appropriate table manners).	**Circle One**
	agree
	somewhat agree
	neutral/no opinion
	somewhat disagree
	(disagree)

This reflects a problem for my **_child_** in the following range (circle one):

mild   moderate   severe   (n/a)

This reflects a problem for my **_family_** in the following range (circle one):

mild   moderate   severe   (n/a)

My child's **food expectations** are **not typical of** his/her **age** (i.e., shows a tolerance for differences in meal preparation and presentation).	**Circle One**
	agree
	somewhat agree
	neutral/no opinion
	somewhat disagree
	(disagree)

This reflects a problem for my **_child_** in the following range (circle one):

mild   moderate   severe   (n/a)

This reflects a problem for my **_family_** in the following range (circle one):

mild   moderate   severe   (n/a)

B. Safety Practices:

My child **does not exhibit** age-appropriate **safe behaviors inside of** the home (e.g., can be trusted around hot surfaces, near open windows, with sharp objects, to answer the door or phone).	**Circle One**
	agree
	somewhat agree
	neutral/no opinion
	(somewhat disagree)
	disagree

This reflects a problem for my **_child_** in the following range (circle one):

mild   moderate   severe   (n/a)

This reflects a problem for my **_family_** in the following range (circle one):

(mild)   moderate   severe   n/a

My child **does not exhibit** age-appropriate **safe behaviors outside of** the home (e.g., can be trusted to stay within agreed-upon areas, to exercise care in navigating the environment, to demonstrate good judgment regarding strangers).	**Circle One**
	agree
	somewhat agree
	neutral/no opinion
	somewhat disagree
	(disagree)

This reflects a problem for my **_child_** in the following range (circle one):

mild   moderate   severe   (n/a)

This reflects a problem for my **_family_** in the following range (circle one):

mild   moderate   severe   (n/a)

My child **does not exhibit** age-appropriate **safe behaviors in school** (e.g., can navigate the school environment, can adhere to a schedule, resists risk-taking behaviors).	**Circle One**
	agree
	somewhat agree
	neutral/no opinion
	(somewhat disagree)
	disagree

This reflects a problem for my **_child_** in the following range (circle one):

mild   moderate   severe   (n/a)

This reflects a problem for my **_family_** in the following range (circle one):

(mild)   moderate   severe   n/a

My child **does not exhibit** age-appropriate **safe behaviors** when engaging **in cyberspace** activities, (ie., texting, Web surfing, game playing, social networking, e-mailing).	**Circle One**
	(agree)
	somewhat agree
	neutral/no opinion
	somewhat disagree
	disagree

This reflects a problem for my **_child_** in the following range (circle one):

mild   moderate   severe   (n/a)

This reflects a problem for my **_family_** in the following range (circle one):

mild   moderate   (severe)   n/a

My child **does not exhibit** age-appropriate **safe behaviors in advocating for him/herself** (e.g., understands when to ask for help, identifies safe/helpful people, communicates his/her own needs effectively).	**Circle One**
	agree
	somewhat agree
	neutral/no opinion
	somewhat disagree
	(disagree)

This reflects a problem for my **_child_** in the following range (circle one):

mild   moderate   severe   (n/a)

This reflects a problem for my **_family_** in the following range (circle one):

mild   moderate   severe   (n/a)

C. <u>Life Skills Practices</u>:

My child **has not acquired** age-appropriate **money management skills** (i.e., understands the purpose of money, the value of coins and bills, the monetary value of material goods).	**Circle One**
	(agree)
	somewhat agree
	neutral/no opinion
	somewhat disagree
	disagree

This reflects a problem for my **_child_** in the following range (circle one):

mild   moderate   (severe)   n/a

This reflects a problem for my **_family_** in the following range (circle one):

mild   moderate   (severe)   n/a

My child **has not acquired** age-appropriate **time management skills** (i.e., allocates time efficiently, meets timelines, and transitions in a timely way from one environment to another).	**Circle One**
	(agree)
	somewhat agree
	neutral/no opinion
	somewhat disagree
	disagree

This reflects a problem for my **_child_** in the following range (circle one):

(mild)   moderate   severe   n/a

This reflects a problem for my **_family_** in the following range (circle one):

mild   moderate   (severe)   n/a

My child **does not participate** as expected in age-appropriate **school/ community activities** (i.e., Boy/Girl Scouts, sports teams, afterschool clubs or other programs).	**Circle One**
	agree
	(somewhat agree)
	neutral/no opinion
	somewhat disagree
	disagree

*This reflects a problem for my **child** in the following range (circle one):*

mild   moderate   severe   (n/a)

*This reflects a problem for my **family** in the following range (circle one):*

mild   (moderate)   severe   n/a

My child **does not complete** age-appropriate **chores/ responsibilities at home** (i.e., household tasks, care of possessions or pets, spontaneously recognizes needs in the home and initiates appropriate actions).	**Circle One**
	(agree)
	somewhat agree
	neutral/no opinion
	somewhat disagree
	disagree

*This reflects a problem for my **child** in the following range (circle one):*

mild   moderate   severe   (n/a)

*This reflects a problem for my **family** in the following range (circle one):*

mild   (moderate)   severe   n/a

My child **does not complete** age-appropriate **chores/ responsibilities at school** (i.e., classroom tasks, care of school-related possessions, spontaneously recognizes needs in the school and initiates appropriate actions.	**Circle One**
	agree
	somewhat agree
	neutral/no opinion
	(somewhat disagree)
	disagree

*This reflects a problem for my **child** in the following range (circle one):*

(mild)   moderate   severe   n/a

*This reflects a problem for my **family** in the following range (circle one):*

mild   (moderate)   severe   n/a

IV. POSITIVE ATTRIBUTES DOMAIN: This section is designed to assist you in generating a list of positive characteristics that most often describe your child at this point in time.

Circle all that apply:

Positive Attributes Domain

Honest	Kind	(Helpful)	Reliable
(Knowledgeable)	(Precise)	(Good memory)	Humorous
(Liked by adults)	(Observant)	(Persistent)	Generous
Nonjudgmental	(Confident in areas of expertise)		(Rule-follower)

Other attributes: —works well alone

—polite to others

—enjoys being helpful in areas of interest

—takes pride in his work

—works well with adults

Appendix H

AUTISM SPECTRUM DESCRIPTIVE PROFILE (ASDP) FORM: PART II

SAMPLE FORM

STEP 1: Using the completed ASDP, Part I, list the bolded descriptors rated as "agree" for the domains below.

I. Social Domain

Relationships	Language	Behaviors
Prefers adults	*Difficulty with conversational exchanges*	*Doesn't relate to emotional experiences*
Bully or be bullied	*Gets stuck on a single interest*	*Exhibits unexpected behaviors*
Difficulty with perspective taking		*Unique perception of fairness*

II. Learning Domain

Organizational	Emotional	Environmental
Attention unpredictably captured	*Inflexible patterns of thoughts and expectations*	*Excessive resistance to change*
Difficulty with discussion-based learning	*Does not work well in groups*	*Absence of interest in others' opinions*

Memory overly focused on details	Focuses on singular interests	
Tendency to compartmentalize	Mood can change unexpectedly/rapidly	
Failure to generalize		

III. Independent Functioning Domain

Self-Care	Safety	Life Skills
	Does not exhibit safe cyberspace behaviors	Hasn't acquired money management skills
		Hasn't acquired time management skills
		Doesn't complete home chores/responsibilities

STEP 2: Using the completed ASDP: Part I, list the entries in the Positive Attributes domain below.

IV. Positive Attributes Domain

knowledgeable	precise	
good memory	observant	persistent
liked by adults	confident in areas of expertise	polite to strangers
enjoys being helpful in areas of interest	takes pride in his work	works well one-on-one with adults
works well independently in areas of high interest		

STEP 3: Create your Autism Spectrum Descriptive Profile. Combine the information obtained in Steps 1 and 2.

John Jones is a 14-year-old, ninth-grade male who lives with his parents and younger sisters. He is diagnosed with Asperger syndrome, a social-communicative disorder. This uniquely affects his emotional and behavioral regulation across social, learning, and independent functioning areas of life.

*Socially, John is the type of child who **prefers the company of adults**. He is often ill at ease with peers because he has **difficulty understanding the perspective of others** and **participating in the give-and-take of conversational exchanges**. It is likely that John will **"get stuck" on a single topic of interest** without awareness of the listener's level of interest in that topic. Additionally, he will have **trouble relating to the emotional experiences of others**, and he may fail to understand their feelings. Because of John's sometimes unusual and **unexpected behaviors** (e.g., hand-flapping when he gets excited), his social presentation makes him a **target for bullying**. As part of his diagnosis, John may have a **unique perception of fairness** which can lead him to retaliate and exhibit **bullying-type behaviors**.*

*In terms of John's learning style, his **attention can be unpredictably captured** by something in the environment not normally of interest to others. He may also be distracted by **his focus on a singular interest or in a particular topic**. John will not easily transition from one task to the next and is **resistant to changes** he does not expect. Because his **memory is overly focused on details**, he can miss the main point of instruction. He learns best when essential facts are emphasized for him and tied to the larger picture. This method of instruction will compensate for his **tendency to compartmentalize and failure to generalize** across learning situations.*

*John has **difficulty with discussion-based learning**. He can become confused and anxious when presented with multiple opinions. Because he has a **inflexible patterns of thought and expectations**, group work can be overwhelming for him and he can **appear to be uninterested in others' opinions**. In order to avoid the kind of frustration that can lead to **rapidly and unexpectedly changing moods**, John requires prior preparation and monitoring for any participation in group processes.*

*Functioning independently can be troublesome for individuals with this profile. Issues of safety commonly arise and more supervision is required. In John's case, he **does not engage in cyberspace activities safely**. Other areas of concern include his **lack of money management skills** which has been exploited by others. His **lack of time management** is also potentially unsafe and can lead to anxiety around issues of punctuality and the ability to meet deadlines. For John, a lack of maturity in social development and a rigid thought process also result in **difficulty with completing chores/ responsibilities at home**. John does not see the communal need for participating in family-shared responsibilities.*

*It is important for the adults in John's life to be aware of his many strengths so that they can promote them to support his success. In fact, John is a young man who is **liked by adults. He is knowledgeable and enjoys helping others in his area of expertise.** He tends to be **observant, persistent, and precise** in executing tasks of high interest. He is **confident in what he can do**. John has a good memory and will **follow the rules** as he understands them. **He is generally polite** when out in the public. John does his **best work alone** or in a one-on-one situation **with an adult**.*

STEP 4: Using the completed ASDP, Part I, list the areas of "severe" concern and the corresponding measure of Family and Child concern for the domains below.

	Family concerns	Child concerns
I. Social Domain	Bully or be bullied	n/a
	Difficulty with Perspective taking	n/a
	Difficulty with conversational exchanges	n/a
	Gets stuck on a single interest	moderate

	Exhibits unexpected behaviors	n/a
	Unique perception of fairness	n/a
II. Learning Domain	Difficulty with discussion-based learning	moderate
	Memory overly focused on details	severe
	Tendency to compartmentalize	severe
	Tendency to generalize	severe
	Inflexible patterns of thought and expectations	moderate
	Focuses on a singular interest	n/a
	Mood can change unexpectedly/rapidly	n/a
	Excessive resistance to change	mild
	Inability to inhibit behaviors and concerns for safety	n/a
III. Independent Functioning Domain	Does not exhibit safe behaviors engaging in cyberspace	n/a
	Not acquired money management skills	severe
	Not acquired time management skills	mild

STEP 5: Create your Treatment Goals, in part, by reviewing the information obtained in Steps 3 and 4.

1. *John is exhibiting bully behaviors. This happens when he perceives that he has been unfairly treated by another child. The goal will be to work on developing skills in communicating his need for fairness. This work will involve training with the parents/guardians so that they can advocate for appropriate school supports.*

2. *John has a fixated interest in animé. This is disrupting his social and learning environments. The goal will be to create a plan with the client and his family to identify appropriate times for engaging in this pastime. Again, this work will involve parent training and the recommendation that they coordinate efforts with the school to create a related plan.*

3. *John does not exhibit safe behaviors when engaging in cyberspace. The goal will be to work with him to understand the dangers and to assist his family to set limits around computer use. The parents/guardians will need help with determining feasible parameters and training in how to coordinate a related plan with the school.*

Appendix I

COLLABORATIVE AGREEMENT BETWEEN THERAPIST AND PARENTS/GUARDIANS

STATEMENT OF PURPOSE: The course of treatment is not always predictable and clear. That is why it is best to begin this process with a written and signed statement of collaboration that can be referred to as the course of therapy unfolds. Defining mutual expectations from the outset is important. This will help to provide a level of comfort for the therapeutic process to flow more efficiently, effectively, and amicably.

I. SESSIONS:

A.	Frequency of sessions:	
B.	Length of sessions:	
C.	Consistent day & time:	

II. TYPICAL STRUCTURE OF SESSIONS:

A. Review of week with parent alone (10 minutes)
B. Review of week and discussion of current issues with child alone (30 minutes)
C. Summary work with child and parents/guardians (10 minutes)

III. POLICIES:

A. *Parent-therapist sessions* will occur on a regular basis, taking the place of a typical session as described above. The frequency of these meetings will be scheduled by the therapist in conjunction with the parents/guardians. Any unscheduled parents/guardians' sessions must be planned in advance to allow adequate notice for the child.

B. *Family sessions* will occur as needed. These must be also planned in advance to allow adequate notice for the child.

C. *Contact outside of sessions* will occur as follows:

1. The therapist's availability to attend school meetings will be:

_____

2. The therapist's availability to attend professional meetings will be:

3. Compensation for attendance, including travel time: _____ per hour.

_____

4. Requests for therapist phone consultation with the parents/guardians and/or the child will be considered. Such requests should be made only when the situation is urgent and cannot wait until the next session. The caller will need to leave a brief summary of the situation and the reason for its urgency. The call will be returned by the therapist and handled accordingly.

5. Professional coverage will be made available when the therapist is on vacation or otherwise away for an extended period of time. As has been previously discussed, this person should be contacted only for urgent matters. However when safety is a concern, care should be sought through the nearest hospital emergency room (i.e., call 911).

6. Phone contact and consultation with school staff and other professionals will require a signed release form describing the parameters of the information to be shared. This will also be true in cases where hospitalization is required and the therapist is involved.

7. The need for nonurgent therapist consultation with the school and other professionals will be determined by the therapist in conjunction with the parents/guardians on a case-by-case basis.

8. At this time, electronic forms of communication will not be used. The therapeutic relationship that is being formed depends upon personal exchanges.

D. *Cancellation of sessions* must be made a minimum of 24 hours in advance. Failure to do so will require a payment of_____. Note that this fee will not be covered by insurance. You may not have the option of rescheduling the missed appointment. If the therapist determines that cancellations are occurring too frequently, in order to continue in treatment, a specific policy to address this issue will be formulated.

E. *Other Policies:* _____

_____

_____

Note: This agreement is not meant to address the limits of confidentiality regarding your child. It is a contract between parents/guardians and therapist that may be modified periodically according to need.

This agreement represents the joint effort of the parents/guardians and therapist to define those guidelines that will best serve the interests of the child.

Parent/Guardian: _____ **Date:** _____

Parent/Guardian: _____ **Date:** _____

Therapist: _____ **Date:** _____

FIRST REVIEW of the Collaborative Agreement

Parent/Guardian: _____ **Date:** _____

Parent/Guardian: _____ **Date:** _____

Therapist: _____ **Date:** _____

SECOND REVIEW of the Collaborative Agreement

Parent/Guardian:_____Date:_____

Parent/Guardian:_____Date:_____

Therapist:_____ Date:_____

MODIFICATIONS to the Collaborative Agreement

New Policy	Date of Change	Initials

Appendix J

COLLABORATIVE AGREEMENT BETWEEN THERAPIST AND CHILD

PURPOSE: We are creating this plan so that we will know exactly what to expect as we work together. Using it will make it easier for us to solve problems. This will be our plan for now.

I. MEETINGS:

A. How often will we meet?

B. How long will our meetings be?

C. What day and time will we meet?

D. Where will we meet?

E. Other meeting information:

II. ORDER OF MEETINGS:

First, I will meet alone with your parents for about 10 minutes.

Second, I will meet alone with you for about 30 minutes.

Third, I will meet with both you and your parents for about 10 minutes.

Other meeting information: _____

III. RULES FOR OUR MEETINGS:

A. Each time we meet, we will start out by deciding what to talk about to best help you.

B. There will be weeks when I will meet with your parents alone for the whole meeting. I will let you know before this happens.

C. There will be weeks when I will meet with you and your family together for the whole meeting. This may mean you and your parents, or it may include other family members. I will let you know before this happens.

D. There will be times when you or I may need to cancel our meeting. I will work this out with your parents. Most of the time, we will follow our meeting schedule.

Other rules for our meetings: _____

_____

IV. RULES FOR OUTSIDE OF OUR MEETINGS:

A. Once in a while, you may see me at your school when I come there for a meeting with your teachers. I will let you know before this happens.

B. Once in a while, you may talk to me on the phone. This would only be for a serious situation and you will need to have your parents' permission before calling.

C. There will be times when I will talk to people at your school or other people who work with you. I will be doing this to help you and cannot always tell you when this is going to happen.

D. We will not be texting or using the computer to talk to each other.

Other rules for our meetings: _____

_____

We both agree to follow this plan as best we can for now. It will help us to understand what to do and what not to do as we work together.

Signed by:_____ **Date:** _____

Signed by:_____ **Date:** _____

Appendix K

THINKING ABOUT SIBLINGS: A CHECKLIST

THINGS TO DO:

Explain the disability:
Choose your words carefully so the child understands.
Do this periodically as the sibling ages.

Allow for typical sibling behaviors:
Take into consideration siblings' ages and stages of development.
Allow for natural sibling rivalry, bickering, and other interactions.

Regularly make time to ask about feelings:
Privately discuss and encourage positive feelings related to the ASD sibling (i.e., pride in accomplishment, appreciation of qualities, shared interests).
Validate feelings of embarrassment, sadness, anger, resentment, jealousy, guilt, shame, and regret related to ASD child. (Consider need for private counseling.)

Routinely provide reassurance:
Let siblings know that you are OK and in control of the care for the ASD child.
Let them know that you are prepared to handle any unforeseen circumstances related to the ASD child.

Express gratitude:
Recognize opportunities to thank siblings for their care and concern for the ASD child.

Celebrate achievements:
Make certain to recognize small accomplishments.

Periodically affirm him/her for being a good person and a good sibling.	Support major achievements; preplan to avoid any disruptions by ASD child.

Plan shared time among siblings:	**Schedule time alone:**
Identify mutually enjoyable activities.	Plan regular outings without ASD sibling, either with other sibs, or with parents/guardians.
Allow siblings to make choices and set reasonable limits.	Focus on ways to give siblings special experiences to look forward to.

Communication with school(s):	**Create an Action plan and an Emergency plan:**
If attending same school, siblings should not be involved in care of ASD child.	Advise sibling of your plan for potential problems with ASD child in social situations.
If different schools, discreetly share info on impact of ASD child on sibling.	Display and discuss a plan in the event of an emergency in the home.

THINGS TO BE AWARE OF:

Change in siblings' behaviors:	**Increased complaints from siblings:**
Look for heightened levels of emotional responses, social withdrawal, or avoidance of usual activities.	Recognize when "fairness" in family decisions is being questioned.
Look for connections that may be linked to the ASD child.	Note when siblings' complaints center on "too much" being expected of them.

Be cognizant of your own actions:
Identify situations in which it appears that you are siding with the ASD child over siblings.
Avoid tendency to justify or minimize ASD child's unacceptable behaviors.

Pay attention to outside factors:
Acknowledge and consider the impact of family variables (e.g., unemployment, divorce, illness, etc.)
Recognize the impact of environmental stressors (e.g., extreme weather, catastrophic events, unpredictable/ threatening incidents, etc.)

Need for professional support:
Consider each individual sibling's need for professional therapeutic support.
Investigate availability of ASD sibling support groups in the area.

Ensure normalizing experiences:
Monitor each sibling for typical participation in outside activities.
Monitor frequency of parental participation in siblings' outside activities.

Siblings' privacy:
Ensure that each sibling has a private space within the home and time to use it.
Make certain that the ASD child does not have access to the private possessions of siblings.

Appendix L

SKILLS AND BEHAVIORS: A CHECKLIST FOR THERAPISTS

Name: _____

Date: _____

Age: _____

<u>Task Accomplished</u>

	YES	NO

1. **Safety Issues:**

   Awareness of directions around home & other familiar places _____ _____

   *current progress:*_____

   _____

   Safe and proper use of cell phone _____ _____

   *current progress:*_____

   _____

   Safe and proper use of Internet & social networks _____ _____

   *current progress:*_____

   _____

   Safe around potentially dangerous objects & products _____ _____

   *current progress:*_____

   _____

   Care in taking risks at home _____ _____

   *current progress:*_____

   _____

Care in taking risks in school & community   _____ _____

*current progress:*_____

_____

Safe behavior around water, woods & outside areas   _____ _____

*current progress:*_____

_____

Navigates community & can safely seek help   _____ _____

*current progress:*_____

_____

<u>Task Accomplished</u>

YES   NO

2. Health & Hygiene
Covers mouth when coughing/sneezing;
uses tissues appropriately   _____ _____

*current progress:*_____

_____

Recognizes & seeks treatment for medical concerns   _____ _____

*current progress:*_____

_____

Demonstrates daily dental care & willingness to visit dentist   _____ _____

*current progress:*_____

_____

Demonstrates bathing/showering practices; hand/face washing _____ _____

*current progress:*_____

_____

Females: proper use of makeup, toiletries, & feminine products _____ _____

_current progress:_____

_____

Males: proper use of toiletries & shaving equipment   _____ _____

_current progress:_____

_____

	Task Accomplished	
	YES	NO

3. Autonomy

Completes household chores; takes care of possessions   _____ _____

_current progress:_____

_____

Independently chooses acceptable clothing   _____ _____

_current progress:_____

_____

**Understands concept of time & adheres
to schedules independently**   _____ _____

_current progress:_____

_____

Awareness and management of money   _____ _____

_current progress:_____

_____

Completes homework and school projects independently   _____ _____

_current progress:_____

_____

Ability to be alone in: the home; neighborhood & community   _____ _____

*current progress:*_____

_____

Independent execution of hygiene practices & toileting needs   _____ _____

*current progress:*_____

_____

Age-appropriate understanding of sexuality   _____ _____

*current progress:*_____

_____

References

Abele, E. (2012, November). *Communication is the key: Language strategies for improving social interaction.* Paper presented at the Harvard Medical School Autism Spectrum Disorders Conference, Boston, MA.

Ainsworth, M. D. S., Blehar, M. C., Waters, E., & Wall, S. (1978). *Patterns of attachment: A psychological study of the strange situation.* Hillsdale, NJ: Erlbaum.

Alberts, A., Elkind, A., & Ginsberg, S. (2007). The personal fable and risk-taking in early adolescence. *Journal of Youth and Adolescence, 36*(1), 71–76.

Anderson, C., Law, J., Daniels, A., Rice, C., Mandell, D., Hagopian, L., & Law, P. (2012). Occurrence and family impact of elopement in children with autism spectrum disorders. *Pediatrics, 130*(5), 870–877.

Asperger, H. (1944). Die "autistichen Psychopathen" im Kindersalter. *Archive for Psychiatric and Nervenkrandkheiten, 117,* 76–136.

Association for Children with a Disability. (2011). *Growing together: A parent guide to supporting siblings of children with a disability.* Hawthorne, Australia: Association for Children with a Disability.

Attwood, T. (2002). The profile of friendship skills in Asperger's syndrome. *Jeni-*

son Autism Journal, 14(3). Retrieved from http://www.tonyattwood.com.au/index.php?option=com_content&view=article&id=71

Attwood, T. (2007). *The complete guide to Asperger's syndrome.* London, UK: Jessica Kingsley.

Attwood, T. (2012, October). Presentation at the proceedings from Asperger's Association of New England Conference, Boston, MA.

Baranek, G., Linn, W., & David, F. (2008). Understanding, assessing, and treating sensory-motor issues. In K. Chawarska, A. Klin, & F. Volkmar (Eds.), *Autism spectrum disorders in infants and toddlers* (pp. 104–140). New York, NY: Guilford.

Baron-Cohen, S. (1990). Do autistic children have obsessions and compulsions? *British Journal of Clinical Psychology, 28,* 193–200.

Baron-Cohen, S. (1991). Precursors to a theory of mind: Understanding attention in others. In A. Whiten (Ed.), *Natural theories of mind: Evolution, development and simulation of everyday mindreading* (pp. 233–251). Oxford, UK: Basil Blackwell.

Baron-Cohen, S. (2001). Theory of mind in normal development and autism. *Prisme, 34,* 174–183.

Baron-Cohen, S., Leslie, A., & Firth, U. (1985). Does the autistic child have a "theory of mind"? *Cognition, 21,* 37–46.

Bettelheim, B. (1972). *The empty fortress.* New York, NY: Simon & Schuster.

Bowlby, J. (1988). *A secure base: Parent-child attachment and healthy human development.* London, UK: Routledge.

Bratton, S., Ray, D., Rhine, T., & Jones, L. (2005). The efficacy of play therapy with children: A meta-analytic review of the outcome research. *Professional Psychology: Research and Practice, 36*(4), 376–390.

Brisbane, H. (2006). *The developing child.* New York, NY: McGraw Hill.

Bromfield, R. (2011a). *Doing therapy with children and adolescents with Asperger syndrome.* Hoboken, NJ: Wiley.

Bromfield, R. (2011b). *Embracing Asperger's.* London, UK: Jessica Kingsley.

Brown I., & Brown, R. I. (2003). *Quality of life and disability.* London, UK: Jessica Kingsley.

Chawarska, K., Klin, A., & Volkmar, F. (Eds.) (2008). *Autism spectrum disorders in infants and toddlers.* New York, NY: Guilford.

Corbett, B., Mendoza, S., Wegelin, J., Carmean, V., & Levine, S. (2008).Variable cortisol circadian rhythms in children with autism and anticipatory stress. *Autism Research, 2*(1), 29–39.

Crissey, P. (2005). *Personal hygiene? What's that got to do with me?* Philadelphia, PA: Jessica Kingsley.

Dix, T. (1993). Attributing dispositions to children: An interactional analysis of attributionin socialization. In F. Volkmar, R. Paul, A. Klin, & D. Cohen (Eds.), *Handbook of autism and pervasive developmental disorders* (3rd ed., pp. 1057–1086). Hoboken, NJ: Wiley.

Donoghue, K., Stallard, P., & Kucia, J. (2011). The clinical practice of cognitive behavioral therapy for children and young people with a diagnosis of Asperger's syndrome. *Clinical Child Psychology and Psychiatry, 16*(1), 89–102.

Erikson, E. (1963). *Childhood and society.* New York, NY: W.W. Norton.

Fattig, M. (2008). Early indicators: High functioning autism and Asperger's syndrome. Retrieved from http://www.disabled-world.com/artman/publish/article_2255.shtml

Fay, W. H. (1980). Aspects of speech. In W. H. Fay & A. L. Schuler (Eds.), *Emerging language in autistic children* (pp. 19–50). Baltimore, MD: University Park Press.

Feiges, L., & Weiss, M. J. (2004). *Sibling stories.* Shawnee Mission, KS: Autism Asperger Publishing.

Ferraioli, S., & Harris, S. (2009). The impact of autism on siblings. *Social Work in Mental Health, 8*(1), 41–53.

Garcia Winner, M., & Crooke, P. J. (2004). *Social Thinking®: A developmental treatment approach for students with social learning/social pragmatic challenges.* San Jose, CA: Think Social Publishing.

Gilliam, J. (2006). *GARS-2: Gilliam Autism Rating Scale* (2nd ed.). Austin, TX: PRO-ED.

Goldstein, S., Naglieri, J., & Ozonoff, S. (2009). *Assessment of autism spectrum disorders.* New York, NY: Guilford.

Grandin, T. (1992). Calming effects of deep touch pressure in patients with autistic disorder, college students, and animals. *Journal of Child and Adolescent Psychopharmacology, 2*(1), 63–72.

Grandin, T., & Duffy, K. (2004). *Developing talents careers for individuals with Asperger syndrome and high-functioning autism.* Shawnee Mission, KS: Autism Asperger Publishing.

Gray, C., & Williams, J. (2006). *No fishing allowed- reel in bullying*. Arlington, TX: Future Horizons.

Greene, R. (2010). *The explosive child*. New York, NY: HarperCollins.

Greene, R. (2012, November). *Understanding and helping children with behavioral issues: The collaborative problem solving approach*. Paper presented at the Harvard Medical School Autism Spectrum Disorder Conference, Boston, MA.

Greenspan, S. I., & Wieder, S. (2006). *Engaging autism: Using the floortime approach to help children relate, communicate, and think*. Philadelphia, PA: DaCapo Lifelong Books.

Haddon, M. (2003). *The curious incident of the dog in the night-time*. New York, NY: Vintage Contemporaries.

Hall, L. (2009). *Autism spectrum disorders from theory to practice*. Upper Saddle River, NJ: Pearson.

Harlow, H. (1959). Love in infant monkeys. *Scientific American 200 6*(68), 70, 72–74.

Havighurst, R. (1971). *Developmental tasks and education* (3rd ed.). New York, NY: Longman.

Hess, E. B. (2009). Play-based intervention with autism spectrum disorders (ASD). Retrieved from http://www.a4pt.org/download.cfm?ID=27847

Higashida, N. (2013). *The reason I jump*. New York, NY: Random House.

Hoffman, M. (2000). *Empathy and moral development: Implications for caring and justice*. New York, NY: Cambridge University Press.

Hudson, J., & Myles, B. (2007). *Starting points*. Shawnee Mission, KA: Autism Asperger Publishing.

Insel, T. (2012). The new genetics of autism-why environment matters. Retrieved from http://www.nimh.nih.gov/about/director/2012/the-new-genetics-of-autism-why-environment-matters.shtml

Ivey, J. K., & Ward, A. K. (2010). Dual familial roles: An Asperger's syndrome case story. *Teaching Exceptional Children Plus*, *6*(3), 1.

Jarrold, C., Boucher, J., & Smith, P. (1996). Generativity deficits in pretend play in autism. *British Journal of Developmental Psychology*, *14*, 275–300.

Just, M. A., Keller, T. A., Malave, V. L., Kana, R. K., & Varma, S. (2012). Autism as a neural systems disorder: A theory of frontal-posterior underconnectivity. *Neuroscience and Biobehavioral Reviews*, *36*, 1292–1313.

Kanner, L. (1943). Autistic disturbances of affective contact. *Nervous Child*, *2*, 217–250.

Klein, M., & Schleifer, M. (Eds.). (1993). *It isn't fair! Siblings of children with disabilities*. Westport, CT: The Exceptional Parent Press.

Konidaris, J. B. (2005). A sibling's perspective on autism. In F. Volkmar, R. Paul, A. Klin, & D. Cohen (Eds.), *Handbook of autism and pervasive developmental disorders* (3rd ed., pp. 1265–1275). Hoboken, NJ: Wiley.

Kroeger, K. A., & Sorensen-Burnworth, R. (2009). Toilet training individuals with autism and other developmental disabilities: A critical review. *Research in Autism Spectrum Disorders, 3*, 607–618.

Landa, R. (2000). Social language use in Asperger syndrome and high-functioning autism. In A. Klin, F. Volkmar, & S. Sparrow (Eds.), *Asperger syndrome* (pp. 125–158). New York, NY: Guilford.

Lenneberg, E. (1967). *Biological foundations of language.* New York: Wiley.

Lessenberry, B., & Rehfeldt, R. (2004). Evaluating stress levels of parents of children with disabilities. *Exceptional Children, 70*(2), 231.

Levine, K., & Chedd, N. (2007). *Replays: Using play to enhance emotional and behavioral development for children with Autism spectrum disorders*. London, UK: Jessica Kingsley.

Levine, K., & Chedd, N. (2013). *Treatment planning for children with autism spectrum disorders*. New York, NY: Wiley.

Lichtenstein, P., Carlstrom, E., Rastam, M., Gillberg, C., & Anckarsater, H. (2010) The genetics of autism spectrum disorders and related neuropsychiatric disorders in childhood. *American Journal of Psychiatry, 167*, 1357–1363.

Linden, W. (2005). *Stress management*. Vancouver, BC: Sage.

Lopata, C., Volker, M., Putnam, S., Thomeer, M., & Nida, R. (2008). Effect of social familiarity on salivary cortisol and self-reports of social anxiety and stress in children with high functioning autism spectrum disorders. *Journal of Autism and Developmental Disorders, 33*(3), 227–234.

Loranger, S., & Kaufmann, W. (2012). The new diagnostic criteria for autism spectrum disorders. Retrieved from http://autismconsortium.org/symposium-files/WalterKaufmannAC2012Symposium.pdf.

Lukas, S. (1993). *Where to start and what to ask*. New York, NY: W. W. Norton.

Madrigal, S., & Winner, M. (2008). *Superflex . . . a superhero social thinking curriculum*. San Jose, CA: Think Social.

Margolis, D., Dacey J., & Kenney, M. (2007). *Adolescent development* (4th ed.). Dubuque, KA: Brown and Benchmark.

Marcus, L. M., Kunce, L. J., & Schopler, E. (2005). Working with families. In F. Volkmar, R. Paul, A. Klin, & D. Cohen (Eds.), *Handbook of autism and pervasive developmental disorders* (3rd ed., pp. 1055–1086). New York, NY: Wiley.

Matson, J. L., Worley, J. A., Fodstad, J. C., Chung, K., Suh, D., Kyung Jhin, H., Furniss, F. (2011). A multinational study examining the cross cultural differences in reported symptoms of autism spectrum disorders: Israel, South Korea, the United Kingdom, and the United States of America. *Research in Autism Spectrum Disorders, 5*(4), 1598–1604.

McIlwain, L., & Fournier, W. (2012). *Lethal outcomes in autism spectrum disorders (ASD) wandering/elopement.* Retrieved from http://nationalautismassociation.org/about-naa/white-papers-articles

Mesibov, G. B., Adams, L. W., & Schopler, E. (2000). *Autism: A brief history. Psychoanalytic Inquiry, 20,* 637–647.

Meyer, D. (2009). *Blood is thicker than water.* Bethesda, MD: Woodbine House.

Meyer, D., & Vadasy, P. (1996). *Living with a brother or sister with special needs* (2nd ed.). Seattle, WA: University of Washington.

Milevsky, A., & Levitt, M. (2005). Sibling support in early adolescence: Buffering and compensation across relationships. *European Journal of Developmental Psychology, 2* (3), 299–320.

Missouri Autism Guidelines Initiative. (2012). Autism spectrum disorders: Guide to evidence-based interventions. Retrieved from http://www.autismguidelines.dmh.missouri.gov/documents/Interventions.pdf

Mossman Steiner, A. (2010). A strength-based approach to parent education for children with autism. *Journal of Positive Behavior Interventions, 13,* 178–190.

Moyson, T., & Roeyers, H. (2012). Quality of life of siblings of children with intellectual disability: The siblings' perspectives. *Journal of Intellectual Disability Research, 56*(1), 87–101.

Myles, B. S., Jones-Bock, S., & Simpson, R. L. (2001). *Asperger syndrome diagnostic scale (ASDS).* Austin, TX: PRO-ED.

Myles, B. S., Trautman, M., & Schelvan, R. (2004). *The hidden curriculum.* Shawnee Mission, KS: Autism Asperger Publishing.

North Carolina Department of Health and Human Services. (2007). *Normal pediatric developmental milestones.* Retrieved from http://www.ncdhhs.gov/dma/capc/Milestones.pdf

Nyman, L.(1995) The identification of birth order personality attributes. *Journal of Psychology, 129* (1), 51.

Orsmond, G., Kuo, H., & Seltzer, M. (2009, Jan.). Siblings of individuals with an autism spectrum disorder; Sibling relationships and well being in adolescence and adulthood. *Journal of Autism and Developmental Disorders, 13*(1), 59–80.

Powell, A. (2002). *Taking responsibility: Good practice guidelines for services – adults with Asperger syndrome.* London, UK: The National Autistic Society.

Richdale, A., & Prior, M. (1995). The sleep/wake rhythm in children with autism. *European Child and Adolescent Psychiatry, 4*(3), 175–186.

Robison, J. (2007). *Look me in the eye.* New York, NY: Crown.

Rogers, S., Hepburn, T., & Stackhouse, F., & Wehner, E. (2003). Imitation performance in toddlers with autism and those with other developmental disorders. *Journal of Child Psychology & Psychiatry, 44*(5), 763–781.

Safer, J. (2002). *The normal one: Life with a difficult or damaged sibling.* New York, NY: Bantam Dell.

Sage, K., & Jegatheesan, B. (2010). Parents socializing sibling relationships in European American and Asian American families of children with autism in the United States. *International Journal of Early Childhood Special Education, 2*(3), 193–213.

Schilling, S., & Schilling, C. (2011). *The best kind of different: Our family's journey with Asperger's syndrome.* New York, NY: William Morrow.

Sigman, M., Mundy, P., Sherman, T., & Ungerer, J. (1986). Social interactions of autistic, mentally retarded and normal children and their caregivers. *Journal of Child Psychology and Psychiatry, 5,* 647–55.

Sigman, M., & Ruskin, E. (1999). *Continuity and change in the social competence of children with autism, Down syndrome, and developmental delays.* Malden, MA: Blackwell.

Sohn, A., & Grayson, C. (2005). *Parenting your Asperger child.* New York, NY: Penguin Group.

Spratt, E. G., Nicholas, J. S., Brady, K. T., Carpenter, L. A., Hatcher, C. R., Meekins, K. A., . . . & Charles, J. M. (2012, Jan.) Enhanced cortisol response to stress in children in autism. *Journal of Autism and Developmental Disorders, 42*(1), 75–81.

Stern Feiges, L. (2004). *Sibling stories: Reflections on life with a brother or sister on the autism spectrum.* Shawnee Mission, KS: Autism Asperger Publishing.

Sterzing, P. R., Shattuck, P. T., Narendorf, S. C., Wagner, M., & Cooper, B. P. (2012). Bullying involvement and autism spectrum disorders: Prevalence and correlates of bullying involvement among adolescents with an autism spectrum disorder. *Archives of Pediatric and Adolescent Medicine, 166*(11), 1058–1064.

Stoneman, Z. (2001). Supporting positive sibling relationships during childhood. *Mental Retardation and Developmental Disabilities Research Reviews, 7,* 134–142.

Tammet, D. (2006). *Born on a blue day.* New York, NY: Free Press.

Teitelbaum, O., & Teitelbaum, P. (2008). *Does your baby have autism?* New York, NY: Square One.

Turnbull, A. P., Brown I., & Turnbull, R. (2004). *Families and persons with mental retardation and quality of life: International perspectives.* Washington, DC: AAMR Books and Monographs.

Volkmar, F. (2005). International perspectives. In F. Volkmar, R. Paul, A. Klin, & D. Cohen (Eds.), *Handbook of autism and pervasive developmental disorders* (3rd ed., pp. 1193–1247). Hoboken, NJ: Wiley.

Wilkinson, L. (2010). *A best practice guide to assessment and intervention for autism and Asperger syndrome in schools.* Philadelphia, PA: Jessica Kingsley.

Willey, L. (1999). *Pretending to be normal.* London, UK: Jessica Kingsley.

Wing, L. (1981). Asperger syndrome: A clinical account. *Psychological Medicine, 11*(1), 115–129.

Wiseman, N. (2006). *Could it be autism?* New York, NY: Broadway Books.

Index